THE
ANGLO-SAXONS
THE VERDICT OF HISTORY

All this was lost on Alice, who was still looking intently along the road, shading her eyes with one hand. 'I see somebody now!' she exclaimed at last. 'But he's coming very slowly-and what curious attitudes he goes into!' (For the Messenger kept skipping up and down, and wriggling like an eel, as he came along, with his great hands spread out like fans on each side). 'Not at all.' Said the King. 'He's an Anglo-Saxon Messenger-and those are Anglo-Saxon Attitudes. He only does them when he is happy.'

Lewis Carroll *Through the Looking Glass (1872)*

THE
ANGLO-SAXONS
THE VERDICT OF HISTORY

PAUL HILL

TEMPUS

First published 2006

Tempus Publishing Limited
The Mill, Brimscombe Port,
Stroud, Gloucestershire, GL5 2QG
www.tempus-publishing.com

British Library Cataloguing in Publication Data.
A catalogue record for this book is available from the British Library.

ISBN 0 7524 3604 X

Typesetting and origination by Tempus Publishing Limited
Printed in Great Britain

CONTENTS

ACKNOWLEDGEMENTS

The Anglo-Saxons: the Verdict of History marks the third and final book in the trilogy of books about Anglo-Saxon history. Inevitably, in a series such as this, a familiar group of people have helped and supported the process throughout. As I was for *The Age of Athelstan* and *The Road to Hastings*, I am always indebted to my wife Lucy who has born the brunt of an Anglo-Saxon passion for longer than is fair.

The Anglo-Saxons has called for some visits to strange places in the English landscape. Curious follies and grand statues erected in memory of Anglo-Saxon kings and queens have been sought out and photographed and for this I am grateful to my parents Richard and Elizabeth Hill for their tireless hunting and gathering.

I am also grateful to the staff at the Royal Collection for helping me secure a copy of a photograph of William Theed's remarkable sculpture of Victoria and Albert dressed as Anglo-Saxons, and also to Emma Gormley of the Houses of Parliament curatorial department, who kindly helped to provided the picture of G.F. Watts's colossal oil painting of *Alfred inciting the English to overcome the Danes*.

As I delved deeper into the photographic collection which had been built up since the compilation of *The Age of Athelstan*, I was reminded once again of those who have helped gather both information and resources for me. Councillor John Bowen of Malmesbury and John Harper of Tamworth, both enthusiastic and knowledgeable men, have provided kindness and valuable information which has been helpful to *The Anglo-Saxons*. Julie Wileman, forever obliging and supportive, knows well the amount of work that goes into volumes such as these having produced her own quality contributions to the world of archaeology. To Julie I am grateful for some of the artistic renditions in this volume.

Lastly, the strength of the material contained within *The Anglo-Saxons* has been dependent upon access to the most obscure and ancient publications. The Saturday staff at the Reading Rooms of the British Library have been most professional in providing for me almost everything I have demanded to see, and although it is part of their daily work, I could hardly have found these works without them.

Paul Hill
Motspur Park
March 2006

PREFACE

Historians were once warned by Herbert Butterfield[1] against writing in a way in which their biases might not be recognised. Whatever political stance one might wish to take on Butterfield's work, this notion must surely remain as an important guide. When a historian attempts to write about the history of an idea the dangers of these biases spilling into the narrative are plain to see. So, perhaps it is wise to reveal at this early stage the present author's stance.

I have long held the view that the achievements of the Anglo-Saxons are something for the modern English people to be proud of. For me, it has never been a question of race, politics or religion, but simply a matter of fascination to learn about the centuries which preceded the Norman Conquest. One cannot grow up within yards of the battlefield of Hastings without wondering what had happened in England before that famous old date. It is, however, a source of sadness that some aspects of the colourful reputation of the Anglo-Saxons have been usurped by groups seeking to promote revisionist views of England's remarkable past. And so *The Anglo-Saxons* is an attempt to restore the balance in favour of an analysis and celebration of how the Anglo-Saxons have been variously treated over the centuries without the recourse to invective or triumphalism this sometimes engenders in people.

It is a story of a remarkably long-lived battle for survival sometimes against a great weight of historical and contemporary opposition. We will read here how history can be twisted to support prevailing myths and how the Anglo-Saxons were used to reinforce English identity during difficult times such as the great split with Rome in the sixteenth century. There are accounts of the activities of many scholars and antiquaries with whom the reader may be familiar, but I have sought to concentrate upon their contributions to the memory of the Anglo-Saxons alone, despite some of them having wider fame in other areas of antiquarian endeavour. It is, of course, necessary to provide the appropriate historical framework for their work and this I hope I have done.

The Anglo-Saxons is not a history of English antiquarianism. It is, however, a demonstration of the power and longevity of the Anglo-Saxon era in the minds of their descendants, a story of a continuing identity in one of Western Europe's most culturally complex countries. Politics, religion, scholarship and art have all had their part to play in the reclaiming of the Anglo-Saxons and I will explore the reasons for it within these pages. But the message is clear. The Anglo-Saxon era (*c.*AD 400-1066) witnessed the birth of England. Of the countless invaders and settlers who beached their ships on the shores of this island, fought wars and farmed the land, the Anglo-Saxons gave the most. Their language and laws survive today in some form as do many of the ancient shires and districts they created. How the Anglo-Saxons rose from the ashes of a seminal defeat to dominate the hearts of so many, how further battles were fought on their behalf, it is my intention to demonstrate.

The book is set out in 10 parts, each containing a series of small essays on chosen themes arranged broadly chronologically. I have chosen these themes to give the reader a wide overview of the issues which prevailed in this thousand-year story, although it remains the case that in some eras, particularly in that of the seventeenth century, a volume of roughly the same size as this could easily be produced from the extant material. A glossary has been included to aid the reader with some of the more obscure terms used in the book and there is also an appendix describing some of the deeds of the more peripheral contributors to Anglo-Saxon memory whose work has not featured in the main narrative. Finally there is a list of resources, many of them available online, which will prove useful to the earnest student of Anglo-Saxon studies.

INTRODUCTION

Anglo-Saxon. One of the Anglo-Saxon race – that is, of the mingled Anglo-Saxons and other Teutonic tribes from whom the English, the Lowland Scotch, a great proportion of the present inhabitants of Ulster, and the mass of the population in the United States and various British colonies are sprung.

Lloyds Encyclopædic Dictionary. Vol I. London 1895

I came across this curious definition, a mere century or so old, whilst browsing a sumptuously illustrated dictionary in an old library. I began to wonder just how a nation of people can possibly aspire to such an imperialistic self-identification at the expense of their neighbours and of distant peoples on foreign shores. Modern dictionaries describe the term Anglo-Saxon with significantly less zeal than our Victorian editor, but their insistence is still that at the root of the notion of an Anglo-Saxon lies an Englishman. As we shall see, this definition was written at around the time the Anglo-Saxons enjoyed their most influential spell in the memory of the English people. For the definition to have evolved into this triumphant rant of 1895, a number of processes must have taken place. One does not arrive at such notions by simply plucking them out of the air.

But this passage from the old dictionary does, however, raise the first question posed in this book: were the Anglo-Saxons English? They had been subjected to a foreign invasion at the hands of a Norman duke and his followers, sanctioned (or so it would seem), by God himself. Then, of course, in a difficult time which stretched for over 200 years according to the traditional view, a new nation was born and a new English identity was forged as England entered the high medieval era and began staking her claim in foreign lands. Very little of this is true, in fact. The Anglo-Saxons remained firmly embedded in the English notion of self throughout those 200 years traditionalists call the Anglo-Norman period.

The Anglo-Saxons marks the third and final book in a series which began with *The Age of Athelstan – Britain's Forgotten History*. The series started with an exploration of a largely forgotten king's deeds which were fundamental in creating what became the Anglo-Saxon state. Athelstan's impact on the story of the Anglo-Saxon revival along with that of his grandfather Alfred the Great, is given consideration below. Then, in *The Road to Hastings – The Politics of Power in Anglo-Saxon England*, we accounted for the decline of the kingdom in its years before the coming of the Normans. Now we must examine the legacy of those Old English centuries, for there are pitfalls everywhere. How did the English regain their Anglo-Saxon identity? Did they ever lose it? Who were the people who made it happen and what were their motives?

The emphasis shifts from era to era of course, but, broadly speaking, the interest in England's Anglo-Saxon past falls into four main areas of endeavour, often with smooth overlaps. There were always strong political reasons for bringing the era into contemporary struggles between king and his subjects and these frequently changed. Also, the religious side of the Anglo-Saxon revival which saw its peak shortly after the Dissolution of the Monasteries, remained a powerful motive for many, but from an early age there seems to have been a scholarly approach reflecting a genuine and earnest interest to find out more about the deeds of kings and bishops. Running alongside these approaches to the Anglo-Saxon past from era to era has been a less overtly political and rather more harmless artistic cultural heritage, which has left its mark in the form of engravings, prints and the grand history painting of the eighteenth and nineteenth centuries. Popular manifestations of the Anglo-Saxons from the nineteenth century onwards are a particular focus of the latter part of this volume.

In the first instance we will examine the prevailing notion of English cultural identity on the eve of the Norman Conquest. Just how did these people see themselves? The most telling aspect of this tale is hidden in the story of some English exiles in the decades following 1066 as they sought foreign lands in which to serve. Theirs was the first great Anglo-Saxon adventure of post-Conquest times. They took their identity with them. Later, in the twelfth century, when men of mixed English and Norman parentage wrote of their nation's history, they did so in a way that shows a new ideal was forming at a time when the erstwhile 'civilising' impact of the Norman Conquest was descending into anarchy and civil war.

As the idea of a new identity grew in the later Middle Ages, helped but not begun by King John's loss of Normandy in 1204, we look at aspects of language, literature and art which recall the Anglo-Saxon area with its strong central power structure, famous law-making and warrior-like nobility.

But then something happened which existed outside the popular imagination and gave the enigmatic movement which we have come to know as 'Anglo-Saxonism' its first pioneers. The sixteenth century saw the beginning in England of an intellectual enquiry into the country's rich heritage. It took the form of the now much-maligned antiquary, without whom we would all be very much in the dark. Alongside this birth of understanding ran the development of the printing press and the overtly political royal interference with the great monastic houses of the age, whose ancient manuscripts – the very records which so fascinated the antiquaries – were dispersed into the hands of private collectors.

This was the beginning of a desperate and prolonged attempt to rescue and interpret documents which revealed England's ancient past. Matthew Parker, the archbishop of Canterbury from 1559-75, charged with developing his queen's independent church would search high and low for Anglo-Saxon manuscripts to prove his case in the aftermath of the great destruction of the monastic libraries in the sixteenth century. The next century saw a continuation of a fascination with the Old English governmental system and also the rise of the cult of King Alfred the Great, but it was the adoption of the Old English era as an example of the type of royal governance expected of the presiding king, where the Anglo-Saxons became a political tool of note. The struggle between king and parliament was perceived by some as a case of the Norman oppressor versus the once free Englishman. For a while, political motivations towards the Anglo-Saxons ran in tandem with genuine intellectual ones. Among the latter was a drive to understand the Old English language, an aspect of a study known as philology. There was a religious and political need for philologists to turn their attentions to the Anglo-Saxons since so much historic material had been written down during the Old English period in the vernacular. Then, bringing up the rear, until it exploded in the late eighteenth and nineteenth centuries, was the movement which manifested itself in the popular imagination: oil paintings, poems, plays, sculptures, monuments and engravings all captured the deeds of kings and celebrated famous moments in the history of the Anglo-Saxons.

The myth encapsulated by our Victorian dictionary editor came about after the philologists and historians had turned into different animals. Although there were hints of it in the seventeenth century, it was not really until the arrival of a Germanic monarchy in England in the eighteenth century and the expansion of the British Empire that the notion of a 'race' of Teutonic people with their attendant characteristics of stoicism, purity and grace came to the fore. Even fledgling America got itself firmly attached to this notion and used the Anglo-Saxons as a cultural identifier against the navies and armies of the old country. The notion of race has begun now to sail into the sunset. It is a welcome departure, for it has clouded modern vision. However, there are some unwelcome vestiges of this movement which at its height saw the most remarkable Victorian claims of English racial supremacy. As the racial myth of the Anglo-Saxons fades, something more genuine must take its place. We must get to the heart of what it is about the Anglo-Saxons that has never allowed them to fully fade from the history books.

And so, *The Anglo-Saxons* brings the efforts of an extraordinary variety of people together, each with differing motives. The work and deeds of monarchs, antiquaries, common lawyers, priests, ministers, archbishops, radical activists, scholars, artists, historians, novelists, playwrights, film-makers and archaeologists are examined here in this book, as we look at the forces which drove the memory of the Anglo-Saxons along this thousand-year journey.

But what of the notion of self-identification? Let us put aside for a moment the triumphant clamour of the Victorian dictionary editor and ask the following simple question: who did the Anglo-Saxons think they were?

I

SURVIVING HASTINGS

WERE THE ANGLO-SAXONS ENGLISH?

The name of England and the appellation of Englishmen, was in use as far back as
in the time of Ine, A.D. 688, but it had never been ratified by a general assembly,
nor indeed could it so long as the kingdom was divided into seven monarchies.

T. Mortimer. *A New History of England*. 3 Vols. 1764-5. p64

Strictly speaking, Mortimer was incorrect. But his assertion is revealing. By the
latter half of the eighteenth century people were stretching English identity
right back to the time of the heptarchy, the seven dominant Saxon kingdoms
of pre-Alfredian England, which saw their heyday in the period between
the sixth and early ninth centuries. There was indeed a loose confederacy
of 'angelcynn', or 'English-kin' at this time, their politics controlled by one
powerful monarch among the seven with the centre of power moving from
one kingdom to another over time. But the question is this: is it possible for
us in the modern age to claim what Mortimer tried to claim, that the English
and the Anglo-Saxons are one and the same people?

The Venerable Bede (*c*.673-735), writing in 731, described the impact of
Pope Gregory the Great (590-604) on the English people in his *Historia
ecclesiastica* thus:

... it was through his zeal that our English nation was brought from the bondage
of Satan to the Faith of Christ, and we may rightly term him our own apostle. For

during his pontificate, while he exercised supreme authority over all the churches of Christendom that had already long since been converted, he transformed our still idolatrous nation into a church of Christ. So we may rightly describe him as our own apostle, for while others may not regard him in this light, he was certainly an apostle to our own nation, and we are the seal of his apostleship in the Lord.

Pope Gregory had of course instigated the mission to convert the early Anglo-Saxons to Christianity in England and had coined a phrase to describe the people of south-eastern Britain at the time of the Augustinian mission. The *Gens Anglorum*, he said, were to be found at the world's corner, in the south-east of Britain. But in that part of Britain, a very different set of words may have been used at the time to describe the inhabitants. These peoples were a mixture of Germanic tribes who, as archaeology has successfully established, were already in a state of such a complex cross-cultural intermingling as to deserve a hybrid identity before they even arrived on the shores of the country that would become England.

As Gregory suggested though, there were indeed many Angles among them. In a famous and often quoted observation Gregory had seen some Angle slave-boys in a Roman market place and was struck by their fair complexion and saw them not as Angles but as 'angels'. But in a way, Pope Gregory's generalisation is unhelpful. King Ethelbert of Kent (*c.*590–*c.*616), the king at the heart of the drama of the Augustinian mission, may have been surprised that his people had all been lumped together under the term 'Angle' when so many of them will have had Frankish or Jutish connections.

In fact, if we take the archaeological evidence of which there is so much spread around the countless cemeteries of the migration-period Germanic settlers of Britain, we can see just how complicated the picture really was. We can identify Anglian, Saxon, Jutish and Frankish influences in the burial rite and discern the regional spread of cremation and inhumation practices. The Angles were particularly strong in the east of England, the Jutes and the Franks in the south-east and the Saxons in the south and centre. But even this description is a generalisation. It masks a multitude of complexities, and so it is interesting to observe how these tribes came to be identified with the Saxons alone in most cases. According to one Gallic chronicler who commented upon the takeover of certain parts of Britain by 'Saxons' around the year 452, there was very little argument about the matter. To him, the Germanic settler of Britain was a Saxon. Bede, however, divided these invading groups into just three, giving us a vision of the migration period in England to which the Oxford School of Victorian historians stuck like glue: these were the Angles, Saxons and Jutes. His *Historia ecclesiastica* was probably responsible for raising the Saxons above their neighbours, although it remains significant that the Welsh and Scottish terms for an Englishman still have the word 'Saxon' at their root.[1] The fact that the Scottish and in particular the Welsh were in closer contact with Saxon groups than others of the Germanic diaspora may also have a bearing on it.

A Byzantine historian, Procopius, had also spotted the influx of new kinds of people into the country that was once known as *Brittia*. Three very populous nations, he said, lived there. They were the *Brittones*, the *Frisiones* and the *Angiloi*.[2] The *Angiloi* would feature again in Byzantine history in much changed circumstances in the eleventh and twelfth centuries, but the point here is that Procopius thought the Angles to be the main cultural identifier amongst this mixture of Germanic tribes in Britain.

Perhaps Bede's most important contribution in this regard was in giving the Gregorian vision a new boost. The *Gens Anglorum* was the work of God. An idea of some sort of unity in the eyes of God could be spread around the Germanic tribes and enable them to distinguish themselves from their neighbours. It was a powerful concept. The Church, it seems, had been instrumental in defining the first phase of Englishness amongst the Germanic groups. How ironic that it should be an acrimonious split with the very same church in the sixteenth century which would serve to define a new English identity several hundred years later. But of course, that new identity would need a machine to drive it, and that machine would be a new Church. The role of the 'church' in any of its forms in the continuing survival of Anglo-Saxon identity is a theme we cannot avoid returning to.

And so the idea of a *Gens Anglorum*, a Christian confederacy of Angelcynn, marched through the centuries of the heptarchy until it married a new concept created by Alfred the Great (871–900). But along the way there had been two kings whose claim to have been the first kings over all England are variously disputed by historians old and new. The Mercian King Offa (757–96), whose power south of the Humber and to the east of the dyke which bears his name was one such candidate. Offa's continental links with Carolingian France in particular and his strong relationship with Rome, revival of mercantile activity and creation of a new monetary system all contributed to the identity of the kingdom over which he ruled. But ultimately it was Wessex that prevailed. The West Saxon King Egbert (802–39), whose campaigns in the west of Britain saw him stamp West Saxon authority over a very wide area, was often accorded the title of the 'first king of England' since his power stretched more or less as far as the modern boundaries of that country, but King Alfred (871–99), for numerous reasons we will examine, won the argument. Alfred's titanic struggles with the Danes continued for much of his reign, and the kingdoms of the heptarchy tumbled one by one to Danish overlordship, but both contemporary and medieval historians saw the taking of London by Alfred in 886 as a seminal moment in the creation of the kingdom of England and in the promotion of a new English identity. The *Anglo-Saxon Chronicle* for that year said that after Alfred had taken London

> all the Angelcynn, those who were not under the subjection of the Danes, submitted to him.

At the end of the ninth century, when King Alfred had managed to fortify Wessex and arrange for the defences of Mercia in conjunction with the Mercian rulers Æthelred (*c.*883–911) and Æthelflead (911–18), the division of the Danelaw was still very much in place. Running roughly in line with Watling Street, it was a cultural and legal divide across the heart of England, separating the Anglo-Saxon from the Danish-held areas and it soon defined itself in terms of different laws, customs and artistic culture. It is even the case that such differences were still very much apparent long after the Norman Conquest.

And yet something profound had happened to the country between the ninth and twelfth centuries and it had little to do with the Norman

Conquest.[3] King Alfred had a political vision and the wherewithal to see it executed. But it required a catalyst and this had come in the form of the ventures of the Danish Great Army who in their political destructiveness provided something of an ethnogenesis for the Anglo-Saxons. A new kingdom was built in the ashes of the Scandinavian fires and out of what little remained of the Old English heptarchy a kingdom was born called the Kingdom of the Anglo-Saxons. It comprised Wessex and the rump of Mercia and it was to be ruled in the first instance from Winchester. Early Alfredian charters style the king as *Saxonum Rex* or *West Seaxena Cinge*, a form of clear self-identification with a Saxon origin. But then, in a letter from the archbishop of Rheims addressed to Alfred, the king is styled as *Regi Anglorum*. For much of the rest of his reign, Alfred was *Angol Saxonum Rex*, a title which reflected the make-up of his new kingdom.

But what are we to make of the legacy of the Danes and the Norse on the identity of the areas in which they settled? These areas are, of course, also in England. From the time of the treaty of Wedmore (878), a treaty which divided England between Alfred's English parts and those of the Danes to the north and during the gradual exchange by the Danish settlers of swords for plough shares, the cultural and linguistic make-up of the midlands and north of England will have been very cosmopolitan indeed. Within a generation or two, children were born to Anglo-Scandinavian parents. Place-name studies bear out the change across these areas of England. Would the son of a Danish jarl and English heiress whose family had settled in Leicestershire see himself as Danish or English? Would it be possible for the cultural affinity of these midland groups to be determined by the successes or failures of a southern English monarchy?

The years between AD 900-21 saw an astounding and sustained campaign of conquest orchestrated by King Edward the Elder (900-21) and for much of that time by his Mercian sister Æthelflead, the Lady of the Mercians. The Alfredian Kingdom of the Anglo-Saxons had become the Kingdom of the English. Between them, the new kingdom expanded northwards like a steamroller and so began an age which saw a now sedentary Danish midland thegnhood choose to offer their allegiance to Edward in the face of a significant threat to their own security from the north. That threat had come from Scandinavia via Ireland, from the Scottish king, and from the resilient kingdom of Strathclyde based around the citadel of Dumbarton. As the Viking Rægnald embedded himself at York and set up a new northern kingdom, the scene was set for another of those great tussles of yesteryear between a changing Northumbria and the kings of the south. Although he could not dislodge the invader, Edward did manage to coerce a famous submission of all the protagonists in 921 and became overlord of them all. And so a dream was awakened in his first son, Athelstan (924-39).

Athelstan, whose accession was opposed at first in Winchester on account of his disputed legitimacy and a Mercian upbringing, literally made a name for himself. If contemporary poetry is anything to go by, his countrymen bought the ideal completely. As the leaders of all the competing polities of the British Isles headed towards a showdown at the mysterious northern field of Brunanburh where Athelstan won a famous victory, a grand vision was expressing itself among the Anglo-Saxons. Their king, after sealing the submission of the northerners at Eamont Bridge in 927, began to elevate himself to a position of authority which surpassed a mere notion of Englishness. The new *Monarchus totius Brittanniæ* staked his claim to hold sway from coast to coast. With him grew an expanding thegnhood. Anglo-Saxon England was now truly taking shape.

Athelstan's brother Edmund (939-46) was described as *Engla þeoden* in 942 and later King Edgar at the head of a great Anglo-Saxon empire was called *Engla cyning* in 975. And so the identification of Anglo-Saxons with the notion of an 'England' continued through what is often described as the Anglo-Saxon Golden Age and through the much maligned reign of Æthelred II (979-1016). Then, by the time of the reign of the Danish King Cnut (1016-36) the country had a very recognisable name, *Engla lond*.

But it is in the surviving evidence left by the teachings of one man where we learn the most about pre-Conquest English identity. In 1014, when Æthelred's kingdom was beset by Danish invasion and the world seemed to some to be entering an era of doom brought about by the sins of the people, Archbishop Wulfstan of York (1002-23) gave a famous sermon entitled *The sermon of the Wolf to the English, when the Danes were greatly persecuting them, which was in the year 1014 after the Incarnation of our Lord Jesus Christ*. In this sermon Wulfstan points out that present troubles were due to present sins and widespread disloyalty amongst senior noblemen, but he also acknowledges that for some considerable time the English have existed as one people.

> Things have not prospered now for a long time neither at home nor abroad, but there has been destruction and hate in every district time and again, and the English have been entirely defeated for a long time now, and very truly disheartened through the anger of God. And pirates are so strong through the consent of God, that often in battle one drives away ten, and two often drive away twenty, sometimes fewer and sometimes more, entirely on account of our sins.

This was Wulfstan's assessment of the reasons for his countrymen's plight, but what of English identity?

> There was a historian in the time of the Britons, called Gildas, who wrote about their misdeeds, how with their sins they infuriated God so excessively that He finally allowed the English army to conquer their land, and to destroy the host of the Britons entirely.

To Wulfstan the Anglo-Saxons had always been the English. They were one people under the law and in the eyes of God. The punishment of the contemporary English was conforming to the same model that the Britons had suffered centuries earlier at the hands of the English. So, if an archbishop of York, a key advisor to both an English and a Danish king was in no doubt about English cultural identity towards the end of the Anglo-Saxon period, then why are we?

Before England was conquered in 1066, it was more than just a patchwork of competing kingdoms. In the form of Edward the Confessor, son of Æthelred, it was headed by the restored member of the most ancient royal line in Europe, the Cerdingas, whose root was in the sixth century. As we will see, the cultural identity of the Anglo-Saxons in the pre-Conquest period expressed itself very clearly in the immediate aftermath of conquest and in the two or three decades which followed, seeing exiled Anglo-Saxons set up something of a New England on the Black Sea coast. The important thing about that episode is that there was a positive identification of the exiles as 'English' by those whom they served and a similar self-identification by the exiles themselves. If there was any doubt in the minds of historians as to whether the Anglo-Saxons were English or not, then this one curious story, seldom told, should set the record straight.

THE STORY OF THE EXILES

In a smouldering Albanian chapel during the heat of battle, some of the last remaining Englishmen of former rank breathed their last, knowing that they had once again fallen prey to Europe's hungriest predator. Some of them will have fought together at Hastings the last time it had happened. But now in 1081, their fortunes were bound together in the Byzantine east in the service of a remarkable emperor, Alexius Comnenus (1081-1118). How had it come to this? Why had these men fled their homeland?

The battle of Dyrrachium (1081) did indeed mark the end for some English exiles. They had joined the famous Varangian Guard, an elite Byzantine Imperial Bodyguard derived from the Great Company of the Old Imperial Guard. The English had been thrown into the fray against Robert Guiscard (c.1015-85) the Sicilian Norman along the Via Egnatia in that unfortunate year. The Normans, who were attempting an assault on the Byzantine capital, had been met by Alexius' forces and the Englishmen in his ranks had come off worse. Their retreat had been cut off and those who were not crushed in the struggle had retreated to a chapel where

> all who could went inside the building; the rest climbed to the roof and stood there, thinking that would save their lives. The Latins merely set fire to them and burned the lot, together with the sanctuary. [4]

Whilst these poor exiles fell, back in England William the Conqueror was taking some time to truly consolidate his hold on a newly won kingdom. There had been rebellions and open warfare in the north and east of England, a recalcitrant earl and a rebel prince of the old royal line to contend with. However, for those Anglo-Saxon aristocrats who had received an indignant demotion, the ties of lordship bondage to which their people had clung for hundreds of years were irretrievably undone. A new enslavement was too much for some of them to take. The twelfth-century monk of St Évroul, Ordericus Vitalis, of whose background we shall examine more shortly, says this of the plight of both high and low born Englishman:

> The petty lords who were guarding the castles oppressed all the native inhabitants of high and low degree, and heaped shameful burdens on them. [5]

Furthermore, in the mid-1070s King Swein of Denmark died. Upon Swein the hopes of the Anglo-Danish aristocracy had rested. For those disinherited Englishmen who chose exile or who were forced to give up their estates, the future might have seemed bleak, and yet it seems that some of them carved out a curious destiny for themselves in a distant land, whilst others had chosen simply to join the Varangian Guard.

Let us examine the fortunes of some of these banished Englishmen, for in their tale is a sub-plot of English cultural consciousness, a theme central to this book.[6] Whatever the view taken by the Normans in William's brave new kingdom, these exiled Englishmen were known to the Normans and to the Byzantine Greeks alike. To the former, they were a menacing presence on the European political stage, a potential standing army whose leaders might decide to return to their homeland in force. But the Byzantines had a different view of their *Inglinoi*, and it developed into a relationship that lasted for hundreds of years.

Ordericus Vitalis is clear as to the cultural affinity of the exiles and to the background of their difficulties.

> And so the English groaned aloud for their lost liberty and plotted ceaselessly to find some way of shaking off that what was so intolerable and unaccustomed.

Attempts had been made by some of the English to seduce the king of Denmark into challenging for the English throne, but despite the fact that the Danish king had indeed sent reinforcements to Harold II on the eve of Hastings and had intervened in the politics of the north, it had not amounted to the overthrow of King William. Ordericus tells us that after this

> others fled into voluntary exile so that they might either find in banishment freedom from the power of the Normans or secure foreign help and come back to fight a war of vengeance. Some of them who were still in the flower of youth travelled into remote lands and bravely offered their arms to Alexius, emperor of Constantinople, a man of great wisdom and nobility. Robert Guiscard, the duke of Apulia, had taken up arms against him in support of Michael, whom the Greeks – resenting the power of the senate – had driven from the imperial throne. Consequently the English exiles were warmly welcomed by the Greeks and were sent into battle against the Norman forces, which were too powerful for the Greeks alone. The Emperor Alexius laid the foundations of a town called Civitot[7] for the English some distance from Byzantium; but later when the Norman threat became too great, he brought them back to the imperial city and sent them to guard his chief palace and royal treasures. This is the reason for the English exodus to Ionia; the emigrants and their heirs faithfully served the holy empire, and are still honoured among the Greeks by Emperor, nobility and people alike.[8]

That the English fled to Byzantium is not in doubt. There are far too many references to it for the matter to be dismissed. There is even mention of a Christian man of noble bearing bringing other nobles from the 'fatherland', impressing the emperor with his military prowess and subsequently being given a command of troops. The man married into a wealthy Byzantine family and built a basilica in honour of the blessed Nicholas and Saint Augustine, a church which some associate with the ruined chapel of Bogdan Sarai in Instanbul.[9] Later sources, particularly the fourteenth-century Icelandic Saga of Edward the Confessor,[10] tell stories of great campaigns and other struggles, but there is one source which is surprisingly explicit about the numbers. The *Chronicon Universale Anonymi Laudunensis* records a group of prominent English coming to Byzantium in 235 ships, arriving at Constantinople in 1075. Some 4350 of these and their families stayed in Constantinople in the service of the emperor, whilst a great many others sailed into the Black Sea to a place called Domapia, six days from Byzantium. Here, they conquered the land and gave it a new name – *Novia Anglia*. The first 'New England' would be here on the shores of the Black Sea, established by the survivors of Anglo-Saxon England's greatest defeat.

They had come to Byzantium by sea, having sold their estates in order to afford to buy their ships, we are told. They had sacked a Moroccan city, landed in Majorca and Minorca and had been to Sicily and Sardinia before arriving beneath the walls of the imperial capital. It seems that the immigrants' first test had been passed with flying colours. As soon as they had arrived in Constantinople they had fallen upon the besieging Seljuk Turks and scattered them, destroying also their fleet in a night surprise. Those who chose not to serve in the Imperial Bodyguard went on to create this *Novia Anglia* on the Black Sea coast. Real events, however, were almost certainly a little more drawn out than the suggestion made in the *Edwardssaga*, but its account is interesting all the same. This time there are 350 ships, which arrived in Constantinople (called Micklegarth here) just in time to save the place from a heathen naval attack. The English continued to perform well for the emperor and Alexius invited them to join the Varangian Guard. This offer was not enough for Earl Sigurd[11] or his men, who craved land and power and not just a career in soldiery. So, the emperor brokered a deal. He knew of land to the north which had once belonged to him, but had recently been wrested from the empire by the heathens. If the English could win that land 'free from tax and toll', they could have it.

Earl Sigurd [Siward] and his men came to this land and had many battles there and got the land won, but drove away all the folk that abode there before. After that they took that land into possession and gave it a name, and called it England. To the towns that were in the land and to those which they built they gave the names of the towns of England. They called them both London and York and by the names of other great towns of England.... This land lies six days and nights sail across the sea to the east and north east of Mickelgarth; and there is the best land there; and that folk has abode there ever since.[12]

Arguments have raged over whether Siward Bearn, the prime candidate for Sigurd, could have managed all this in the 1070s as is suggested by the date of the arrival of the English in the *Chronicon Universale Anonymi Laudunensis,* or even shortly after the succession of Alexius Comnenus in 1081 as is put forward by the *Edwardssaga*. Siward, according to John of Worcester, was in prison until 1087. It has led some to suggest that the saga is really recalling a later arrival, perhaps in the 1090s of Siward and his men, the suggestion being that they arrived in Byzantium into a world where there were already exiled Englishmen in the Varangian Guard and that Siward's was a later, though notable influx. It would mean that the first wave of Englishmen probably arrived not during the reign of Alexius Comnenus, but during that of Michael VII (1071-78). It is no surprise that the *Inglinoi* are first mentioned in an exemption document of *c.*1080 and to the Sicilian Normans they were known as 'Waring' a word similar to 'Varangian'. But the story of Earl Siward is not the same as the story of those who joined the Guard. It seems that his arrival with anything between eight to twelve other men of former rank and their retinues, should indeed be placed in the early 1090s. The earl perhaps had accepted exile after his release from prison. At this time Constantinople was under great threat by both land and sea. To the north the Pecheneg horsemen, long a scourge of Byzantium, were in open revolt and were not defeated until April 1091. By sea, the Turks under their leader Tzachas were besieging the city and it is probably these forces against whom the fleet of the English was pitted in the first instance. We will return to the adventures of Siward and his countrymen, but first we must consider the institution in which so many exiled Englishmen found a spiritual home, the Varangian Guard.

Anna Comnena has given us a glimpse of what the English Varangians might have looked like, particularly in battle. They had a habit of wearing their two-handed swords on their shoulders and had distinctly shaped shields and heavy armour. It is a description which rings true of the Anglo-Danish housecarle of the later eleventh century and the reference to those 'swords' probably indicates the presence upon their shoulders of the famous Dane-axe. Their loyalty to their lord it seemed, went unquestioned. But now their lord was a Byzantine Emperor. They regarded his protection as a family tradition, a sacred trust and inheritance which Anna says was handed down from generation to generation. Such was the strength of the Germanic bond of lordship. It was an allegiance which they would not break, nor ever would they brook the slightest hint of betrayal towards their lord.

But what of their compatriots who sailed out of Constantinople for six days and nights and landed on the shores of the Crimea and along the north-east coast of the Black Sea? Theirs is a history never told. And yet we have some tantalising glimpses into the whereabouts of this first 'New England'. By around 1100, the Byzantine records show that the once great empire had indeed regained some influence in the region around the Crimea and the Sea of Azov.[13] The lands had been under the rule (or at least under the punitive taxation) of the Turks. The Danishmend[14] Emir Melik Ghazi, much to his annoyance, is recorded as being no longer able to levy taxes in the Greek cities along the east coast of the Black Sea. Melik, according to a letter written by Theophylact of Occhrida to Gregory the Taronite (who was responsible for much of the military campaigning in this area), was bent on seizing all the lands as well as control of the sea. An anonymous letter from about 1095 also suggests that the Black Sea had been ridden of a piratical force, and it is proposed that the English may have been responsible for it.[15]

But where had the English settled? There exist some naval charts of the Black Sea coastlines drawn up by Catalan, Genoese and Venetian sailors between the fourteenth to sixteenth centuries. These 'portolans' as they are called, show some curious settlements whose names are now lost. On the Crimea there were settlements at Varangolimen and Vagropoli (near Sugdaea on the great silk-route). Both settlements, by their very names, are thought to be indicative of a Varangian presence. Near the mouth of the river Don the presence of Varangido Agaria (sometimes Agropoli) may allude to the same sort of thing. Further east, on the north-east shores of the Black Sea there existed perhaps the most compelling evidence for the English settlement. Londina, sometimes known as Londia or Fluslondin is the possible candidate for London, the name which the English are traditionally thought to have brought with them. The area was described as the river Lontia in 1534 and it may be the case that the settlement had given its name to the geographical feature. Also in this region was the settlement of Susaco (sometimes Susacho), a completely alien-sounding name in this area. It is possible that this place was named after its Saxon founders.

As to what the English did for several centuries on these distant shores, we are poorly served for evidence. Clearly, there had been a sound strategic and political reason for the establishment of Varangian garrisons in the area. There is even some tantalising evidence to suggest that it was not just directly for the empire that the English served. Some 'Varangians' seem to have sought service with the Georgian King, David II, and fought for him in 1121. These will have been second and third generation Englishmen, the sons and grandsons of the vanquished from Hastings. It is likely that these men had come to David from their settlements around the Black Sea coast.[16] But, the most appealing reference to the continuing existence of the English exiles comes from the quills of a number of Franciscan friars whose mission had sent them near to the lands of the English in the thirteenth century.

On their way to visit the Mongols in 1246-47, a mission of Franciscan friars sent by Pope Innocent IV left Kiev and ventured through the lands of Cumania (held by the horse people known as the Cumans) and headed east. It was a dangerous mission, but the friars had time to observe their surroundings. Benedict the Pole, one of four, described the political geography of the peoples to his right and left as he went through these strange lands to the north of the Black Sea. One of the areas on his right he described as the land of the Saxi,[17] *terram Saxorum*, whose inhabitants seemed to have surprised the friars by their very existence. They should not have been there. Mentioned elsewhere as *antiquorum Saxorum*, these folk were Christians and not, as one might expect, Muslims. Furthermore, they were obviously different to their neighbours and the friars ascribed this difference to their gothic ancestry, a possible misinterpretation of their Anglo-Saxon origins. Plan Carpini, another friar, suggested that the Saxi were one of the few who had yet to submit to the Mongols. They dwelt in scattered strongholds along the coast and one of their cities, as is firmly suggested by at least two documents, successfully withstood a Tartar siege. They had built engines says Carpini, engines which destroyed all the

Tartars' siege machines so that they could not approach the city. Then the Tartars tried to undermine the city by excavation and some indeed made it inside and started fires which were hurriedly put out by the inhabitants. This, the invaders paid for with their lives. The enemy subsequently ran out of energy and retired from the siege.

So, by the time of the writing of the *Edwardssaga* in the thirteenth century, it was apparent to the author that the English were still out there somewhere on the coast of the Black Sea. Quite what eventually happened to them is a mystery. Perhaps they were forced by circumstance to come to terms with their enemies who will surely have outnumbered them, but perhaps for a while at least, some of the very first 'New Englanders' may have seen off the thirteenth and fourteenth centuries and still kept to their native ways, maybe even to their native tongue.

For the most part, however, life for the exiles would have been quite different from how it had ever been in England. As the English were falling at Dyrrachium, thousands of miles from home, and as Sigurd's men and their families were learning to speak a foreign language, the old country was changing, too. It was embarking upon its great medieval adventure. Soon, Norman would marry Saxon. Within just a few generations there would be a new type of Englishman, often called by historians an Anglo-Norman. How soon did the Anglo-Norman become an Englishman? Some of these people, born of a union between Saxon and Norman, would express their sentiments in their writings, feeling no less English than those who had gone before them, and the transition to a wholly native identity happened quicker than most people have thought. We must now return to England to examine how this new consciousness worked and who its key players were.

'THE NATIONS ARE SO MIXED'

The twelfth century in England is a good example of cultural identity in flux. In fact, at the dawn of the century Europe was entering what can be described as one of its most cosmopolitan eras. If a man spoke French he could make himself understood in certain social circles from the crusading outposts of the eastern Outremer states, through Italy and Sicily to the western shores of the British Isles.

It is important to realise that, the Norman Conquest of England notwithstanding, England would still have been heavily influenced by the political, philosophical, religious and scholarly changes which were taking place across the whole of Europe at this time. There is little point in arguing that things would have been so very different if there had been no Norman Conquest. This would be to deny the nature of the changes across twelfth-century Europe. Identities were being fused everywhere. The Norman Conquest of England had been but one, albeit clear and sharp, example.

That said, something was happening to cultural identity in England for which we have literary evidence. The new aristocracy was beginning to see itself as part of a wider and more historic pattern of Anglo-Saxon dominance in lowland Britain. This notion is borne out by what they read and what was said about them by contemporaries.

Recent enquiry has established that the descendants of the Conqueror's men saw themselves as English earlier than is traditionally thought, although this is not to say that they were not proud of their Norman lineage.[18] The seminal date of 1204 when King John lost Normandy has been seen as a convenient point at which to draw a line under the Anglo-Norman period, but it is an entirely misleading date. Already, by the 1170s, if the often mentioned statement by Richard FitzNigel is to be believed, things were very much in the melting pot:

> Nowadays when English and Normans live close together and marry and give in
> marriage to each other, the nations are so mixed that it can scarcely be decided
> (I mean in the case of freemen) who is of English birth and who of Norman.[19]

In fact, Walter Map, writing in the twelfth century, tells us that King Henry I (1100-1135) instigated the policy of enforcing intermarriage between the English and the Normans and this is likely to have been a significant catalyst in the process. Yet it remains the case that cultural identities are not changed or formed by royal prerogative alone. Wider influences must have been at work. Besides, it was noted by Archbishop Lanfranc (d. 1089) that

Anglo-Saxon women who lived in fear of forced marriages, often ran off to join convents. The benefit here was that the Church and not the Norman suitor inherited the woman's land.

By the 1090s, the writer of the *Anglo-Saxon Chronicle* was referring to the unpopular William Rufus, king of England (1087-1100) as 'our king', a statement of plain truth of course, but who in this case are 'we'? We might recall that such a term was used by the chronicler for none other than the usurper King Harold for the year 1066. Also, although it is true to say that by the 1090s, only one Englishman remained in office in 16 bishoprics, it is also true to say that there was soon to be a revival in the cults of saints who had been popular in the Anglo-Saxon era. The initial assault on the Anglo-Saxon saints had been spearheaded by Archbishop Lanfranc who seems to have viewed them with suspicion. To others in Norman cloth, the old saints of England had been rough, illiterate or uncouth. Lanfranc, who openly doubted the sanctity of many of the Old English saints, dropped St Elphege and St Dunstan from the Canterbury liturgy, something quite unthinkable in the years before the Conquest. Similar revision took place elsewhere, particularly at St Albans, where the first Norman bishop more or less tore up the list.

But the attack on saints was not a wholesale affair. Some of the ancients continued to be revered beyond the Conquest. Osyth, Audrey, Modwenna, Edmund and Alban were among the number. Edward the Confessor's fame, himself half-Norman, would of course march into the thirteenth century where it continued to gather speed. The Norman aristocracy, whether it liked it or not, was becoming a local one. It could not sustain for long a completely alien approach towards the worshipping of saints, at least not at the local level. Besides, there is ample evidence in a medieval collection of English saints lives known as the *South English Legendary* which contains some fascinating evidence to suggest that not only did the English saints continue to be popular after the Conquest, but they were used as a projection of Anglo-Saxon identity.[20] There were over 25 manuscripts of this medieval work in circulation in the thirteenth and fourteenth centuries and if it reflected popular opinion regarding the Anglo-Saxon saints, then it reveals there was a very clear idea of what the Norman Conquest had meant to the average Englishman. The Lives which feature in the *South English Legendary* include those of St Oswald, St Alphege, St Edmund and St Wulfstan (1008–95). Wulfstan's Life is shot through with anti-Norman sentiment and describes him as 'the truest Englishman' and somewhat augments the stance which the real Wulfstan of Worcester took against the Normans. Interestingly, at the death of Edward the Confessor, the author states that Harold had taken the throne 'with treason', and that William had sought to obtain it through strength of force and wickedness more than hinting that both pretenders to the throne on Senlac ridge had no right to be king of England.

So, if the Norman attack on saints was only partially successful, then the assault on the personal names of England must rank as very successful indeed. Williams, Henrys and Roberts would prevail at the expense of the holders of Old English and Danish names such as Edward, Toki, Alfgar and the like. The example frequently quoted is that of a young man born in the area of Whitby around 1100 as Tostig. He grew up to taunts and bullying about his name and consequently changed it to the rather more acceptable William.[21] This must have happened almost everywhere. When we come across a William of the twelfth or thirteenth century, how can we be certain that Norman blood flowed through his veins? The answer is that we cannot.

So, in this England with its changing names, mixed marriages and a changing identity, what would the historians, many of whom were born of mixed stock, make of the Anglo-Saxon past? Just how far had the Norman Conquest changed the concept of Anglo-Saxon history?

2

MEDIEVAL ENGLAND
LOOKS BACK

THE TWELFTH-CENTURY HISTORIANS

The monk Eadmer of Canterbury (d.*c.*1124), writing of Archbishop
Lanfranc's striking out of numerous Anglo-Saxon saints from the liturgical
calendar of Christ Church, remarked that Lanfranc was but a 'half-fledged
Englishman'. English by birth, Eadmer is the first of all those who follow
here to write not just about his country's history but about contemporary
events. In his writing he captures some of the attitudes of an early Anglo-
Norman world.

At Christ Church in Canterbury, Eadmer compiled a biography of
Archbishop Anselm (*c.*1033-1109) which necessarily included a large
amount of historical narrative, as Eadmer felt the need to stretch things
back into the Anglo-Saxon era to justify his work. The *Historia Novorum
in Anglia*, a work whose influence was felt both at Worcester and Durham
and was read by William of Malmesbury, another great historian who
features here, begins with a prophecy from the tenth-century archbishop
of Canterbury St Dunstan. Dunstan had said that the country would meet
with disaster because of King Æthelred's sins. Whilst heavily emphasising
the primacy of Canterbury, Eadmer goes on to suggest that both the
Danish and Norman Conquests were fulfilments of the prophecy of
Dunstan. Eadmer leaves us in no doubt as to where he stands on the fate
of his countrymen at the hands of the Norman Conqueror, although we

would have benefited from knowing the details if only Eadmer could
have been bothered to supply them:

> William, thus having been made king, what he did to the English leaders who
> managed to survive so great a slaughter, as it could do no good to mention, I omit.[1]

It is a view shared by William of Malmesbury. Referring to the fateful date
of 14 October 1066, the day of the battle of Hastings, he says

> That was a day of destiny for England, a fatal disaster for our dear country as she
> exchanged old masters for new.[2]

Sharing a similar evolution of thought with Henry of Huntingdon (d. 1155),
William of Malmesbury adopts a position on the nature of the Normanising
influence in England which changes with time. By the time he writes his
Historia Novella, a history of his own times (1126-42), the notion that the
Norman Conquest had been a civilising force for the English had all but
disappeared. There was now, he says, fearfulness all around as the country
descended into civil war and barbarism. Of mixed parentage himself, having
a Norman father and an English mother, he was nevertheless damning of
the Anglo-Saxons for neglecting their past. No one since the Venerable Bede,
whom William greatly admired, had written a history of them, he said. William
of course, would be different. He went to extraordinary lengths to get his
evidence. Travelling widely to hear stories and visit ancient places, William's
efforts put us in mind of the great itinerant historians of the later centuries
such as William Worcestre and John Leland. William of Malmesbury wrote
down the things he saw and heard, sometimes even gathered on his own
doorstep, leaving us with a profound feeling that despite the grumble about
the English not recording their history properly, there was a great respect
for the Anglo-Saxon rulers of the past amongst the man in the streets of
England.

Henry of Huntingdon, a contemporary of William, was born in around
1088 at Little Stukeley. His father Nicholas, a Glanville, was probably related
to the great Glanville family who had inherited vast estates in East Anglia

after the Conquest. Nicholas was a clergyman, but his union with an unknown English heiress to the estate at Little Stukeley was not altogether unusual for its time. He was appointed in around 1075 to the archdeaconry of Huntingdon by the Norman bishop of Lincoln, Remegius. Both the Glanvilles and Remegius were Normans, having their roots in the pays de Caux area to the north of Le Havre. But the boy would grow up to be an Englishman. His story is an ideal example of what must have been taking place in similar families across the country.

Henry followed in his father's footsteps. Nicholas had also been a canon of Lincoln cathedral and it was here that he sent the young Henry for his education. This experience brought Henry into close contact with people who had a part to play in the running of the Anglo-Norman state. He lodged with the bishop of Lincoln, Robert Bloet, who had been chancellor to King William II (1087-1100) and who was still an active contributor to the pool of advice received by King Henry I (1100-35). Bloet appointed Henry to his father's archdeaconry at Nicholas's death in 1110. Henry also became canon at Lincoln. His closeness to the leading men of the Anglo-Norman kingdom is something which gives his testimony about earlier history a real ring of authenticity and closeness.

Early in 1123 Henry was deprived of Bloet's companionship when the bishop died in the middle of winter. The next bishop of Lincoln, who may well have been an Anglo-Saxon or an Anglo-Dane, was Alexander 'the Magnificent'. Alexander soon noticed Henry's exceptional Latin writing skills and perhaps more so his prolific poetry. He must also have been aware of his keen grasp of the history of his country, the nation Henry describes as 'this, the most celebrated of islands, formerly called Albion, later Britain, and now England'. And so it was Alexander who asked Henry to write his *The History of the English People*. Alexander's request must have been made shortly after his appointment. In his prologue, Henry flatters his master in a passage which strongly suggests a native or at least non-Norman origin for Alexander:

> ... and at your command, Bishop Alexander, I have undertaken to narrate the history of this kingdom and the origins of our people, of which you are regarded as the most splendid ornament.

Henry was closely tutored by Alexander, who advised him to use as his source for the early period Bede's *Historia ecclesiastica* and for the period after 731 when that work ends, he told Henry to use material from chronicles preserved in ancient libraries. Henry also worked from a now lost copy of the *Anglo-Saxon Chronicle* similar to the version kept at Peterborough and occasionally from one similar to that at Abingdon. His work also shares one or two similarities with a version used by another twelfth-century historian, John of Worcester.

Henry's *History* is important for a number of reasons. Firstly, it was widely read by others for a very long time after it was written. Secondly, it contains within it some nuggets of handed-down memories such as his recollection that he had heard very old men talk about the infamous St Brice's Day massacre when he was a boy. This massacre had come about because of an order sent by King Æthelred that on St Brice's Day (13 November) 1002, all the Danes in England were to be murdered at once. The order was only partially carried out, but the tale reveals something to us. Henry would have been recalling a period in his own life around the mid to late 1090s. The men he overheard would have been sons of the witnesses to this event. They were still talking about an event in the Anglo-Saxon past nearly 100 years after it had occurred. Moreover, the most important aspect of this memory is surely that they will have been talking about the event in English. Henry therefore, must have spoken English as a boy.

Henry's *History*, like others of its era, acknowledges the immorality of the English and how they deserved their punishment in the eyes of God, but it also expresses regret that the English were still ruled by the Normans at the time of his writing. Henry took the view that the Norman Conquest was indeed a form of punishment for the English. His work goes from describing a *Gens Normannorum et Anglorum* to barely mentioning a division between Saxon and Norman by the mid-1140s when he revised his work. Also, Henry was fond of using the collective 'we' or 'our' when referring to the recent military feats of the Anglo-Norman monarchy or aristocracy. Let us take for an example the account of the battle of the Standard which took place in 1138. It was a struggle between the Anglo-Normans and David, king of the Scots, which took place on Cowton Moor near Northallerton in Yorkshire. Henry's account of it is preceded by a rousing speech from Ralph, bishop of the Orkneys. It is the sort of speech which is similar in tone to others written around the same time. William the Conqueror's speech before the battle of Hastings, and another speech at the battle of the Standard attributed by Ailred of Rievaulx to Walter Espec, a Yorkshire baron, both contain bellicose exhortations about the military prowess of the Norman people. Henry's rendition of Ralph's speech, which begins 'Noblemen of England, renowned sons of Normandy, before you go into battle you should call to mind your reputation and origin ...' goes on to outline every conceivable Norman achievement: the conquests of Apulia, of England, exploits in Jerusalem and Antioch, and the general military prowess of the Normans. It is, however, a literary device. But when Henry finishes his account of Ralph's speech, he tells us that 'Every *Englishman* answered and the hills and mountains echoed, "Amen, Amen!"'. And at the victorious Anglo-Norman conclusion of the struggle, Henry says that 'our men were victorious'. The English were beginning to claim shared rights now over the martial prowess of their erstwhile deadliest enemies!

Another of our twelfth century-historians, Ordericus Vitalis, shares a personal tale similar to Henry and William's but it contains within it the very essence of the meaning of the union between England and Normandy to a young man of mixed parentage. Born at Atcham near Shrewsbury in 1075, Ordericus was the son of Odelerius d'Orleans who had come to England with Roger de Montgomery, the earl of Shrewsbury. The boy, whose mother was English, studied in his early years at Shrewsbury but was soon sent to Normandy, becoming a monk at St Évroul. He seems to have considered himself as something of an exile. He did, however, visit England again on a number of occasions, visiting Crowland Abbey for five weeks in 1115 and later returning to visit Thorney and Worcester.

Ordericus' work *Ecclesiastica Historia* was a grand-scale narrative history. In it, he regarded England and Normandy as both politically and culturally wed, but he was not without his opinions and biases. He clearly admired the community at Crowland and gave praise in his work to Waltheof, their secular Anglo-Saxon patron as well as inserting a life of St Guthlac, their patron saint, into his work. His love for the English saints and his concern about the oppression of English monks are expressed very clearly, but it is perhaps his admiration for Guitmund of La-Croix-Saint-Leufroi which is most revealing. Guitmund, who had refused a presentment in England, had written to William the Conqueror telling him why. Guitmund was writing from England at the time, just before his departure for France. The letter is included by Ordericus in his work. Guitmund sets out his stance to the king by first of all saying that he felt to old and frail to take office in England, but it soon becomes very clear what Guitmund had thought about the Norman Conquest of England:

> I cannot see what right I have to govern a body of men whose strange customs and barbarous speech are unknown to me, whose beloved ancestors and friends you have either put to the sword, driven into bitter exile, or unjustly imprisoned or enslaved ….
>
> It is a fundamental law for men of religion to abstain from all plunder and refuse to accept booty even when it is offered as a reward for just service … I am sorely afraid I deem all England the spoils of robbery and shrink from it and its treasures as from consuming fire.[3]

But there is a reverse side to all this. Ordericus is quite clear about the effects of the Norman Conquest on the English and states that because of churchmen's high reputation Guitmund's letter had stirred up something of a hornet's nest among those Normans who had stood to gain from the dispossessed Englishmen. But Ordericus, like so many of his contemporaries, accepted the Norman Conquest on religious and moral grounds and on this matter he does not shift. The English he said, were degenerate apostates and effeminate to boot. Had he spent a little more time in the secular castles of twelfth-century England he may have observed that the descendants of the Conqueror wore their hair long and adopted many of the mannerisms of their Anglo-Saxon predecessors.

After Ordericus had visited Worcester, he reported that he had seen a monk called John writing a Latin history of England. Bishop Wulfstan of Worcester, before his death in 1095, had asked one of his monks to write the work and there has traditionally been some confusion over the identity of the author. The monk Florence was for a long time the favoured candidate for the authorship of the work, but John acknowledges Florence's contribution whilst recording his death in 1118 and had told Ordericus that the instruction to write the work had come directly from Wulfstan. John's work, written very much in the Worcester tradition is very pro-Anglo-Saxon in its outlook, as one might expect, and in its account of later Anglo-Saxon history gives a little more insight into developments than the main text of the *Anglo-Saxon Chronicle*.

But, for a slightly different slant on things, Ailred of Rievaulx (abbot from 1147-67), provides some very interesting and revealing interpretations. Ailred, a Northumbrian, was brought up in the house of King David of the Scots (1124-53). He promoted King David as chief representative of the ancient line of English kings stretching back through Edgar (who Ailred tells us was to the English what Charlemagne was to the French), Athelstan and Alfred. This was suggested because David's mother was St Margaret, blood relation of Edgar the Ætheling, the last descendant of Cerdic to have the briefest of tastes of life as an English king in 1066. It is an interesting argument, since it brings to mind the very essence of the protracted succession crisis which led to the great showdown on Senlac ridge in 1066. That argument, long since put to bed by Norman propaganda on account of the fact that it had been the Normans who had looked after the exiled Edward and his luckless brother Alfred, sons of Æthelred, did not convince Ailred, who clearly knew of the political potency of the claim of the ancient house of Wessex.

A measure of just how far the Anglo-Saxon past had come to be accepted among the twelfth-century nobility can be found in the work of Gaimar. His *L'Estoire des Engles*, produced in the 1130s for Constance, the wife of Ralph FitzGilbert, a great Norman Lincolnshire landowner, was written in French and had a great appeal to the Francophone secular elite. It gave them a sense of belonging. Within its pages we find stories of great English heroes such as Hereward the Wake, a particular favourite of Gaimar's. We know less about Gaimar than we would like. His sympathies might seem to betray him as an Englishman, but what is clear is that there was an audience for his work. That these people read in French and thought of themselves as part of an English culture cannot be doubted.

Gaimar's audience was also interested in a certain work which did not paint the Anglo-Saxons in a good light at all. Geoffrey of Monmouth, about whose *Historia Regum Britanniae* more ink has been spilled than on any other twelfth-century work, had a remarkable imagination. He also had an even more remarkable impact on post-Conquest Anglo-Saxon identity. Quite how widely Geoffrey's monumental work was read around the Norman dominions of Europe, we will never know, but there was clearly something in his *Historia* which appealed to the Norman mind. It propelled Geoffrey to near superstardom both in his own time and afterwards.[4]

Geoffrey was born in Wales in about 1100 and died in 1155. His heritage is unclear, but his father was appropriately named Arthur although it is not known if his 'Britishness' had its roots within the realm of Brittany or Wales. From about 1129 Geoffrey was a secular Augustinian canon at St George's College in Oxford Castle. He wrote his *Historia* at Oxford in around 1138-9,[5] having already written the *Prophesies of Merlin* in 1135. Walter, archdeacon of Oxford, had said he had given Geoffrey a book written in the 'British language' and Geoffrey's *Historia* was the Latin translation. Closer inspection of Geoffrey's *Historia* reveals a number of sources and not just one, however.

It is clear that Geoffrey wanted the Welsh and the Bretons to consider themselves as from a common heritage and above this the Normans could enjoy their rightful place as moral custodians of the legend. The Anglo-Saxons and their achievements were more or less dismissed. In short, Geoffrey's *Historia* was a powerful piece of medieval propaganda. Covering a period of over 2000 years, the *Historia* included accounts of the reigns of 99 kings in Britain, the first of whom it was said was Brutus of Troy. Of Brutus's arrival upon what would have been the Bronze Age shores of southern Britain he says:

> At that time the name of the island was Albion, and of none was it inhabited, save only a few giants.

The *Historia* goes through the British kings up to Cadwaladr in the seventh century AD, but it gives over one fifth of the whole work to the story of Arthur, complete with all that we have come to expect of this talismanic figure. William of Newburgh, writing later in the century, said of Geoffrey that he had made the little finger of Arthur thicker than the loins of Alexander the Great. He was not the only complainant. It may have been Ailred of Rievaulx who in 1142-3 wrote in his *Speculum Charitatis* that novices 'weep more readily over fictitious tales about someone (I know not whom) called Arthur than over pious books.'[6] But it was the figure of Arthur which sold the work not only to the hearts and minds of the Norman establishment, but to almost the whole of Christendom. In fact, another scholar named Alfred, or Alured of Beverly, finally found himself forced to turn to the *Historia* against his will after admitting that everyone was talking about it and he was ashamed to say that he had not until that time read it.

The *Historia* greatly influenced other writers such as the later twelfth-century Master Wace and the early thirteenth-century English writer Layamon, a parish priest of Areley-Kings near Worcester, who wrote his own *Brut*. Layamon's was a romantic and semi-mythical view of early British history which would run alongside the various more earnest accounts of English history with some degree of discomfort. The tone is unusually anti-Saxon in its perspective, something which has puzzled historians since it was written in English. It does, however, end with a praising of the Angles, who Layamon claims were 'untouched by Saxon guilt'. The Angles, he said, had given their name to England. But Layamon's royal lineages would be used again and again in later centuries. Llywelyn ap Gruffydd and Edward I both justified dynastic claims based on his writings[7] and Henry Tudor delivered to Richard III a genealogically backed-up argument stretching back to Brutus after Richard accused him of having no right to the throne of England.

Geoffrey's passion for the western histories is clear to see. He speaks in scathing terms of the Saxons who first came to Britain and caused trouble and death. When Henry of Huntingdon saw the *Historia* at Bec, he was truly amazed at the scope of the work, but both he and William of Malmesbury, renowned and progressive historians of English affairs, were to be given a stark warning by Geoffrey:

Howbeit their [the Welsh] kings who from that time [after Cadwaladr] have succeeded in Wales I hand over in the matter of writing unto Caradoc of Llancarfan, my contemporary, as do I those of the Saxons unto William of

Malmesbury and Henry of Huntingdon whom I bid be silent as to the kings
of the Britons, seeing that they have not that book in the British speech which
Walter, archdeacon of Oxford, did convey hither out of Brittany ....

It is a passage which follows on from the very end piece of the *Historia*. In
his summary of the fate of the Britons, now turned Welsh, he gives us a
hint at the rise of the English under their most powerful of all monarchs.
That such a biased work could even include a nod in the direction of the
Kingdom of the English in the form of the following statement is testimony
not to Geoffrey but to the man about whom he is talking.

[The Saxons]… thus throwing off the sovereignty of the Britons, held the empire
of all England under their Duke Athelstan, who was the first to wear the crown
amongst them.

It is as near as Geoffrey can get to acknowledging the great power
struggles of the tenth century which saw King Athelstan capitalise on the
achievements of Alfred and Edward the Elder and set up an English empire
in Britain for which one of his successors, King Edgar, would take most of
the glory. From then on, the Britons had degenerated and the Saxons had
risen. So Geoffrey, in his wisdom, stopped writing about it.

Fantastically popular throughout the medieval world, Geoffrey finally
went out of fashion – though was by no means lost – when a new form of
historical enquiry gathered pace in the sixteenth century. This, the era of
the first antiquaries, was governed by very different agendas to that which
was held by Geoffrey and we will look at them later in this volume. But for
now, we might muse upon the notion that Geoffrey of Monmouth did for
Arthurianism what William Stukeley did for druidism.

So, Anglo-Saxon identity did more than just survive the twelfth century, it
was completely rebuilt. There were sympathetic and unsympathetic historians,
but even in the works of the most anti-Saxon writers there were grudging
admissions here and there. How, then, would people put the idea of the
Anglo-Saxon past to practical or demonstrative use? The popular memories
of the period will be examined shortly but there is also the idea of Anglo-

Saxon England as expressed through constructive historical justification carried out by monastic communities who felt that without reference to the Anglo-Saxon past they would be under threat from the new order.

FORGING IDENTITIES

The twelfth century in England was a time when the forging of charters and privileges was so widespread as to be virtually the norm as opposed to the exception.[8] It is argued that not only was the Anglo-Saxon period being used in the twelfth century to consolidate the ancient rights and privileges which it was felt were under threat, but that the feeling was so strong that a tradition of creative writing more or less grew around groups of communities giving them a sense of their own identity. One Peterborough 'cartulary', for want of a better word, will serve to prove the point. The document in question, the *Relatio Heddæ,* which survives in the *Liber Niger* of Peterborough and elsewhere, includes an account of the foundation of Peterborough 'written' by the Abbot Hedda, Peterborough's second abbot, in the seventh century.

Peterborough, it should be noted, was the producer of the longest-lasting version of the *Anglo-Saxon Chronicle*, version E, which in the twelfth century began to contain references specific to Peterborough itself which were particularly acerbic towards a certain Abbot Henry. Clearly, the community were worried about something and needed to justify and express themselves in a difficult time. We might recall that Peterborough had a strained relationship with the Norman monarchy after sending their new candidate for the abbacy in 1066 to the young Edgar the Ætheling in London whom they thought should be king after Harold's death, and not to the newly arrived victorious Duke William.[9] But if the Peterborough scribe's words are to be believed, there was a great feeling of Peterborough's Anglo-Saxon independence, which in this case seems to have stretched itself as far back as the pagan period in an attempt to frighten off poor Henry:

1127 … This same year he [King Henry I] gave the abbacy of Peterborough to an abbot [who] was called Henry of Poitou.... Let it not be thought remarkable, the truth of what we say, because it was fully known over all the land, that immediately after he came there ... then soon afterwards many men saw and heard many huntsmen hunting. The huntsmen were black and huge and loathesome, and their hounds all black and wide-eyed and loathesome, and they rode on black horses and on black billy-goats. This was seen in the very deer park of that town and in all the woods there were from that same town to Stamford; and the monks heard the horns blow that they blew in the night. Honest men who kept watch in the night said that it seemed to them there might well have been twenty to thirty horn blowers. This was seen and heard from when he came there, all that Lenten-tide right up to Easter. This was his entrance: of his exit we cannot yet say. May God provide!

1131 ... May Christ take measures for the wretched monks of Peterborough and for that wretched place! Now they need the help of Christ and all the Christian people.

1132 ... This year King Henry came to this land. Then came Abbot Henry, and accused the monks of Peterborough to the king because he wished to subject that minster to Cluny, so that the king was well nigh lured and sent for the monks. And through God's mercy ... the king then knew that he acted with treachery.[10]

The strength of feeling in and around Peterborough cannot be underestimated. The recourse to pagan hunting rituals (the use of goats and blackness is particularly associated with Woden) is quite another matter. But it does demonstrate a feeling of threat and insecurity which may go along way towards explaining the inclusion in the *Relatio Heddae* of the spurious material surrounding its foundation which apparently dated from the time of the great pagan King Penda's son Paeda who accepted baptism at what was then the community of Medehamstede. There is also a seventh-century bull from Pope Agatho and a 'refoundation' charter endorsed by King Edgar dating from the time the monastery was refounded by Bishop Æthelwold during the tenth-century reform movement in the 960s. All of this points to Peterborough's proud conception of its own Anglo-Saxon past and its relationship with the old monarchy. Also, its relationship with the papacy as expressed in these paranoid insertions probably gave the community some crumbs of comfort at the time.

So, that is one example of how the medieval monastic mind used the Anglo-Saxon period. Peterbourough is by no means the only example, but it is one of the more colourful. Monks at St Albans, Westminster and Ely were all up to much the same sort of thing, helping these fine old institutions forge a meaningful English identity. Meanwhile, outside the confines of these religious institutions, the people's language had been changing. Even the men who terrorised Abbot Henry on horseback across the flat lands around Peterborough in the name of Anglo-Saxon identity were beginning to talk a different language. It is time to look at the nature of the survival of Old English, for it is in the English language that the secret of the success of the lasting appeal of the Anglo-Saxons lies.

CHANGING VOICES

Thus come, Lo! Engelond into Normannes honed,

And the Normans ne couþe speke þo . bote hor owe speche

& speke frenss as hii dude atom . & hor children dude also teche

So þat heiemen of þis lond . þat of hor blod come

Holdeþ alle þulke speche . þat hii of him nome

Vor bote a man conne frenss . me telþ of him lute

Ac lowe men holdeþ to engliss . and to hor owe speche yute.

Robert of Gloucester. *c*.AD 1300 (7,538–43)

It is a subject which arouses passion. We have already touched upon the interest of post-Conquest scholars in some Old English historical documents, but what of the survival of the language itself? To follow the fortunes of English after the Norman Conquest is to some extent to follow the adventure of the Anglo-Saxons themselves as expressed by the material left to us written in the changing English language. The specifics of the changes to the language are covered by a number of scholarly volumes based on hundreds of years of philological study, but for the purposes of the present volume, we must concentrate on the impact of those changes and the motivations of those who sought to understand them. People still seek to impress upon us how the English language was transformed in England after the Norman Conquest. The dominance of the Norman French tongue in the upper classes of English society in the Middle Ages is hardly a matter for dispute. We have seen that it was precisely for this audience the historian Gaimar was writing in the twelfth century. This fact, plus the obvious preponderance of Latin texts in officialdom should not, however, lead us to believe that Old English, as a form of literary standard, had completely died out.

Firstly, as far as the *spoken* word was concerned English continued to be used at all levels including that of the scholarly Latin writers of the age, as Henry of Huntingdon's own recollections of overheard conversations reveal. In fact, the case for the defence of English as a continually evolving language as spoken by English men and women before and after the Norman Conquest and right up to this very day is best served by an example. Below is an exercise published in Mitchell and Robinson's *A Guide to Old English*. It is designed to show that with some creative borrowing from the Old English lexicon (and creative it must be), it is possible to construct entire sentences which have essentially the same appearance in Old English as they do in Modern English. The pronunciation would have been different in Old English times, and it is difficult to imagine anyone ever coming out with the following passage, without being closely questioned by his friends, but here it is all the same:

> Harold is swift. His hand is strong and his word grim. Late in
> life he went to his wife in Rome.
> Is his inn open? His cornbin is full and his song is writen.
> Grind his corn for me and sing me his song.
> He is dead. His bed is under him. His lamb is deaf and blind.
> He sang for me.
> He swam west in storm and wind and frost.
> Bring us gold. Stand up and find wise men.[11]

However, the inclusion of the example in the current context serves only to demonstrate the similarities between an ancient form and modern form of the same language, and whilst it is successful in doing so, it does not help explain the great changes which took place in English. It is important to understand these changes, since it was the case that when scholars of a later age had good cause to revisit ancient documents written in the Anglo-Saxon period, they had to do so armed with some of the disciplines of the philologist. In other words, Old English had to be learned by the men of medieval England. The above exercise in fact recalls a philosophy of interpretation which Samuel Henshall tried to expound in 1797. He had suggested that both the old and modern forms of the English language could actually sound the same if spoken in a certain way, whereas in the above example, they have been made to *appear* similar. But Henshall's *The Saxon and English Languages Reciprocally Illustrative of Each Other* received poor reviews, particularly in the *Gentleman's Magazine*, where Richard Gough, himself a noted antiquarian and Anglo-Saxon scholar, claimed Henshall simply did not have the qualifications to make such observations. But Henshall was at least trying to simplify an argument. Old English and Modern English were one and the same language. But in his over-simplification, he had ignored too many of the fundamental changes.

In Anglo-Saxon times English appears to have been split into four different dialects: Nothumbrian, Mercian, Kentish and West Saxon. These differences are mainly identifiable due to their variant spelling arrangements. After time, and perhaps as a result of the political rise to dominance of the West Saxon line of kings over the whole of Britain in the tenth century, the standard written language for the most part was the West Saxon dialect. This dialect in itself had an earlier form dating from around the time of Alfred (c.900) and a later form dating from around the time of Ælfric (c.1000). The point here is that English was already a clearly evolving language. In fact, case endings and inflections were already changing at the time of the Norman Conquest to the extent that there was an increasing reliance on prepositions and word order at the expense of noun inflexions (which had grown in form at the time of the Danish settlements of the north of England). Thus, it would become that much harder to read a piece of Old English and make sense of its structure as time went by. The standardisation of word order in sentence construction and the abandonment of all but a few inflexions after the Norman Conquest made the language more recognisable to modern eyes and ears. The influence of Norman French (itself a variant form of French) will have had something to do with this. Also, the introduction of a whole new set of loaned words from the French will have greatly enhanced the lexicon. In fact, the impact of French upon the vocabulary of English was profound.

But for all we have said about the changes in the language, there remain some intriguing signs that Old English did indeed have an active afterlife beyond 1066. Old English writing from the period after the Conquest is far from unknown. In fact, between 1066 and c.1200 there are over 50 surviving manuscripts written in Old English and a further 100 with Old English glosses or annotations. One man in particular has left enough evidence, enigmatic though it is, to suggest that people could work with and were still working with Old English. His disposition has given him the posthumous name 'the tremulous hand' of Worcester. He annotated some 20 surviving Anglo-Saxon manuscripts and provided around 50,000 glosses, usually Latin and rarely Middle English to Old English words. He is known to have copied a manuscript of Ælfric's Grammar and Glossary, too. Quite what his role was at Worcester is a mystery, but it is thought that he was probably engaged in some kind of pastoral or teaching work which will have freed him from the constraints of Latin and allowed him to work in the vernacular. But it remains the case that he needed to have learned Old English to have understood it properly. The canonisation of St Wulfstan at Worcester in 1203 may well have provided the springboard for the work of the tremulous hand. It is not necessarily the case that the scribe was a very old man with a memory of the old language from his youth. For this to have been the case he will have to have been unusually old at the time of his writing. It is more likely that his shaky hand was due to some sort of nervous affliction. However, his work is a remarkable and rare example of how Old English manuscripts could still be understood, with some effort, at the beginning of the thirteenth century.

So, if the spoken and written language was changing in medieval England, what of the memory of the Anglo-Saxon monarchs? Had there been anyone from that era who had stuck in the minds of the man in the street? It is argued that the institution of the Old English monarchy was still very much in the memory of the medieval mind.

THE MEMORY OF KINGS

Concerning this king, there is a vigorous tradition in England that he was the most law-abiding and best-educated ruler they have ever had.

William of Malmesbury. *Gesta Regum Anglorum*

The words of William of Malmesbury directed his reader to the legend of King Athelstan. William knew the story of King Alfred's grandson better perhaps than any other medieval historian, for Athelstan had been buried in Malmesbury and more or less called it his spiritual home. William even tells us that he had gazed upon the face of the king himself within his tomb. It is a piece of writing which captures two important aspects of the way in which the medieval mind viewed the Anglo-Saxon past in England. First, there was the extraordinary power of some of the kings, especially those who came immediately after Alfred, who had seen their influence extend beyond the borders of ancient Britannia into pastures new. Secondly, there was a preoccupation with the role of the monarchs as givers of law, sometimes expressing itself in the form of referrals to the old trials by ordeal. But this idea of the Saxons as great law-makers was a notion which eventually became linked to the powerful assertion that the Anglo-Saxon kings, in particular Alfred the Great, had been responsible for the notion of the common law.

All of these ideas were expressed by people in the medieval period in a number of ways: through poetry and song, and through a variety of legal and governmental documents. Malmesbury, however, gives us that rare insight into the view of the 'man in the street' as it were. There is no doubt at all that the Anglo-Saxon period of history loomed large in the minds of every-day medieval folk.

The fascination with King Athelstan[12] was not confined to the streets of Malmesbury of course. Writers such as the thirteenth-century Layamon recalled the king's great law-making capabilities and compared him to King Ine (688-726), another earlier Saxon king with a strong record in legislation. Indeed, the creation of the shires of England and the setting of the names of towns in Saxon runes are attributed to Athelstan. Moreover, the wide-scale issuing of law codes was not seen in medieval times in the way we might see it today. We might suppose, knowing what we know of the great struggles against pagan disorder in the ninth and tenth centuries, the codes were symbolic of a government struggling to keep the peace, but to the medieval mind they were symbolic of a great strength in kingship, of a ruler protecting his people. That strength of course, was borne of wisdom.

Alfred the Great and Athelstan had been wise rulers. This much was accepted in medieval times. The poem *The Owl and the Nightingale*, for example, written in around 1250 contained a great many Alfredian proverbs and included Alfred's words of wisdom to his son Edward the Elder among other things. In the Anglo-Norman poem *Gui de Warewic* of *c.*1230 the tale of Athelstan's struggle against the Danes is recounted for its contemporary audience. A champion, Gui, is chosen to fight against the Danish champion in traditional style. Although Athelstan is wise here, he tends towards indecision in this poem and here we begin to see the beginning of that particular king's demise in the minds of medieval writers as his well-remembered power becomes more and more abused in later works. The medieval poem *Athelston*, for example, written at the end of the fourteenth century, has the king as an almighty yet somewhat tyrannical ruler. Here, the audience is being warned of the dangers of an overmighty king. It would have been a message that made much sense to them, given that the reigning king of the time would have been Richard II (1377-99). So, wisdom, power and its potential abuse, preoccupied the medieval mind when it looked to the Anglo-Saxon past.

But there was one important medieval document, which was seized upon hundreds of years later in the seventeenth century, which displayed the power of a king and helped outline the nature of the ancient constitution, giving rise ultimately to the theory of the Norman Yoke. *The Mirror of Justices* is attributed to Andrew Horne and was written in around the 1290s. It places Alfredian power in the heart of London, an idea which the St Albans school of medieval historians were keen to promote. Here, in London Alfred convened his 'parliaments' twice a year according to Horne. Here, too, the form of appeal for treason could be found 'in old rolls of the time of King Alfred'. *The Mirror* was written to emphasise the sanctity of law and the falseness of judges which is why it includes the story that in one year, Alfred had had 44 judges hanged for giving false judgements.

The *Modus tenendi Parliamentum*, another popular legal document, also recalled the great law giving powers of the Anglo-Saxon period, this time referring to Edward the Confessor. In fact, as far as Rome was concerned it had always been Edward the Confessor who represented the more acceptable and powerful symbol of Anglo-Saxon kingship since it was he who conveniently, through his parentage, helped bridge the uncomfortable gap between the Anglo-Saxon and Norman periods. For this reason, and because his cult was propagated widely in the thirteenth and fourteenth centuries, Edward the Confessor has remained to this day a popular figure in the notion of Anglo-Saxon kingship.

But the idea of Anglo-Saxon kingship as expressed in material of the medieval era is given an airing in the metrical *Chronicle* written around 1300 by Robert of Gloucester. The *Chronicle* is written in Middle English and although it is a history of England, it is obsessed with the ideas surrounding the nature of kingship and government. Robert, who will have grown up during the baronial revolts of the mid-thirteenth century and who will have seen the constitutional aspects of English kingship hotly debated in political circles, treats the Anglo-Saxon era as a place in which to find the ideals or models of correct governance for his medieval audience. Robert's grievances centre on a desire for his 'Engelond' to return to a form of greater freedom for its people and for its traditional laws to be taken as the standard to underpin this freedom.[13] Robert was also aggrieved that the ecclesiastical role in medieval governance was being overlooked by the contemporary king. For his time, Robert of Gloucester was progressive. These issues would surface again in the great constitutional struggles of the early seventeenth century, but to witness them creating such an emotive piece of work in the late thirteenth and early fourteenth centuries might permit us to pose the question how much similar material from this era is lost to us and to what extent these issues occupied the minds of educated medieval Englishmen. Robert holds up King Alfred as an exemplar of kingship, paying particular attention to the importance of the young Alfred's visit to Rome and his anointing by the pope there. For Robert, Alfred was of the legitimate line of Cerdic, the very root of the English monarchy. The legitimacy of the sons of Cnut and of both

Harold II and William I is dismissed in an argument echoing that of Ailred of Rievaulx which centres on the rightfulness through blood lines alone of the claim of the young Edgar the Atheling, who was the son of Edward Ætheling the Exile, the son of the great Edmund Ironside. However, by recounting the fabled death-bed prophecy of Edward the Confessor, containing a vision of a green tree cut in half with branches which eventually meet up again symbolising the union of Saxon and Norman, Robert reconciles the argument in traditional fashion and concedes that the Henry III, the monarch at the heart of the current invective, is in fact through the marriage of Henry I to Matilda of Scotland (a descendant of Edgar) a legitimate monarch. It is the classic English art of compromise.

But there is clearly much wrong with Henry's monarchy and Robert is in no doubt as to where to lay the blame. The overbearing nature of the French-favouring monarchy goes back to the reigns of William the Conqueror and his sons. Magna Carta, or at least its later ratifications made during the reign of Henry III (1216-72) is referred to as a 'good old law' and Henry is castigated for having let these newly agreed liberties slip. But it is not just these lost liberties Robert wants restored. He even goes as far as saying, as surely Earl Godwin had said before him, that the 'French' (referring of course to the Normans) should simply leave England. Leaving aside this last xenophobic observation, there must surely have been in medieval England a great many people who shared Robert's general views about not only the impact of the Norman Conquest, but about the fact that England's monarchy and its legal mechanisms had their root in an Anglo-Saxon past. The men who struggled to demonstrate just this point in the sixteenth and seventeenth centuries were not creating an argument without its own historical evolution. The very fact that Robert was writing for a presumably wide audience and also in English provides testimony for the suggestion.

But not every king of Anglo-Saxon England survived with reputation intact into the medieval period. The reputation of King Æthelred II (979-1016), deserved or undeserved, began its decline before 1066 and the poor morale suffered by his countrymen during the Viking attacks on England is attributed by the scribes of the *Anglo-Saxon Chronicle* to the king himself. It is a theme picked up on by the author of the *South English Legendary* who opts for the popular belief that the king was a coward in the field of battle and suggests to us that he was not the brightest of leaders.

> So simple he was and so milde
> 150.61

> Of bataile he nolde noðing do
> Bote huld him ever stille
> 150.65

It is the exception which proves the rule. Æthelred's reign, as we know, was a very long and complicated one beset with threats from abroad; a complete political change in direction brought about by a Norman marriage alliance and internal struggles for power across the kingdom. Although in modern times there are more apologists for this king than was previously the case, the case against him in the medieval period and later seems to stem from a nationalistic notion that he had not done enough to protect England in time of crisis. In other words, the unfair argument against Æthelred would appear to have been a very Anglo-Saxon one.

SOME ACCIDENTAL ANGLO-SAXONISTS

Regardless of Æthelred's poor reputation, there was clearly an overwhelmingly positive identification with the Anglo-Saxon period in medieval England. It was reflected in both popular culture and in people's reflections on matters of law and religion. Towards the end of the medieval period there is some evidence for the existence of what should perhaps be described as 'proto-antiquarianism'. There were those whose interest in antiquity was of course motivated by their present concerns for their own cherished institutions, but whose work provides another insight into the continuing usefulness of the Anglo-Saxons.

A little like they had felt in the twelfth century, the monastic communities of the fifteenth century began to feel under threat from various quarters.

There were the secular canons, Lollards and litigious neighbours, tax collectors and interference from church administrators. One fourteenth-century monk even went as far as writing a tract which 'proved' that monasticism went back in time a good deal further than St Augustine's institution of the Regular Canons.[14] All this prompted a desire to reach back once again into the Anglo-Saxon past to provide proof of some sort of legitimacy for these monastic houses during difficult times. The idea was simple. The further back you could go, the more legitimate was the title you had to your privileges and rights. Consequently and certainly in legal terms, the more edified you felt. Of course, there were blatant forgeries of various charters in circulation, some scarcely with their ink dry, but the histories which were written in this era represent on the whole earnest attempts to provide, however political the motivation, a sense of continuity from the Anglo-Saxon to medieval eras, much the same as it had been in the twelfth century.

This does not mean, however, that even the most thoughtful scholars of their day did not have an occasional flight of fancy. Writing primarily to defend the privileges of St Augustine's at Canterbury, Thomas Elmham (d.*c*.1420), a veteran of Agincourt, revealed his knowledge of Old English by supplying a Latin translation of an Anglo-Saxon charter and further revealed an interest in an old tale which allowed him to demonstrate St Augustine's privileges. The tale, known as the tale of *Domne Eafe's Hind* went like this. There was a Minster on the Isle of Thanet of which Domne Eafe was the founder and the first abbess. After it had been destroyed by the Danes, Cnut had given its lands to St Augustine's. The old legend was that King Edgar had promised to give the Minster the area delineated by the course of the hind running across the island, but for his own selfish reasons a thegn named Thunor had tried to stop-up the hind. The ground opened up and swallowed him. In Elmham's day, the great pit into which Thunor had sunk could still be seen. So, there was still physical evidence for this divine intervention and this was part of Elmham's argument. Like many such tales from the monasteries in this era, Elmham's is a parochial one which picks the relevant material from the Anglo-Saxon past and places it within the framework of a contemporary political or legal struggle, but as we have already seen with the activities of the monasteries in the twelfth century, it is by no means unusual. If this time-honoured habit of dipping into the Anglo-Saxon past for selfish reasons was still prevailing in the fifteenth century for the monasteries, then on the secular side of things, something a little different seemed to be afoot.

John Rous (1411-91), John Hardyng (1378-1465) and William Worcestre (1415-c.83) were three figures with slightly differing motives whose contributions bore more resemblance to the pioneering work of John Leland and his contemporaries than to the historians of the monasteries. There was still a kind of parochialism in their approach and an amusing tendency towards reckless speculation and the acceptance of legend as historical evidence, but their efforts are important nonetheless.

Rous, who was educated at Oxford and became a chaplain to the earl of Warwick, was motivated by an objection to the enclosure movement to write his *Historia Regum Angliae*. His work, including two Warwick Rolls, demonstrated a keen interest in the histories of both Warwick and Oxford, places with which he was familiar. Writing around 1477, on the history of the earls of Warwick, he begins with the legendary forebears of the earls, the ancient British. He goes through the subsequent eras including some very fine depictions of these figures in armour and costume. In fact, his approach is revealing. The Anglo-Saxon earls he draws in shortened mailcoats with no plate armour showing a rare insight into the history of the development of body armour most unusual for its time. In his *Historia* Rous depicts Æthelflead, the Lady of the Mercians, in a costume which he knows is historic, but which bears more resemblance to the costume shown on the effigy of Catherine, wife of Thomas Beauchamp, earl of Warwick (1329-69), an effigy with which Rous would have been familiar. John Rous was also one of the first writers to assert King Alfred's claim to be the founder of Oxford University, thus sparking a debate over an issue which we will shortly observe continued for many centuries with particular attention paid to it in the seventeenth century. The date of the foundation of Oxford University, he said, was 873. It had been made at the behest of St Neot who wished for the establishment of a place of learning for grammar, the arts and theology. Three halls had apparently existed: Parva Aula (in the High Street), Aula Minor (in the north of the city) and Aula Magna (again, in the High Street). Much, it should be said, would be made of all this in years to come.

John Hardyng's 'antiquarianism', if that is what we should call it, was mainly refined to extensive historical research exercises to explore England's relationship with Scotland at a time of strife between the two. In fact, Henry V (1413-22) sent him to Scotland in 1418 where he stayed for three years. Another veteran of Agincourt, Hardyng endured many difficulties for much of his life, particularly on his Scottish travels. He was a great manipulator of history. Some of his papers on the England and Scotland debate were works of pure fiction, but he managed to produce a rhyming *Chronicle of England*, shot through with Arthurian legend, which between the 1430s and 1460s changed its story to please his various patrons and kept the legend alive.

William Worcestre, who had also been motivated by the desire to please a king by urging him to prosecute his claim to the throne of France, was only able to concentrate on wholly antiquarian matters towards the very end of his life. He had been the hard-working secretary to Sir John Fastolf, whose estate kept Worcestre busy even after Fastolf's death. But there was something new in the way that Worcestre did it. His approach foreshadowed the great Itineraries of the sixteenth and seventeenth centuries. In 1478, he began a journey motivated by pure historical interest which took him from Norfolk to London and then to St Michael's Mount in Cornwall. The next year he was in Norfolk again and the year after that he went from London to Glastonbury where he made enquiries for the chronicles of King Arthur. He recorded churches and inscriptions along the way and if his Itinerary is the father of those of the subsequent centuries, so his interest in topographical observations would be repeated too. Whilst Worcestre's contribution to the memory of the Anglo-Saxons remains limited to the topographical and architectural observations he made on his journeys, his approach in the form of the country's first real itinerant antiquary is of great importance. There would soon come to pass the greatest destruction of England's historical resources in the form of the Dissolution of the Monasteries and the break-up of the great monastic libraries. It would take men of the same energy as Worcestre to piece together the jigsaw of early English history after all this destruction, but their motives would be very different. Before we examine these first pioneers of a movement which has come to be called 'Anglo-Saxonism', we must first understand the drama of the Dissolution and what it meant to the historical record of the country.

3

THE RISE OF THE SCHOLARS

THE DISPERSAL OF THE MONASTIC LIBRARIES

It is difficult to overstate the impact of the great upheaval in English political and religious life in the sixteenth century. The country's monarch was in the process of masterminding an independence from Rome during an era of humanism, increasing intellectualism and, as it would prove to be, the divisive printing press. There would be a great interest amongst the confident English protestant community in the manuscripts which had been housed by the monastic libraries. Within these exclusive places resided the means by which Protestantism could be justified. Ancient Anglo-Saxon texts demonstrated insular peculiarities in English Christianity. This interest, coupled with the notion held by Protestants that the monasteries were corrupt and wicked places, would be the driving force behind the creation of an entirely new form of historical enquiry. The English antiquary was born.

The royal commissioners who were appointed to visit the monasteries to begin dismantling their wealth started their work in 1535, although some dispersal of books had already taken place as early as 1530. Legal clearance in terms of the appropriate acts of parliament arrived in 1536 and there was another visitation to the monasteries in 1538, after which time 12 houses still held out. But on 23 March 1540, Waltham, the last of them all, fell. At this time when the Church was undergoing its greatest ever change in England, there grew a fascination among some men with the history of England.

The interest was, of course, spurred by the Dissolution of the Monasteries and the subsequent uncontrolled circulation of many manuscripts, few of which came home to rest in libraries and many of which were used as scrap or found inserted in the bindings of other books. But enough material saw the light of day and was being read for the first time by a new set of eyes.

The scale of the destruction was colossal. Worcester held over 600 books at the time of the Dissolution and a mere fragment survived representing around one per cent of the total. At first, the monastic libraries were rather passed over by those whose remit was to rob the Church of its riches. They preferred to take portable or actual wealth instead of material of intellectual value. But the libraries of early sixteenth-century England had been by far the largest repositories for books of any kind in England notwithstanding the recent increase in printed material around the country which Caxton's invention of the printing press had made possible in 1476. These places contained the necessary service books and liturgical documentation used in daily ecclesiastical life, but also included on their shelves the great histories of the earlier medieval periods and the writings of influential churchmen such as Ælfric, abbot of Eynsham (c.955-c.1020), a great writer of homilies, saints' lives, treatises and most importantly of all, a great translator of biblical material into the vernacular.

It is argued that from about 1350 the standard of monastic scholarship in England was lagging behind that of the continent.[1] In Italy, for example, there were scholars who regularly trawled the monastic houses for ancient literature, but on the eve of the destruction of the monastic libraries no such English equivalent had yet become active. So, when the attention of the destroyer was turned upon these libraries, the loss to posterity was immense.

A great private collector of monastic manuscripts, John Bale (1495-1563) found himself very much embroiled in the turmoil of the Reformation. He was a former Carmelite friar who subsequently rejected Catholicism and became a radical preacher in London in the 1530s, taking his opportunity to attack Catholic iconography wherever he saw it. In 1540, after his patron Cromwell had fallen, Bale fled abroad and continued to write of the corruption of the Catholic Church. Later in his career he went to Ireland where his missionary zeal and anti-Catholicism earned him the title 'Bilious Bale'. But outside of Bale's writings about the struggles of his time, he was also a prolific playwright and historian. He had even managed to give King John an extraordinary makeover presenting him as a man who loved his people and who, of course, had defied the pope. He wrote the *Actes of Englysh Votaryes* of 1546 and 1551 and worked closely with John Leland (1506-52) whose *New Year's Gift to Henry VIII* Bale printed and prefaced. Bale seems to have had an eye for the historic value of these manuscripts despite the fact that he was clearly motivated by Protestantism to pursue them. True history and true Christianity were inextricably linked and they were to be found in the ancient texts. Bale also believed that preserving the books might mean that the view held abroad that England was in some way a 'barbarous nacyon' would be allayed. Despite the fact that he recommended the use of the printing press in the copying of the ancient manuscripts in order to disperse them to a wider audience now that they were out in the open, Bale urged that there should be:

> In every shyre of England but one soleyme lybrarye, to preservacyon of those notable workes and preferrement of good lernynges in our posteryte.

Bale also commented that some of the laymen who purchased the great libraries had done so purely with the intention of turning them into a source for scrap paper:

> A great nombre of them whych purchased those supertycyous mansyons, resrved of those lybrarye bokes, some to serve theyr jakes, some to scoure candelstyckes, and some to rubbe their bootes.

He lamented that the books and manuscripts were turning up in odd places unrecognised and uncared for. They were to be found

> ... in stacyoners and bokebynders store houses, some in grosers, sope sellers, taylers and other occupiers shoppes, some in shyppes ready to be carried over the sea into Flaunders to be solde.

John Aubrey (1626-97), the famous antiquary, said that on one day in the sixteenth century leaves of illuminated manuscripts from the despoiled abbey at Malmesbury could be seen fluttering like butterflies down the streets of the town, a story almost certainly told to him by his grandfather Isaac Lyte (1577-1660). The glovers of the town of Malmesbury were using manuscripts to wrap their goods in, without a care for what they might be.[2] But Isaac Lyte's sorrow was other men's delight. The very fact that ancient manuscripts were now in open circulation meant that there were some individuals whose curiosity could be satisfied by the noble art of collecting. These people to whom the epithet of the first Anglo-Saxon scholars can be applied varied a little in their motives, but were not few in number.

THE FIRST GENERATION

As early as 1533, John Leland, who was the chaplain and librarian to Henry VIII received his own royal backing for his antiquarian activities having asked the king in his own words to 'peruse and dylygentlye to searche all the libraryes of monasteries and colegies of thys youre noble realme.' Leland shared Bale's concerns about the break up of the historic material from the monastic libraries and tried in vain to alert Cromwell to the matter as early as 1536.

As King's Antiquary, Leland found himself in a position which had neither predecessor nor successor. As such, out of his contemporaries like Bale, John Prise (c.1502-55), Robert Talbot (c.1505-58) and Robert Recorde (c.1510-58), Leland was the only early antiquary with official royal backing. His two main works, the famous *Itinerary* and his *Collectanea*, reveal a passionate and energetic man. He travelled around the country describing his travels and the historical things he saw. Commenting on the magnificent Malmesbury Abbey, just a few years before its destruction, he noted that it was 'a right magnificent thing'.

Leland was also a collector of manuscripts. However, we do not quite know what exactly got into the collection he was in the process of establishing before his death. At Henry VIII's death Bartholomew Traheron oversaw the weeding out of a number of unspecified manuscripts, although it remains probable that many of Leland's collection found their way into the collections of the second generation of antiquaries of the sixteenth century. Leland's activities supply us with a certain amount of information for the early years of the dispersal of the manuscripts. The letter he wrote to Cromwell on 16 July 1536, and his *New Year's Gift* to Henry VIII in 1546, and John Bale's own preface to the 1549 version of the *Gift* provide us with insights as to the importance and concerns of Leland in the preservation of ancient material. In fact, letters from Bale to Matthew Parker (1504-75), archbishop of Canterbury, and from Parker to William Cecil (1520-98) reveal a great desire from the Protestant community to preserve the written material of the former monastic libraries.

Leland was a dedicated man. Bale tells us that Leland learned the ancient British tongue in the course of his studies as well as Old English (which he called 'Saxonyshe') and there is no good reason to doubt this, although Old English notes that can be found in Leland's hand are but a few. There are a few jottings in the *Collectanea* and his interest in this regard seems to have been restricted to topographical place-name issues which presumably will have helped him in his travels.

It is difficult to imagine where English antiquarianism would be without John Leland. Sadly, after 1547 he was to make little more contribution to the discipline and it was said of him 'by a most pitiful accident he fell beside his wits'. His descent into madness notwithstanding, Leland's achievements were lasting. There were many who came after him who will have been clutching the very books which had passed through Leland's hands.

Robert Talbot, whose valuable notebook survives in the collections of Corpus Christi College, Cambridge, was an avid early collector and antiquary. He had been the Cathedral Treasurer at Norwich and was made prebendary in 1547. At least 10 Old English manuscripts are thought to have passed through his hands including gospels, the work of Bede, *Orosius*, the *Anglo-Saxon Chronicle* and a number of homilies. His transcriptions of his material indicate that there were other things he saw which have subsequently been lost. A little like Leland, his annotations reveal an interest in the names of places and a keen topographical eye, but there are also one or two religiously motivated annotations which foreshadow the work of the forthcoming generation of Anglo-Saxon scholars of the era of Matthew Parker.

As for the Welshman Robert Recorde, to some his efforts in ancient matters may seem insignificant when compared to his contribution towards mathematics and astronomy. But Recorde's interest in Old English was intensive and on one occasion it happily coincided with his other occupation. Not only did one of Recorde's manuscripts contain an abridged version of Matthew Paris's *Chronica maiora* to which he supplemented the account of the years 449-871 by adding into the margins 25 extracts from two Old English texts (the *Anglo-Saxon Chronicle* version C and the West Saxon genealogy which prefaces the Old English translation of Bede's *Historia ecclesiastica*), but he also seems to have taken an interest in the Old English text *Orosius*. This latter describes the visit to Alfred's court of the Scandinavian sailor and trader Othere, whose great voyages in the northern seas around and beyond the coasts of Norway and Sweden are packed with navigational detail which would raise the eyebrows of any astronomer. Recorde is known to have mentioned to the Muscovy Company, on the occasion of their own successful charting of north-eastern waters, that he had known of no other such useful work since the days of Othere's travels. It is an interesting revelation in the context of these early days of Anglo-Saxonism, since it hints at the possibility that there were others like Recorde, who had reason to read and absorb the texts of Old English manuscripts, but who may not have left us with a record of their activities.

There was an attempt made under the reign of the Catholic Mary Tudor (1553-58) to further the cause of the preservation of the ancient manuscripts from the monastic libraries, but it was not an effort which had royal backing. Instead, the impetus came from the mathematician, magical occultist and intellectual John Dee who later became a close advisor to Queen Elizabeth I (1558-1603). On 15 January 1556 he presented *A Supplication for the Recovery and Preservation of Ancient Writers and Monuments* to Queen Mary in which he proposed to establish a commission to search the country for manuscripts which could then be researched under royal authority. A new royal library, Dee insisted, would do the queen no harm at all, neither in this life or the next. But it fell on deaf ears. Dee was just a little ahead of his time, but not by much. For all his dalliance in strange intellectual pastimes concerning the occult, Dee had seen something which others would shortly see. The manuscripts of ancient England were not simply tools for a political or theological campaign, but were in fact a valuable learning resource in their own right.

PARKER AND HIS CIRCLE

It was probably as a result of the collecting activities of Talbot that both Leland and Recorde found themselves adequately furnished with material. When these three died in the 1550s, there was a brief gap to the 1560s when the next generation of pioneers began their work in earnest. The collecting instinct very much characterised the work of the Parker era, but there were new and important themes surrounding the motivations of these men. An intense interest in Old English legal texts and in versions of the *Anglo-Saxon Chronicle*, were accompanied by an approach designed to extract historical religious precedent from Anglo-Saxon texts as Matthew Parker (1504-75), the archbishop of Canterbury, looked to consolidate his *Ecclesia Anglicana*.

The advancing technology of the age also made this generation of Anglo-Saxon scholars the first to print contemporary editions of Old English texts. Laurence Nowell (*c.*1520-*c.*1570), William Lambarde (1536-1601), Matthew Parker and John Joscelyn (1525-1603) were the main players on the stage of an extraordinary academic drama. Behind this group people like John Foxe (1516-87), who worked closely with Parker, were promulgating religious works of Protestant zeal which claimed among other things that it was Rome that had shifted ground on important doctrinal affairs and that the Protestant view was more in keeping with the origins of Christianity in England. In 1563, Foxe published the first edition of *Acts and Monuments of these Latter and Perillous Dayes, touching Matters of the Church*, which soon became known as *The Book of Martyrs*. It was a widely read work centred upon the persecution and martyrdom of Christians. Foxe was keen to point out that the Catholics had rubbed out what they could from Latin texts to support their case, but had left alone the Old English ones because they 'knew them not'. He edited Matthew Parker's *The Gospels of the Fower evangelists translated in the olde Saxons tyme out of Latin into the vulgare toung of the Saxons, newly collected out of Auncient Monuments of the sayd Saxons, and new published testimonie of the same*. People, said Foxe, were deliberately misunderstanding the past. 'New thynges were reported for old' and without the proper elucidation of the ancient Anglo-Saxon texts it seemed that 'Truth hath lacked witnesse, tyme wanted light'. So, a growing sense of nationalism and an overt religious necessity provided the motor for the age of Matthew Parker. Who then, were the key figures in this revolution of scholarly endeavour and what did they publish?

Laurence Nowell, a keen traveller and cartographer, began exercising his interest in Old English studies in 1562. He had joined the house of William Cecil, Queen Elizabeth's Secretary of State, serving as a tutor to Cecil's ward the young Edward de Vere. Cecil's own motivations in the revival of the study of Anglo-Saxon texts was that he was anxious to secure historical material which would help him feed the growing nationalism and supply for himself background material which would strengthen Queen Elizabeth's position. By 1567 Nowell had sailed for the continent, but he had left behind a great deal of his work. He had transcribed a number of Old English manuscripts and compiled his *Vocabularium Saxonicum*, a dictionary of some 6000 entries which amounts to the earliest contribution to Old English lexicography. Unlike many others of his generation, Nowell had a passion for Old English poetry and his signature and the date of 1563 are to be found on the manuscript of the famous Anglo-Saxon poem *Beowulf*. His hand is also to be spotted on the *Exeter Book*. Mainly though, his work concentrated upon the legal side of matters and he transcribed Alfred and Ine's law codes. In fact, Nowell's transcription of these laws plus his additions of variant material rank as the earliest critical appraisals of Old English legal affairs. His appreciation that the preservation of ancient laws might have some use in the present preceded the notable interests of the numerous early seventeenth-century constitutional lawyers and in this regard Nowell deserves to be seen as a pioneer, way ahead of his time.

Nowell's friend William Lambarde came from a slightly different background but was no less important. Trained at Lincoln's Inn, this lawyer turned historian was one of the earliest county historians, devoting himself to a *Perambulation of Kent* in 1576 in which he investigated many aspects of the ancient kingdom and, like his predecessors in the study of English history, once again gave due attention to topography and place-names. On his departure from England in 1567, Nowell had left his research material and transcriptions with Lambarde, who was not a man to simply store them away. Instead, he added to the material in his possession and even provided additional entries for Nowell's *Vocabularium*.

With his legal training it was hardly surprising that Lambarde picked up on the legal work of Nowell. He soon set about completing the material he had before him and by 1568 he published it as *Archaionomia, sive de priscis Anglorum Legibus Libri*.[3] The work covered over 12 Old English law codes with Latin translations and went a long way towards improving the standing of Alfred and the West Saxon tradition at the expense of other kingdoms, notably Kent. At around the same time as Lambarde was pulling together Nowell's work, John Day, a printer of Aldersgate, was making his own piece of history. At the behest of Matthew Parker, he published in 1566 *A Testimonie of Antiquitie, Shewing the Ancient Fayth in the Church of England Touching the Sacrament of the Body and Bloude of the Lorde here publikely preached and also receaued in the Saxons tyme, aboue 600 yeares agoe*. Here, for the first time Day had used a special Anglo-Saxon font in his printing process. It would be used again. *A Testimonie* was a work packed with meaning for Parker.

The lasting impact of the industrious efforts of Matthew Parker upon English history cannot be overestimated. As for his approach to the old Anglo-Saxon texts, much the same could and should be said. Between 1566 and 1574 he was involved in one way or another in the publication of nine of them. Ably assisted by his Latin secretary John Joscelyn, Parker applied himself with great energy and after the dust of the Dissolution had settled his endeavours to track material down earned him the sobriquet 'Nosey Parker'. Clearly, the archbishop was a man on a mission. On 4 July 1568 Parker had written to Cecil to ask him to get letters from the Privy Council to allow him permission to write to private owners of ancient manuscripts. He wished to have the power to demand that they temporarily hand over their documents for inspection and that they should only have them back on the proviso that they would preserve them. He saw in the Anglo-Saxon literary heritage the potential to prove that Canterbury and Rome were permanently split, that the position of the new English Church was firmly rooted in pre-Conquest history. In *A Testimonie* the preface to his readers points out exactly where he is getting it all from: 'Thou hast here ... written in the Old Englyshe or Saxon speech ... a testimonye of verye auncient tyme' which demonstrated 'the judgement of learned men in this matter, in the dayes of the Saxons.'

Parker's doctrinal concerns were what drove him to become the great preserver of ancient manuscripts. The true nature of bread and wine at the Eucharist, the legality of clerical marriage, and the use of the vernacular in ecclesiastical writings were the three main issues he campaigned over and his stance on these was outlined in Day's publication of *A Testimonie*. Here, Parker referred himself on the issue of transubstantiation to one of Ælfric's Easter homilies and deduced that the Anglo-Saxon Church had not necessarily taken transubstantiation at face value. *A Testimonie* also included some Old English versions of the Lord's Prayer and the Ten Commandments. Parker stated that he thought there was nothing at all new in teaching the English people the articles of their faith in their own language. Nor was he prepared to accept criticism on the subject of celibacy. He pointed out that it had only been from the time of Archbishop Lanfranc (1070-89) that the issue had arisen. Parker, being married himself, had extra reason to prosecute this difference with Rome.

But the archbishop, who is often connected purely with a religious zeal in his work, was in fact concerned with the study of Anglo-Saxon history as a whole. He is known to have revealed to his readership that he thought there was great merit in the study of Old English documents if people were to better understand the history of English institutions in general. It is an aspect of Parker's wider appreciation of Anglo-Saxon history which is not often acknowledged.

John Joscelyn's interests in all this seem to have been two-fold. He certainly had a keen eye for the Old English language and like Nowell he paid close attention to the variant versions of the *Anglo-Saxon Chronicle* (which, unlike Nowell, he annotated with his own hand). Furthermore, he heavily contributed to Parker's *De antiquitate Britannicæ ecclesiæ & priulegiis Cantuariensis* in which he penned extensive biographies of the archbishops of Canterbury.

Joscelyn's Old English language interests were intense enough to lead him, along with John Parker the archbishop's son, to write an Old English Grammar, which was passed from Cotton to William Camden (1551-1623) and subsequently never heard of again. His contribution in the form of the compilation of word lists was more lasting. His extensive studies of ancient manuscripts led to a two-volume dictionary of over 20,000 entries. The dictionary found its way into the famous library of Sir Robert Cotton where it provided inspiration for a number of scholars of the next generation. Joscelyn and his associates had provided a platform for Anglo-Saxon studies. The *Ecclesia Anglicana* had lifted the Anglo-Saxons from the 'also-rans' of British history and given them a role from which there was no turning back, but their adventure was far from over.

THE ELIZABETHAN SOCIETY OF ANTIQUARIES

A number of our Anglo-Saxonists were closely associated with the Elizabethan Society of Antiquaries, the forerunner of its early eighteenth-century cousin. The society, which ultimately sputtered to halt in the early seventeenth century, is of particular note to us here because it demonstrates in its surviving evidence the direction of historical enquiry at the time. Founded around 1586, the same year as Camden published his *Britannica*, the institution known as the College of Antiquaries, full of 'persons of great worth', comprised mainly gentlemen. There was an honourable exception to this rule, however, in the form of John Stowe (1525-1605). Stowe, a Londoner who made a transcription of Leland's *Itinerary* in 1576, was a studious man who seems to have gained a reputation he did not quite deserve. He worked on a summary of the *Chronicles and Annals of England* and a number of other works, but Spelman, when writing to William Dugdale (1605-86) in later years said of him 'we are beholding to messrs. Speed and Stowe for stitching up our English history'. It was an oblique and sarcastic reference to Stowe's trade as a tailor.

Poor John Stowe aside, the society counted among its membership some significant figures who, with their emphasis on ancient charters and law codes, would define the nature of historical enquiry for generations. Their approach to their work represented the very beginnings of what in the next century would become the great debate over the Ancient Constitution. They included Robert Cotton (1571-1631); Henry Spelman (1562-1641); Francis Tate (1560-1616); William Camden (1551-1623); Francis Thynne (c.1545-1608) and Arthur Agarde (1540-1615). The occupations of the gentlemen, however, were not particularly diverse. Their professional interests coloured their research, but their group approach is interesting all the same. Most of them were at one time or another lawyers, many of them were knights and two of them were noblemen. Essentially secular in nature they engaged themselves, perhaps for the first time in English history, in group research within a structured and formal environment. For some time they held their meetings at Derby House which since 1555 had become home to the College of Heralds who were important members of the society themselves. After 1590, however, they met at the home of Sir Robert Cotton, who although still young at the time was to have a seminal influence on the course of historical preservation of manuscripts in England. Camden was there too, often imposing himself on proceedings, but always there was a formalised approach to the issue of historical research which had not been there in the previous few decades.

Surviving accounts of the topics discussed at the Elizabethan Society of Antiquaries reveal the obsession. The history of land tenureship and land division was a favourite subject as well as the nature of the antiquity of some of the great offices and titles of England. On 27 November 1590 they sat to discuss 'Of what Antiquity the name of Dux or duke is in England & what is the estate thereof' and 'What is the Antiquitye and exposition of the word Sterlingorum [sic] or Sterling', subjects which in each case would have propelled the discussion back to a time before the Norman Conquest. The next year, however, saw a debate upon the very essence of the Anglo-Saxon argument as members sought to establish how the ancient shires of England had been created and who had been responsible for it. Thynne argued convincingly, using William of Malmesbury and the now discredited Ingulf as sources, that King Alfred had been responsible for it all. This was a notion which would pervade history for centuries to come. But in the same room there sat some dissenters to the idea. One Thomas Talbot argued that Alfred cannot have been in a position to make such sweeping reforms across his kingdom, although others took a more strident view and suggested the whole thing went back to before even Alfred. It does not matter who was right or wrong, the important thing is that it was being discussed by learned men. It is our first example of the discussion of issues which came to split the entire country in just a few decades time.

The meetings were not very frequent however. There were three more in 1591, one in 1592, four in 1594, one in 1595, one in 1598 (the gap here being attributable to an outbreak of plague in London), five in 1599 and five more in 1600. Of the last meetings a record of 13 February 1600-01 survives entitled 'The Antiquity, use and Ceremonies of Lawful Combattes [sic] in England' revealing once again the professional concerns of a majority of the membership.

The society's preoccupation with the antiquity of the laws, customs and institutions of England and with the principal of precedent in historical politics had defined them. In fact, it was precisely this approach which got the members into hot water when Spelman tried in vain to re-convene the society in 1614. Spelman had noted that the king had quickly developed 'a mislike of our society'. When we examine what happened next in the battle between the king and his subjects, this statement will not surprise us.

Despite their disposition to concentrate upon historical precedent and not to look into the more important question of historical contexts,[4] the society did at least understand the importance of dedicated research. It even went as far as proposing an 'Academy for the Study of Antiquity and History Founded by Queen Elizabeth' in *c*.1600. It was a visionary concept. Public documents were to be brought into public possession, the right to access them guaranteed. Sir Robert Cotton's own library would have formed the basis of such an academy had it ever seen fruition, but unfortunately it did not. However, as an example of how far the study of English history had come in a few short decades its mere proposition speaks volumes. As the progress of the Society ground to halt amid royal suspicion in 1607, Spelman among others was beginning his journey into developing historical contexts for his arguments. In short, a new age of historical scholarship was dawning and the Anglo-Saxons would continue to play a role at the centre of it all.

4

THE COMMON MAN SPEAKS

THE ANGLO-SAXONS AND THE ANCIENT CONSTITUTION

There may or may not be something hidden in the evidence for the struggles between king and commoner in the decades surrounding the English Civil War. It may be the case that the remonstrances of the common man against the so-called Norman Yoke had a deeper and longer popular memory than we might assume. But we must make no mistake about it. The Anglo-Saxons were used in an overtly political way during this period and those who used them felt passionately about it. These were not issues debated in the parlour or at a debating society. These were issues fought over in the courtroom and on the battlefield. Blood would be spilled. A country was at war with itself.

England in the seventeenth century found itself right at the very heart of European political thought. The first major country of the western world to have its own revolution so to speak, the English argument was heard over the world. In terms of the ways in which the Anglo-Saxons were being used, there was a vital shift from what had gone before. Instead of a philosophical argument, it was being pointed out that the effects of the Norman Conquest were so tangible in contemporary life and so related to legal issues in the seventeenth century that they could be brought into a constitutional struggle. Anglo-Saxon England became a heavily politicised subject thrust into the heart of the debate about the future of a nation against the background of a perceived overbearing and absolutist monarchy in the form of James I (1603-25) and Charles I (1625-49).

There had been rumblings of anti-Normanism in the previous century and we must consider the notion that because these enigmatic notices of discontent had emanated from the illiterate classes, we may have been denied a great deal of written evidence which might suggest that in the centuries before the seventeenth the issue was just as sore as it evidently would become. Thomas Starkey, writing in the 1530s in his *Dialogue between Pole and Lupset* has his characters discuss the tyranny of Norman rule and the fact that matters pertaining to the common law were always discussed and deliberated upon in French. Pole even went as far as declaring it to be a shame 'to be governed by the laws given to us of such a barbarous nation as the Normans be.'[1]

But by the seventeenth century there were several arguments going on. First, there was the theory of the Ancient Constitution which claimed that the common law of England was a pre-Conquest idea and that the Saxons had ruled through representative institutions.[2] Then there was the counter argument given by the royalists that William the Conqueror had ruled by right of conquest and therefore the king, his descendant, had the perfect right to impose arbitrary taxations on things like property. Secondly, there was the theory of the Norman Yoke which pitted the common man against crown, Church and landed gentry as well as the monarch. Then, on the more radical wing came those who believed that ancient or not, all current and prevailing laws were the badge of the Norman Conquest and that they should go. It was a certainly a colourful time.

So, what was 'the Ancient Constitution'? It was an idea that became something of a mantra for the Whig movement. The theory was simple enough. Before 1066 the English people had existed in a more or less free and equal state and most importantly of all had been governed by those representative institutions. After the Conquest, the liberty of the English had been taken away from them and tyranny had been the replacement. Ever since, or so it seemed, the English had struggled against the tyranny to restore the balance. Both Sir Edward Coke (1552-1634) and John Pym (1584-1643) took the view that in Old English times, the power of the king had been limited and so it should be again. They saw the Norman

Conquest as having broken a natural political discourse between the king and his people but they also saw something of a restoration of those people's rights in Magna Carta, a regaining of equilibrium, so to speak.

But here we see the great paradox of Anglo-Saxonism. It was entirely possible for those who opposed the monarchy on the grounds of the Norman Yoke argument to express their Anglo-Saxon identity in terms of the disinherited or the fettered captive. Whereas, there were royalists in the form of John Spelman, King Alfred's first biographer, and William Somner, a loyalist Anglo-Saxon scholar who could claim that the mandate for the monarchy also had its roots in the Anglo-Saxon period. Alfred the Great, for example, could and did become the darling of both Whig and Tory alike. It is a theme we will return to when we look at the American representation of the Anglo-Saxons and examine the ways in which the enemies of the British monarchy used their own Anglo-Saxon links as justification for their actions. The Anglo-Saxons were proving to be most versatile.

The work of a number of lawyers formed the basis for the argument of the Ancient Constitution. Coke was, of course, among them. Lord Chief Justice of the Common Pleas from 1606-13, Coke had written many legal reports between 1600-15. In 1621 he had told the House of Commons that the common law had already been in place before the Norman Conquest, picking up on a theme he had stressed many years earlier to Queen Elizabeth I. But it is in his *Institutes of the Laws of England* (1628) that his greatest contribution to this debate was made, much to the consternation of Charles I. Here, Coke reviewed early English laws in his preface to the eighth part of the work. He was keen to point out that the Norman kings and those dynasties which followed them had ruled with frequent references to the confirmation and upholding of the laws of Edward the Confessor. In his preface to the ninth part *The Mirror of Justices* is also woven into the argument as is the legislative record of King Alfred and his creation of the shires of England. The message was clear. Coke had brought into the fray the twin notions of government by representative institution and the continuity of the common law. Even the security of one's own property was safeguarded by the common law, he argued.

So, on the one side you had patriotism, Protestantism, the continuity of the law and the defence of representative institutions, whilst on the other you had conservatism, royalism and absolutism. But the theory of the Ancient Constitution itself had a fault line running down its middle. There were those who took the view, like Philip Hunton in his *A Treatise on Monarchy* of 1643, that the year 1066 had not been a particularly significant one in terms of the law, arguing that there had been a good deal of continuity particularly on the matter of trial by jury and basing this whole notion on the fact that William the Conqueror had been accepted as king by the people. But there were radicals who saw things differently. There had indeed been a breach in continuity in 1066 argued Henry Parker, among others. From that time the English people had struggled to restrict the power of the monarchy and restore their ancient rights. Magna Carta was held by some to be an example of such a struggle. Both views did, however, see the common law and the Ancient Constitution as an Anglo-Saxon beast. Taken to its extremes the argument was eventually pushed, not by the common lawyers or parliamentarians, but by the common man to the point that the very law itself represented the oppressive boot of the conqueror.

Parliament, of course, won the Civil War. It found itself in a position to use the old argument of ruling by right of conquest to do a number of things, but for some it did not do enough. Nathaniel Bacon's *Historical Discourse of the Uniformity of the Government of England* (1647 with a continuation in 1651) was one of the more significant publications during the interregnum. Bacon argued that the Normans had made royal government too aristocratic. He also said that from a distance the Anglo-Saxon form of government might look like a monarchy but when it was closely inspected it revealed itself to be a democracy. Inevitably, Bacon implicated by association the descendants of the Norman lords who had become 'the chief instruments of keeping kings above and people beneath'. The Anglo-Saxons had indeed had a monarchy, but Bacon deliberately played down the extent of its power. It was necessary for him to do this. For John Hare, Bacon and for the Levellers the Norman tradition was one of an overbearing monarchy. Although this institution was indisputably an Old English one, the notion of tyranny by any of the Old English kings could not be stomached for one moment. Bacon went as far as he thought he could go in acknowledging the existence of an Anglo-Saxon monarchy, but seemed to relegate their status to that of field commanders during difficult times, an ideal way of inspiring respect whilst reducing the actual role played by the kings in Anglo-Saxon society.

Sir Henry Spelman had been another to throw his weight into the argument by writing a tract upon the *Ancient Government of England* and another entitled *Of Parliaments*. But it was John Selden (1584-1654) who gained a reputation for being an expert on the Ancient Constitution, helped in part not just by the quality of his research, but by its sheer volume. In 1607 Selden wrote his *Analecton Anglobritannicon* which was published in 1615 and that same year he had written *England's Epinomis* which was not published until 1683, but his most consummate approach was in his 1610 publication entitled *Jani Anglorum Facies Altera* which dealt with the progress of English law down to Henry II (up to 1189). Selden, whose earliest patron had been Sir Robert Cotton, was a remarkable intellectual whose legal and parliamentary activities got him into some hot water. He was the architect of the Protestation of the Commons in 1621 which had asserted to King James the rights of parliament over the monarch. Selden paid for all this with a brief period of incarceration during which he evidently worked on a version of Eadmer's *Historia*.

One other man, Robert Powell, deserves mention, for it is he who bridged the gap between those who went before him and the arrival on the scene of Spelman's son John whose claim to be the first real biographer of King Alfred has a great deal of foundation. Powell, who wrote his own *Life of Alfred* in 1634[3] was also a keen legislative historian. Just before Coke died in 1634 he was able to read and approve Powell's massive treatise on the origins of ancient law in which Powell suggested that things such as the division of the shires and the appointment of judges had their origins in Alfredian times and he suggested that other aspects of the English law could even be traced as far back as Moses.[4]

THE LEVELLERS

Is it tolerable ... that after such privileges conferred on us by heaven we should have our spirits so broken and un-Teutonised by one unfortunate battle as for above five hundred years together and even for eternity, not only to remain but contentedly to rest under the disgraceful title of a conquered nation and in captivity and vassalage

to a foreign power? … Our language could be mistaken for a dialect of Gallic….
We cannot move but we hear the chains of our captivity rattle.

John Hare. *St Edward's Ghost or Anti-Normanism*. 1642 (published in 1647)[5]

The idea that the Norman monarchic government was too aristocratic appealed to the radical Levellers. To them, the aristocracy was an alien imposition on the English. Hare was not short of a bit of humour on the matter, despite the strength of feeling the subject aroused: 'If we contemplate the heraldry and titles of our nobility, there is scarce any other matter than inventories of foreign villages.'

Hare was quite radical in his demands. He certainly did not want anyone to refer to William I as 'the Conqueror' and he insisted that the present monarchy abandon its claim to rule by right of conquest. Those titles of the Norman aristocracy must be repudiated and their rights to English possessions must be denied too. Moreover, any laws which had their origins in Normandy but were in use in England should be abolished in favour of a return to those of Edward the Confessor (whose laws the Normans had always claimed they were upholding). French words which had crept into English must also be banned. It was a very powerful and appealing message and like a lot of reactionary political rhetoric, it was surprisingly, yet deliberately, easy to understand. The fact that Norman laws still remained in England even after the parliamentary victory in the Civil War bothered Hare greatly. So, too, did the fact that the lawyers of the land were all of Norman descent. Hare berated parliament for not capitalising on its victory and ridding the English people of these laws and lawyers. The mood in the country was changing. It was not just the monarchy who was the enemy: it was the whole Norman Yoke. Parliament it seemed, was not listening. In Essex in June 1647 a thousand people came to Sir Thomas Fairfax, Lord General of the New Model Army, with a petition claiming that despite the great victory they were still plagued by Norman laws. So, the people were no longer appealing to parliament, but to the army!

Nothing quite like this had ever happened in England before. The Levellers have often been ascribed the accolade of being Europe's first socialist movement, but to take things this far is to misunderstand them. The importance of their activity is in the fact that they did not only use the past to demonstrate what rights had been lost, but actually projected a new future into the debate by suggesting rights they thought should exist. They wanted new laws which were to be made clearer and less open to scandalously bias interpretation by those qualified to read and understand them. The Anglo-Saxons were, of course, used as their trusty weapon in the argument. Furthermore, they had their own publishing machine. A weekly newspaper, *The Moderate*, ran from July 1648 until it was banned in October 1649. It helped in co-ordinating Leveller supporters across the country. John Lilburne, a charismatic Leveller leader had a head full of radical ideas. As a young man he had cherished his copy of John Speed's *History of Great Britain* and he had been aware of many of the works on early English history already in circulation. The upshot of his keen interest in pre-Conquest history was that the people in the movement could paint any picture they liked of Anglo-Saxon history on what for their audience might be a relatively broad and blank canvas. Coke's defence of the common law and his views on Magna Carta, which were inherently conservative in nature, were swept aside by the Levellers. The influential early Leveller pamphlet of July 1646 *Remonstrance of Many Thousand Citizens* spelled out the Leveller position and it was overtly radical:

Ye know the Laws of this nation are unworthy of a free people .... Magna Carta itself being but a beggarly thing, containing many works of intolerable bondage.... The Norman way for ending of controversies was much more abusive than the English way, yet the Conqueror, contrary to his oath, introduced the Norman laws and his litigious and vexatious way amongst us. The like he did also for the punishment of malefactors, controversies of all natures having before a quick and final despatch in every hundred. He erected a trade of judges and lawyers, to sell justice and injustice at his own unconscionable rate and in what time he pleased, the corruption whereof is yet remaining upon us to our continuing impoverishing and molestation.

So, the common law it seemed, was the invention of the foreigner, a downright imposition on the ordinary man. It did not help that matters pertaining to legal claims were still even now in the 1640s, being drawn up or even discussed in either Latin or Norman French. In fact, it was the unhappy case for the common man that an indictment was not even legally valid unless it was read out in court in Latin. To the Levellers, this alien chit-chat in court, and the production of unfathomable legal documents represented a symbol of their captivity. If the bible had been translated into English, why could not the laws by which the common man was supposed to be governed?

The Leveller claims were somewhat unrealistic, but for their time they did express a real desire for a form of freedom which many felt had been denied them for centuries. We must not forget the changes which the nation had recently gone through and for John Lilburne, William Walwyn and Richard Overton, the principle movers and shakers in the movement, anything might have seemed quite possible. The *Remonstrance* even proclaimed an expectation for men to be freed from all the unreasonable laws made since the Norman Conquest. Throughout the following year of 1647 their views found favour with all sorts. The soldiers of the New Model Army, who regarded themselves as 'instruments to recover the lost liberties of a nation', expressed their own grievances about many matters including the popular gripe about laws being written and spoken in another language. Lilburne subsequently published an extraordinary invective known as *Regal Tyranny Discovered*. Here, he poured forth on a mixture of assumptions which laid the blame for almost every malevolent force in contemporary society. The monarchy was oppressive, the House of Lords was arrogant and, moreover, was packed with 'the lineal issue and progeny' of 'robbers, rogues and thieves'. The lawyers too played their part in national misery with their greed. All of these evils could be traced back to the invasion and subsequent conquest of a 'free nation' by a usurper from Normandy. Even contemporary lords owed their position to the thief who stole Englishmen's land. Everything conspired against the common man. He was driven by the iron Norman Yoke to Westminster to make his pleas in a foreign tongue. Lilburne had once taken Coke's line on Magna Carta thinking it to be an example of the English struggle to regain lost freedoms, but even this had gone now. The mainstream of the common law was too corrupt. There was too much Normanism in the system. The purist form of justice should not come from the judges, but from the juries, that great and indisputably Anglo-Saxon institution.

In fact, Lilburne endeared himself to very few people in high places, not least to Cromwell himself, and ended up facing a trial for treason in 1649. This is what he had to say to the jury:

> You Judges that sit there, being no more, if they please, but Ciphers to pronounce the sentence or their Clarks to say Amen, to them, being at the best, in your Original, but the Norman Conqueror's Intruders; and therefore you Gentlemen of the Jury [are] my sole judges, the keepers of my life.

Lilburne was not alone in his anti-Norman rhetoric. Richard Overton and William Walwyn, the two other great Leveller pamphleteers, had spread their word too. But for Gerard Winstanley there was yet another gripe to be had with the Normans and his view came to be recognised as that of another radical movement, the Diggers. Winstanley in 1649 wrote the following passage:

> Lords of Mannours stole the land from their fellow creatures formerly in the conquests of Kings, and now they have made lawes to imprison and hang all those that seek to recover the land again out of their thieving murdering hands.[6]

The Diggers' main goal was land reform. There did exist, however, in the seventeenth-century countryside some very recognisable vestiges of post-Conquest oppression and they came in the form of basic land tenure. A great many of the English peasantry held their plots through a system known as base tenure. This effectively meant that they did not own their land, but held it as copy holders. Frankly, it put them at the mercy of the lord of the manor who at any time might take his land back or more importantly drastically increase fines when it suited him. The lord would also insist on the swearing of oaths of fealty and the doing of homage in return for the right of tenancy. Feudal tenures had gone for the gentry, but the peasant was still held captive to his lord in this way. The demand, and indeed the instruction, was for people not to do homage for their land.

Elsewhere in the countryside there was an issue which seemed to have Norman meddling at its core. This was the issue of enclosure. The system of open field farming which relied upon the late Anglo-Saxon institution of the village organisation had continued for centuries after the Norman Conquest and its longevity was a testimony to the Anglo-Saxon spirit. Now, these field systems were being split up and parcelled out under the ownership of those who meant nothing and owed nothing to an institution that was at once the most widespread and parochial in England.

The Diggers' arguments are perhaps understandable, but the demand that private property in land must be abolished was too difficult even for common lawyers to bear. To be fair to the Diggers, they did not seem to think it would work anyway. They even published a warning which turned out to be strikingly correct just three months into the proclamation of the republic that the Norman gentry and their monarchy would rebound in due course. And indeed, in 1657 a second chamber was established and in 1660 a king reigned once again on the throne of England.

Despite the fact that the monarchy was restored in 1660, there were some aspects of the great debate on the ancient constitution which had stuck in the favour of the Anglo-Saxon side of the argument. And in 1688 as the Ancient Constitution was becoming a Whig talking-point, there came the end of absolutism. Much blood had been spilled on the issue and it did not entirely die down in the years which followed. But the theory of the Norman Yoke found itself in the centuries to come wholly subsumed by socialism and here it ran a wider course than before. The Whig theory of continuity of institutions and of law, of Germanism and the curious love of the perceived free democracy of the Anglo-Saxons had begun. But here, in the closing decades of the seventeenth century the Anglo-Saxons had been at the heart of the greatest political fight they had ever encountered. Now we must examine how the scholars at the great universities used the Anglo-Saxons and what they made in particular of one very important king as we enter another era of earnest scholarship and frantic debate.

5

COLLEGES AND KINGS

THE GREAT OXFORD DEBATE

The seventeenth century saw a great increase in the contribution to Anglo-Saxon studies by the universities, in particular by Oxford and Cambridge. Oxford had for some time claimed that King Alfred was their founder and they would make a great deal out of it in this era. We will recall that the fifteenth-century historian John Rous had stated that King Alfred was the founder of Oxford University. He was not the first to claim it by any means. Ranulph Higden, a monk from St Werburgh's in Chester, had said the same thing in his *Polychronicon* and also attributed the move to the will of St Neot. Asser had said that one eighth of the kingdom's income was set aside for the upkeep of a school for the youth of the kingdom and Higden claimed this to be the Oxford stipend. As well as Higden and Rous there is also the claim of the early fifteenth-century *Liber abbatiae* of Hyde Abbey in Winchester. Here, the date given for the foundation is 886, the same year in which Alfred reclaimed London from the Danes. Oxford, it is said, comprised St Neot himself as doctor of theology, Grimbald as professor of divinity, Asser as regent in grammar and rhetoric and John of St David's as reader in logic, music and arithmetic with another John bringing up the rear in geometry and astronomy.

Whilst the claim will have meant a great deal to the medieval scholars at Oxford, it was not used in anger until the fellows of University College in *c.*1380 had reason to prove their title to some Oxford property whereupon they petitioned King Richard II and got what they wanted. Once it was successfully used, it became something of trump card. But it was not until the 1590s that the claim reared its head again. This time it was a battle between Oxford and Cambridge over the antiquity of the dates of their foundation. Henry Savile had sent William Camden a passage concerning Alfred and Oxford which he said had come from an Asser manuscript he possessed. The passage revealed how Grimbald had got himself into a spot of bother at Oxford. He had come from Francia to assist Alfred in his campaign for a learning renaissance and had become embroiled with the 'old scholars' already established there over issues relating to teaching methods. Alfred had to personally step in and resolve the matter whilst Grimbald retreated to Winchester to cool his heels. Grimbald's technical argument, should we ever recover it in full, is not half as important in our current context as the notion that there might have been a community of scholars long established at Oxford by this time. Camden leapt at the opportunity. Being an Oxford man (Magdelen College, Broadgates Hall and finally Christ Church), he considered this passage as proof that the date of Oxford's foundation went back a long way and might even precede Cambridge's claims that their own university had been founded by Sigeberht of East Anglia in the seventh century. So, in his 1600 edition of his famous *Britannia*, he printed it. Battles raged over the authenticity of the piece, but the point is that it gave Oxford a great deal of impetus which it took into the next century with great enthusiasm, decorating its halls with engravings, portraits and busts.[1]

The Cambridge claim to greater antiquity is about as spurious as the Oxford one. It is based on the story of St Felix of Dunwich (d.647) who was a Burgundian priest who travelled to England in 640 and was subsequently sent to East Anglia where King Sigeberht allowed him to establish a see at 'Dommoc'. Bede suggests that between them a palace and church were built and that Felix founded a school 'in which boys might be taught letters'. But is not the accuracy of either the Cambridge or Oxford claims which is the point here. The fact that both institutions were looking for legitimacy in the Anglo-Saxon past and seemed to feel that only the Anglo-Saxon past could provide it, is of greater significance.

THE MARCH OF SCHOLARSHIP

Meanwhile, earnest scholars were paying frequent visits to a famous library. Of all the private collections of Anglo-Saxon books and manuscripts Sir Robert Cotton's was perhaps the most widely read. He had been collecting since 1588 and over the years had managed to accrue the *Lindisfarne Gospels*, *Beowulf*, the illustrated copy of the *Old English Hexateuch* and five of the seven versions of the *Anglo-Saxon Chronicle* as well as many other fine documents. His library moved around over the years, but started at Blackfriars and from 1622 presided within Cotton House in the Palace of Westminster.

Cotton was very open about letting other scholars use his library. He was assisted by Richard James (1592–1638) who provided content lists and worked on some transcriptions. Some notable people who came to Cotton's library included James Ussher (1581–1656) and John Selden who, like others of their time, would glean what they could from the material for their own legal or theological purposes.

William L'Isle (*c.*1569–1638) was also a visitor. Having previously held a fellowship at Kings College, Cambridge, he resigned his position and gave himself up to a passion. In 1623 he published *A Saxon Treatise Concerning the Old and New Testament* which included a translation of Ælfric's letter to Sigeweard, about which L'Isle waxes lyrical in his preface. The purpose of its inclusion was to demonstrate that Ælfric, by his own admission, had translated a great many books into the vernacular, a subject of heated debate in the new post-Reformation church. L'Isle was a great believer in the strength of the Old English language in helping scholars to understand important theological matters and decried the fact that the study of Old English was still being largely ignored by the descendants of the Anglo-Saxons. So, in his preface to *A Saxon Treatise* he made an impassioned plea to his readers and placed himself in the imaginary position of King Alfred observing the modern world with some degree of horror at what he saw. The 'complaint of a Saxon king' went thus:

> … I perceiue there the nation which once I gouerned, which hath also many Kings, both before and after a Norman interruption, descended of my bloud,

to make so small account of our writings and language…. Haue I translated with my own hand the godly Pastorall of saint Gregory, with many his learned Homilies; yea the whole Bible it selfe; haue I sent copies of them all to my Churches, with many Mancusses of gold, for the helpe and incouragement of my Pastors, and instruction of my people; that all should be lost, all forgot, all grow out of knowledge and remembrance? That my English in England, neede to be Englished; and my translation translated; while few now, and shortly perhaps none, shall be able to do it?

L'Isle need not have worried too much. The study of Old English was on the rise, though had not yet burst into the mainstream. His own efforts would not be in vain and the king he was so fond of will surely have looked down upon him with delight. The vernacular texts of the Anglo-Saxon period fascinated L'Isle. He set about collecting together all the biblical texts in Old English he could find with a view to publishing them as the *Remaines of the Saxon English Bible*, but he did not complete the project. L'Isle, the owner of the Peterborough version of the *Anglo-Saxon Chronicle*, was also unable to complete a grand idea to publish an edition of it which would have been a first in the history of Anglo-Saxon studies. Similarly, Gerard Langbaine (1609-58) provost of Queen's College, who was like minded, was also beaten to it by an extraordinary scholar.

Abraham Wheelock (1593-1653) was a man of firsts in many respects. In 1639 he became the first incumbent of a lectureship related to the study of the Anglo-Saxon period. The lectureship was in British and Saxon Antiquities. It had been a long-term goal of Sir Henry Spelman to establish such a lectureship and it was he who eventually ended up endowing it for the study of 'domestic antiquities touching our church and reviving the Saxon tongue'. Spelman and his son John were both dedicated Anglo-Saxonists. Whilst Sir Henry had been visiting Cambridge to study Old English manuscripts which might be useful for his work *Concilia Ecclesiastica Orbis Britannici*, he discovered to his amazement that the place was full of them. He knew then that there was a need for someone to be employed full time to deal with this work and the librarian and lecturer in Arabic, namely Abraham Wheelock, was given the task.

Wheelock's remit was to give two lectures a term and also be available on two afternoons a week for anyone wishing to learn Old English. He seems to have found his new subject tough going, more so than with his Arabic studies. But by 1643, Wheelock's work had borne fruit in a grand style. He published a huge edition of Bede's *Historia ecclesiastica* to which a version of the *Anglo-Saxon Chronicle* was appended. The next year it was re-issued with Lambarde's *Archaionomia* into which Wheelock dropped further legal texts not known to its original author.

Whilst Anglo-Saxon studies had risen to the respectable heights of a university lectureship in the form of Wheelock's post, an ancient king was being reborn. Alfred the Great, whom we have already observed was having a great impact on the minds of the university scholars, was to be used and reused century after century by different people for a variety of different reasons. The comparison between the founder of the English monarchy and his seventeenth-century descendants was too seductive to some writers to be ignored.

KING ALFRED IS REBORN

The journey of Alfred the Great through history has been a remarkable one. In the early days, a little like the memory of his grandson Athelstan, people had reason to recall the nature of the power and the great legacy of church revival and learning. Alfred had been a great legislator and had impressed with the sword, too.

The kings of the kingdom of the Anglo-Saxons, and later the kings of the kingdom of the English had been stern law-makers, active warriors and energetic in government. But above all they had made their power felt. And so, for Alfred at least, a strong cult was more or less achieved in his own lifetime. The chronicler Æthelweard wrote highly of Alfred and his offspring in the late tenth century and for different and obvious reasons Ælfric hailed him as a good Christian king. Our twelfth-century historians brought some new material to light, such as the story by William of Malmesbury about the king entering the Danish camp disguised as a minstrel and the touching description of the building of Alfred's church on Athelney Island. Malmesbury, however, whilst not including the two famous stories of Alfred breaking bread with a passing pilgrim at Athelney and the burning of the cakes, did give us something which stuck in the minds of historians for centuries. Alfred had divided his kingdom into shires and tithings to aid his people in the fight against lawlessness. Again, this is probably truer of the reigns of his son and grandson than it was of Alfred, but the acknowledgement stuck fast and we have seen that it was a debating point at the Elizabethan Society of Antiquaries.

In the twelfth century Ordericus Vitalis had noted Alfred's claim to have been the first to 'hold sway over all of England'. Others, such as Henry of Huntingdon were just as impressed with Alfred, but did not accord him the accolade of being the first king over all England, preferring instead, as many would do afterwards, to give the title to King Egbert (802–39).

The following century, Alfred received the attentions of the St Albans school that included the notable historians Roger of Wendover (d. 1236), John of Wallingford (d. 1214) and Matthew Paris (c. 1200–59). Generally speaking, these men clung to the notions promulgated in the twelfth century, but added new ideas. Wendover earnestly tried to put together Alfred's story from a variety of sources and felt sure that the date of the taking of London from the Danes in 886 had been a seminal moment. This, he thought, was the end for the heptarchy and the beginning of the new Alfredian order. It would be a tough job for a modern historian to prove Wendover wrong.

Matthew Paris, to whom we owe an early depiction of the Anglo-Saxon heptarchy of kingdoms, placed Alfred at the very centre of that world in the middle of a diagram of the same in his *Chronica Majora*. He also refers to the king for the first time, as 'the Great'. Many legends continued to resound about Alfred in the Middle Ages; one such was that the royal regalia of the fourteenth century had in fact been brought back from Rome by the king. Alfred is known to have gone to Rome and to have brought many items back with him.

By about 1300 a picture had formed clearly in the minds of English scholars, helped by documents such as *The Mirror of Justices*. The king had been a great Christian warrior-intellect. He had personally handled a religious revival and re-organised administrative and legal affairs, founding a new kingdom with great and extended powers. And so, with Robert of Gloucester's metrical *Chronicle* written at the turn of the fourteenth century, the juggernaut rolled on. This time it was backed by the weighty observation that Alfred had gone to Rome and had been anointed by Pope Leo and that this had given the monarch a legitimacy like no other. Nor was that the end of the papal connection. Henry VI (1421-71) attempted to get Alfred, whom he regarded as the first monarch of all England, canonised along with another candidate Osmund of Salisbury. In a letter of 1441 written to Pope Eugenius IV he set out his case, but only Osmund, and then after a few years, got the nod. This disappointing result notwithstanding, the episode is important in that it is a rare and unambiguous example of the view taken in medieval times by an English monarch of one his Anglo-Saxon forebears. One cannot but assume that the failure in this case of Henry VI was due to the still powerful cult of St Edward the Confessor with its symbolic span across the Saxon and Norman divide. Perhaps Rome felt this to be the most appropriate model.

Later, when Matthew Parker published Asser's *Life* in Latin in 1574 with an abstract from Bale, the king was once again termed 'the Great' reintroducing Matthew Paris's terminology. It also included a Latin translation of Alfred's will and the prefaces to Alfred's translation of Gregory's *Pastoral Care*. A little later, as we have seen, William Camden brought the Grimbald incident into the fray and started something which has not stopped to this very day. But it was not all legal, academic or religious motivations which brought the memory of Alfred alive again. There was also bubbling away under the surface a popular feeling of admiration towards the king for which we are served by a little evidence. One wonders how much material representing the same sort of thing is lost to us. The *Ballad of Alfred and the Shepherd*, variously titled in its several manifestations has all the hallmarks of a song handed down from generation to generation and comes complete with the full cooking disaster.[2]

During the early seventeenth century, Alfred's relationship with the contemporary monarchy came to the fore. Robert Powell's sycophantic

Life of Alfred, in which up to 70 pages were devoted to a direct comparison between Alfred and the contemporary king is but one example. In around 1640, however, a work was completed which ranks as one of the first great historical biographies. John Spelman was a close advisor of Charles I. He began his great work in the 1630s and wrote some of it from the royalist camp at Oxford. Based at Brasenose College at this time, one of the 'Alfredian' foundations, Spelman produced something extraordinary.

John Spelman's *Life of King Alfred the Great,* dedicated to a young Charles, Prince of Wales, was published first in a Latin translation and then later in its English form. In 1678 Obadiah Walker, Master of University College Oxford, included notes and appendices from his colleagues and a section on coins with a variety of engraved copper plates in his *Ælfredi Magni Anglorum Regis Invictissimi Vita Tribus Libris Comprehensa a Clarissimo Dno Johanne Spelman.* Some of his preparatory works, including his plates, still exist at Oxford, abandoned when Walker fled the place. Walker's Roman Catholic sympathies led to a dramatic flight from office in 1688. He was expelled from his post and was even imprisoned for a few years, living in relative obscurity in London thereafter, although he managed to continue to contribute to Anglo-Saxon studies in the form of numismatics with the help of his friend John Radcliffe.

The English version of the *Life of Alfred the Great by Sir John Spelman Kt* of 1709, was published by Thomas Hearne (1678-1735), under-librarian at the Bodleian. Walter Charlett, the master of the college at the time, did not particularly take to the copy that was presented to him preferring to promote, when it came, the 1722 version of Asser's *Life,* by Francis Wise. Charlett objected to a choice of portrait of the king in the work but was most likely put out that it was not dedicated to him. Hearne, a clever and vociferous scholar, replaced Walker's notes and inserted a strident defence of Camden's disputed Grimbald passage in a bid to take a swipe at Cambridge. This much notwithstanding, the Spelman *Life* was an extraordinary contribution for its time. In his dedication, Spelman explains that Alfred's memory had gone missing:

> I here preſent unto YOUR HIGHNESS a REPAIRED IMAGE of one of your
> Anceſtors. Not according to the perfect Life and Beauty: for it was never ſo well
> taken.

The standard of research and the quality of presentation in the book are very high indeed and there is a clear attempt to back arguments up with evidence. There are extensive footnotes to each page including aspects of language and topography. In short, it makes good reading, even today.

The work is divided into three books. Book One concentrates on Alfred's military struggles, Book Two on his legal and political administrative work and Book Three on his reputation and private life. As for the great debate over the foundation of Oxford, Spelman, a Trinity College, Cambridge, man, was a little more careful. He opted for an accepted foundation of Oxford by King Alfred but did not push the argument put forward by Camden that there had been a longer association going back before Alfred. Spelman, partially basing his arguments on the *Mirror of Justices*, was responsible for a vision of Alfred which would take the king through to the next century and beyond. Alfred had revived learning and education in his kingdom, he had ruled over a free Christian people, had been an administrator without parallel and had created trial by jury and been the originator of common law. Moreover, he had not allowed himself to be dictated to by Rome and had always wisely listened to his council.

On the lighter side, there are one or two amusing sweeping statements in the *Life* which are nevertheless interesting for the very early date at which they were published. One cannot help but wonder to what extent some of these issues, to which we shall return, had been the accepted opinion for some considerable time before Spelman sat down to write.

> Now we must know that the five great Plagues or Scourges, wherewith they remember this island to have been afflicted, that is to say the *Romans*, *Picts* and *Scots*, *Saxons*, *Danes* and *Normans*, this of the Danes (with whom our Ælfred had ſo much to do) is judged to have been beyond compariſon the most miſerable.

> Book I, p3.4

Spelman seems to have chosen the Danes as the greatest of all the foreign violators of English liberty. It is a stance which makes perfect sense considering the subject matter at hand. It would have been difficult to

89

completely destroy the Normans bearing in mind all that had happened in recent decades and for whom the book was written.

On the subject of the arrival of the Saxons in Britain after the fall of Rome, Spelman suggests that it happened in waves and not in one giant invasion, a vision ahead of his time:

> … and augmenting evermore with new Arrivals, made good unto themselves ſuch portions of Land as was necceſſary, … planted themselves in Colonies, and each Colonie grew at length into a little kingdom.

> Book I. p6

The author does, however, opt for the driving out of the native Britons by the incoming Saxons and this was a view which in the late eighteenth and nineteenth centuries transformed itself into a vision of Anglo-Saxon annihilation and conquest of the native inhabitants of Britain.

Perhaps the most intriguing thing about Spelman's work is the length to which he goes throughout it to stress the dynastic links of the contemporary monarchy with the line of Alfred. This is of course quite possible to do thanks to the union of the Norman line with the remnant of the house of Cerdic in the twelfth century. Spelman triumphantly finishes his work with a direct message to his reader:

> … whom his majeſty, now Reigning, receiving the Monarchy whole and entired, does, notwithstanding the threefold Alienation [the three times the crown passed into foreign hands], to this day continue, both in Right and poſſeſſion, the Lineal Heir and succeſſor of him that was the first Imperial Founder of *English* Monarchy.

The restoration of the monarchy did much for Alfred. Popular culture, this time with a heavy political spin, reared its head again. In 1659 R. Kirkham wrote a drama entitled *Alfred, or Right Re-Enthroned* which portrayed a victorious Alfred after the battle of Edington being re-crowned and a direct comparison was drawn with the symbolic restoration of the monarchy under Charles II.

Meanwhile back at Oxford, the Alfredian revival continued unabated. And it was beginning to be represented in a visual dimension. An early sculpture of Alfred first bears mentioning. Robert Plot (1640-96),[3] soon to be first keeper of the Ashmolean, had presented in 1682-3 a life-sized statue of the king for an empty niche over the entrance to the University College dining hall. It was to provide the counter balance for a statue of St Cuthbert which Walker had placed in the niche over the chapel door. Both were taken down in 1802 and Alfred was moved to the master's garden where the piece suffered greatly over the years.

And so Alfred would enter the eighteenth century as an Oxfordian royalist with a considerable scholastic backing. Before we examine how his character was seized by opposing sides of the contemporary political debate during the extraordinarily long eighteenth century, we must first assess the general climate of historical writing at the time, paying particular attention to the way in which the Anglo-Saxons were variously portrayed.

THE FIRST HISTORIES

The seventeenth century witnessed some serious attempts to assess the history of England which were produced on a relatively wide scale if not immediately published after they were written. There had, however, been earlier attempts. Among them, was the extraordinary work of Polydore Vergil (c. 1470-1555). Vergil had come to England from Urbino to seek the patronage of King Henry VII (1485-1509). The Tudor dynasty viewed the Anglo-Saxon story with some suspicion and gave the legend of Arthur the sort of credence once accorded by none other than Geoffrey of Monmouth. Henry's first son had even been given the name of the ancient British figure. So, it would have come as a surprise to Tudor readers to learn of Vergil's stance on the issue. Henry VII had asked Vergil to produce a history of England. Vergil had finished it by 1513, but it was not published until 1534 when it contained a dedication to Henry VIII (1509-47). Vergil's treatment of the Arthurian myth was surprisingly sceptical. In fact, he seemed keener to point out an Anglo-Saxon contribution, mentioning that King Ine of Wessex had made his kingdom tributary to Rome and had fined every house a penny. This, of course, was the origin of the Peter's Pence and while it would seem that Vergil had understood early Anglo-Saxon history to a remarkably detailed degree, it should not be forgotten that collecting Peter's Pence had once been his job.

Raphael Holinshed had produced a *Historie of England* in 1577 which it seems William Shakespeare had found of some use, but in 1586 Camden (who we might recall taught himself Old English) produced his monumental *Britannia*, which among a great many other things cast doubts upon the sanctity of the Arthurian legend. During the 1590s, although they were not histories as such, some other works appeared, further underlining a growing intellectual interest in the history of the Anglo-Saxon period. In 1592 Lord William Howard produced his version of the Chronicles of 'Florence' of Worcester and in 1596 Sir Henry Savile reproduced the works of William of Malmesbury, Henry of Huntingdon, Roger of Howenden, Ethelweard and Ingulf. It is perhaps worth pointing out that despite the fact that the Anglo-Saxons were beginning to fare well in the histories written around this time, the old Brut myth of the origin of Britain still had its supporters. One man in particular was fanatical in his opposition to the Anglo-Saxons. Richard Harvey wrote in his preface to his *Philadelphius* in 1593 the following invective:

> If I omit some histories of Saxons I do but my dutie: what I have to do with them, unless it were to make them tributary to Brutans.... Let them live in dead forgetfulness like stones ... let their names be clean put out, and not come among the righteous. When men play the part of beasts, let them goe among the numbers of cattel a Zoography and keep their fit place.... Arise, ye sons of Ebranke, and ye kinsmen of the true ancient Brutans and make those stone hearted creatures know that they are made to be your servants and drudges: let not any double forked toonge perswade you that Brutanie is under any part of the earth.

And in support of the Brut approach, he had this to say:

> It is manifest, that some of written more of Brut then behoved them, but some have behaved themselves unkindly to against Brutans, and done less for them, then they should.

But in the early seventeenth century, against a background of uncertainty
and argument about the Ancient Constitution, the more enquiring histories
began to roll in thick and fast from all sides of the political divide. One of
the earliest of these seems to have been one of the more influential. Richard
Verstagen's[4] (*c.*1545-1620) *Restitution of Decayed Intelligence in Antiquities* (1605)
was one of the many inspirations for the appreciations of the Germanic side
of England's history as represented in Viscount Cobham's sumptuous gardens
built at Stowe in 1733. Verstagen, an Englishman of Dutch extraction, was
educated at Christ Church, Oxford. He too, was not a fan of the Arthurian
myth, but his objection to it was not as strong as his love affair with the
Germanic aspects of the history of the English people. It is an extraordinary
read for its time. The 1628 version's title page reads as follows:

A

RESTITUTION

OF

DECAYED INTELLIGENCE

In antiquities.
Concerning the moſt noble and renow-
ned English Nation
By the ſtudie and trauell of R.V.
Dedicated vnto the Kings most excellent Maiestie

Verstagen's dedication to King James makes interesting reading for it is
another bold statement of the relationship between contemporary and
Anglo-Saxon monarchy. The king, he says is 'deſcended of the chiefest
bloud royall of our antient English-Saxon Kings.' Verstagen was clearly a
Germanist who long preceded the great Germanists of the late eighteenth
and nineteenth centuries. At the very opening of his book, he concentrates
on the ways in which the contemporary English were referred to by their
British neighbours. The common defining word for the English in all of
the non-English languages, he says, was 'Saxon'. It is this argument, he says,
which proves a Saxon is an Englishman and to be perfectly frank, it his hard

to disprove. But if we wanted to know where Verstagen stood on Germanic matters, we need look no further than the title for Chapter Two:

> How the antient noble Saxons the true ancestors of Englishmen, were originally a people of *Germanie*, and how honourable it is for an Englishmen to be defcended from the Germans.

Verstagen also offers us an insight to the way in which he viewed the Saxons' political and personal characteristics: they were 'free, liberall and cheereful of mind.' *A Restitution* also includes chapters on the pagan idols of the early Anglo-Saxons and here was the inspiration for the grove of pagan deities which later embellished the grounds at Stowe. There was also an attempt to describe the etymology of Saxon names and to look at the derivations of 'terms of contempt' in England, such as 'knave', 'scold' and 'thief', to name a few. For some reason, less ink has been spilled over Verstagen's efforts by modern writers on the subject than on his contemporaries. His work, which later attracted some criticism, was nevertheless ahead of its time.[5] Importantly, for the development of the notion of the place of the Anglo-Saxons in the political and constitutional history of the country, Verstagen says first of all that they had been identified by Pope Gregory as one people in the eyes of God. Egbert had been the first true king of England and Alfred had instigated the division of his kingdom into shires.

John Clapham's (1566-1618) *The History of Great Britain*, published in 1606, towed a similar line without the overt Germanism. It covered the Anglo-Saxons in the first two books of its second volume, re-telling, without a great deal of straying from the accepted story, the tale of Hengist and Horsa and their struggles with the Romano-British authorities, and of course the era of King Arthur which it treats with a small amount of respect. But in its full title, the work expresses the view long held by many historians in England since medieval times that it had been King Egbert and not King Alfred who had founded the nation:

> The Historie of Great Britannie. Declaring the Successe of times and affaires in that Iland, from the Romans first entrance, until the raigne of EGBERT, the

West-Saxon prince; who reduced the Severall Principalities of the Saxons and
English into a Monarchie, and changed the name of Britannie into England.

Clapham is perfectly clear on the matter of the establishment of England.
Egbert, he says, had commanded that several provinces should bear but one
name jointly, that of Angles-Land. The Angles, Clapham argued, were the
true English.

John Speed (1552-1629) produced a visually attractive history in 1611
with the title *The Theatre of the Empire of Great Britaine & The History of
Great Britaine Under the Conquests of the Romans, Saxons, Danes and Normans.*
Dedicated to King James, and using Sir Robert Cotton's coin collections
as decorative devices, the work had another visual aspect: Speed included a
retrospective heraldic history for the Anglo-Saxons both for the kingdoms
of the heptarchy and for each of the kings from Edgar onwards. Speed,
whilst telling us that Egbert was the first king of all England, also tells us
that it was a matter of some degree of controversy in his own time and
that Alfred, in the minds of some of his contemporaries, had also a been a
candidate.

The First Part of the Historie of England by S. Daniel, published in 1612, was
an effort in prose from a poet. It is memorable for one thing. It is notably
pro-Norman in its stance. Alfred the Great comes off quite well, being
described as a 'mirrour of Princes', but the Anglo-Saxons as a whole were
not given much credence. Whilst Daniel's approach was one which was not
uncommon, he nevertheless found time to muse upon the old Brut legends
and decried the 'heroycall of miraculous beginnings' of such works. Another
work, which gave the Anglo-Saxons only a cursory visit proved to be very
influential among the upper classes and went through nine editions by
1696. Sir Richard Baker (1568-1645), High Sheriff of Oxfordshire between
1620-1, wrote his *Chronicle of the Kings of England* from prison in the 1630s
and dedicated his work to Charles, the Prince of Wales.[6] Not everyone in
the seventeenth century, it would seem, assigned to the Anglo-Saxons the
lofty position they would eventually assume.

John Milton's history is still read today. *The History of Britain, That Part
Especially Now call'd England. From the First traditional beginning, continu'd to the*

Norman Conquest is a thoroughly researched and influential work. Although not published until 1670, it was written in the late 1640s during the period of the Commonwealth. It is not particularly controversial in the sense that it does not stray too far outside what were the accepted tenets of opinion for its time. In fact, it even has a Trojan beginning to it. But we can discern Milton's distrust of some of the sources. He is particularly scathing of Geoffrey of Monmouth for example, whom he acknowledges as unreliable and fanciful. On the whole, the work is a somewhat dry read comprised of excruciatingly long sentences of difficult construction. But this was simply the way Milton did things. His earnest approach was apparent in his work. Whilst he did not offer many opinions about the characteristics of the Anglo-Saxons, he thought the life of Alfred perfectly fit for an epic poem, and he did at least cover the period in some detail. The reign of Æthelred II, he said, was particularly 'ill-governed', a view to which many historians would cling long after Milton had died. Perhaps his most revealing statement in the work, which has a very thorough index as one might expect of its author, is the notion at the end that the English had 'had to take the yoke of an outlandish conqueror'. Milton clearly saw the Norman Conquest as a bad thing for the country and at the end of his volume he took the same line, perhaps understandably in view of his religious position, as Henry of Huntingdon had done all those centuries before, suggesting that the Conquest had come as a result of some sort of divine intervention for the punishment of the sins of the English Church.

Earnest scholarship is not, unfortunately, a term which could be applied to Thomas Rymer's 1691 offering to the memory of the Anglo-Saxons, although its very existence is testimony to the strength of the appeal of the Anglo-Saxon period in the early modern age in popular literary form. *Edgar, A Tragedy* is a play written in excruciating rhyming couplets with an almost unfathomable plot involving the Danes, the king of the Scots, King Edgar and his intriguing wife. But it is important nevertheless as the first of a number of such popular interpretations which, during the eighteenth century, would proliferate and export themselves into the parlours of the educated classes. The descendants of *Edgar* would, however, be no easier for modern eyes to read.

The century turned on a more serious note with the publication of William Temple's *An Introduction to the History of England* (1695). Another

1 Worcester Cathedral. The importance of the Worcester tradition cannot be underestimated. Bishop Wulfstan (1008-95) was one of the few to survive the Norman Conquest. From here, some of the great histories of the twelfth century were written and in the thirteenth century, the 'tremulous hand' of Worcester edited his ancient texts

Left and above: 2 and *3* Malmesbury Abbey. John Aubrey (1626-97) the famous antiquary lamented that on one day in the sixteenth century leaves of illuminated manuscripts from the despoiled abbey at Malmesbury could be seen 'fluttering like butterflies' down the streets of the town. During the twelfth century William of Malmesbury had written his influential *Histories* which recalled the great kings of Saxon England

4 John Dee (1527–*c*.1609). On 15 January 1556 Dee presented *A Supplication for the Recovery and Preservation of Ancient Writers and Monuments* to Queen Mary in which he proposed to establish a commission to search the country for manuscripts. Dee was concerned at the destruction of ancient texts, but his pleas fell on deaf ears

5 Laurence Nowell (*c*.1520–70) on the left and William Cecil (1521–98) on the right. Nowell, a traveller, cartographer and antiquary was ably supported in his Saxon studies by Cecil whose aim as Queen Elizabeth's Secretary of State was to strengthen her position

6 William Camden (1551–1623). Camden was one of the most famous antiquaries of his age. He published his *Britannia* in 1586, a historical survey of the country, and took a keen interest in the Old English language, learning it from Nowell

THE ARRIVALL OF THE FIRST
Anceſtors of Engliſh-men out of *Germany* into
Bruttaine.

7 The Landing of Hengist and Horsa in Kent, from Richard Verstagen's influential *A Restitution of Decayed Intelligence in Antiquities, etc* (1628), as reprinted in Mortimer Wheeler's *London and the Saxons* (1935). Verstagen tried to portray the Saxons in the costume he thought appropriate 'because these gentlemen were the very first bringers, and conductors of the ancestors of English-men into Brittaine …'

8 John Lilburne (*c.*1614–57). Lilburne was a political agitator associated with the Levellers who campaigned for basic freedoms at the time of the Civil War. Lilburne complained in court that the judges were merely the descendants of the Norman conquerors and that it was the jury, with its constitutional roots in Anglo-Saxon England, which was of more significance. He demanded to make his pleas in English

9 Elizabeth Elstob (1683–1756). One of England's foremost female Old English language scholars. Elstob had to battle against prejudice to get her transcripts and observations on Old English literature published. Despite a later life of obscurity, she is still remembered for her pioneering work

THE
RUDIMENTS
OF
GRAMMAR
FOR THE
Englifh-Saxon Tongue,

Firft given in ENGLISH:

WITH AN
APOLOGY
For the Study of
NORTHERN ANTIQUITIES.

Being very ufeful towards the underftanding our
ancient *Englifh* POETS, and other WRITERS.

By ELIZABETH ELSTOB.

Our Eartbly Poffeffions are truly enough called a PATRIMONY, *as derived
to us by the Induftry of our* FATHERS; *but the Language that we
fpeak is our* MOTHER-TONGUE; *And who fo proper to play the Cri-
ticks in this as the* FEMALES.
In a Letter from a Right Reverend Prelate to the Author.

LONDON,
Printed by *W. Bowyer :* And Sold by J. BOWYER at the *Rofe*
in *Ludgate-ftreet,* and C. KING in *Weftminfter-hall,* 1715.

---

10 Elizabeth Elstob's *Rudiments* included a scathing attack on those who sought to belittle
the Old English language. Such people, she had concluded, were 'light and fluttering wits'

11 Lord Bathurst's 'Alfred's Hall' was conceived in 1721. An extraordinary folly-cum-picnic shelter in the grounds of Cirencester Park, this building eventually took its Alfredian name when it was pointed out to Bathurst that it was around this area that the famous king had stayed before the battle of Edgington in 878

12 Ashburnham House, Westminster. In October 1731 a fire broke out in this famous collection of ancient manuscripts gathered by Sir Robert Bruce Cotton (1571-1631). To some, it might have symbolised the end of an era in Anglo-Saxon studies, but there would be further revivals in the years to come

13 Thomas Jefferson (president of America from 1801-09). Jefferson was a champion of Anglo-Saxon language and culture, even using them in his argument against the old country. To him, and to Benjamin Franklin, the Anglo-Saxon migration into Britain during the Dark Ages bore a close resemblance to America's own recent experience

This page: 14, 15, 16 and *17* Viscount Cobham's *Temple of British Worthies* at Stowe, *c.*1733. Cobham, an opponent of Walpole, included a magnificent bust of King Alfred in this remarkable building set within the grounds. Alfred (whose bust is included in these two close-up pictures) it seemed, could bat for any side in the political arguments of the eighteenth century

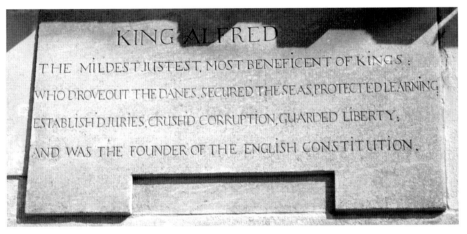

KING ALFRED
THE MILDEST JUSTEST, MOST BENEFICENT OF KINGS :
WHO DROVE OUT THE DANES, SECURED THE SEAS, PROTECTED LEARNING,
ESTABLISH'D JURIES, CRUSH'D CORRUPTION, GUARDED LIBERTY,
AND WAS THE FOUNDER OF THE ENGLISH CONSTITUTION.

Opposite and this page: 18, 19, 20 and *21* Henry Hoare's 'Alfred's Tower' was conceived in 1762 and was completed 10 years later. Hoare, a wealthy banker, built the monument just yards from the site of Egbert's Stone where Alfred is thought to have once rallied his troops. It is a massive 160ft high and contains 1.2 million red bricks

Left and below: 22 and *23* Jeremiah Dixon (1726–82) of (Chapel) Allerton and Gledhow, built a fantastic Gothic castle on Tunnel How Hill overlooking Leeds in 1769. It was known as 'King Alfred's Castle'. It was still there until 1949, a classic reminder of the romantic appeal of King Alfred to the eighteenth-century mind. *Photographs courtesy of Leeds Central Library*

Old Castle Ruins, Meanwood.

24 In 1834 the Houses of Parliament had burned to the ground. From 1841 Sir Charles Barry's new building was being erected and a select committee was soon appointed to ponder the internal decorations of the Palace of Westminster. Numerous competitions were held for artists to adorn the walls with historical themes in which the Anglo-Saxons made several conspicuous appearances

25 G.F. Watts (1817–1904), Alfred inciting the English to resist the Danes (1846–7). This award-winning painting, entered for one of the competitions to decorate the walls of the new Houses of Parliament, was 'dedicated to patriotism and posterity' according to its painter. Watts received a £500 prize for it. *Picture courtesy of the Palace of Westminster Collection*

"ALLURED TO BRIGHTER WORLDS, AND LED THE WAY."

26 William Theed the Younger (1868), *Queen Victoria and Prince Albert in Saxon Dress*. At the height of Imperial self-confidence and acknowledging the English monarchy's Germanic root, Theed produced what must surely have been inevitable, a sculpture encapsulating a whole generation of thinking about contemporary links between the English monarchy and the Anglo-Saxon past. *Photograph courtesy of The Royal Collection © 2005, Her Majesty Queen Elizabeth II*

27 Unveiled in 1877, this statue of Alfred at Wantage is inscribed thus: 'Alfred found learning dead, and he restored it; education neglected, and he revived it; the laws powerless and he gave them force; the Church debased, and he raised it; the land ravaged by a fearful enemy, from which he delivered it. Alfred's name will live as long as mankind shall respect the past'

Anglo-Saxon Remains found at Fairford, Cᵒ Gloucester.

Left: 28 'Anglo-Saxon Remains Found at Fairford, Gloucester'. From W.M. Wylie's influential report on the *Fairfield Graves* (1852). From the middle of the eighteenth century archaeology had a growing role to play in the recovery of the Anglo-Saxons

Below: 29 Tamworth millenary celebrations in 1913. Many towns in England saw great opportunities to mix civic pride with a celebration of the Anglo-Saxons. Here, Æthelflead, the Lady of the Mercians, leads a procession which includes her nephew Athelstan and her daughter. Sinister monks bring up the rear

30 Statue of Æthelflead, the Lady of the Mercians, with her charge Athelstan gazing up at her. This beautiful sculpture in the grounds of Tamworth Castle was carved by Edward George Branwell and designed by Henry Charles Mitchell. It was unveiled during the celebrations of 1913.
Photograph by Paul Barber

Above right and right: 31, 32 Two modern references to a famous Anglo-Saxon king in Malmesbury. A commemorative plaque set in the pavement recalls Athelstan's impact on the people of the town and a local garage carries the king's name

Left: 33 George Hickes (1642-1715), one of the great philologists of his era, was buried in the churchyard of St Margaret's in Westminster. Hickes, together with Humfrey Wanley (1672-1726) produced such an impressive work in the form of *Antiquæ Literaturæ Septentrionalis Libri Duo*, that it nearly brought other research in the field to a standstill

Below left, below right: 34, 35 Westminster Abbey in the modern age. A favourite of Edward the Confessor's, Westminster Abbey has seen it all. It is the burial place of many people who have had an influence on the resurrection of the Anglo-Saxons and once provided the theatre for the dramas of January 1066

supporter of the claim of Egbert, Temple has some interesting things to say on the Norman Conquest. It was a just and good thing, he says; Harold had been a usurper and in England there had been many 'happy circumstances' derived from William's invasion, although these are not fully outlined. Although the Anglo-Saxon period is well covered, the omissions reveal that Temple was not really prepared to delve any deeper than what he thought were accepted facts. The tenth-century rise of the English under the descendants of Alfred, the single most important era in the whole of English history is scarcely there at all. The accurate memory of Anglo-Saxon England it seemed now required a little jogging.

The resurgence of the Anglo-Saxons in these new history books was in some places countered by the old argument between the British and English schools of thought. There was also a resurgence of interest in native British history around the time of the Act of Union in 1707. In fact, it was in that year that E. Lhuyd published his huge work entitled *Archaeologia Britannica, giving some account Additional to what has been hitherto Publish'd, of the Languages, Histories and Customs of the Original Inhabitants of Great Britain: From Collections and Observations in Travels through Wales, Cornwal* [sic], *Bas-Bretagne, Ireland and Scotland.* The Act of Union had given some people the chance to establish a British identity in their historical arguments and it is no accident that it is only from around this time and no earlier that the native inhabitants of the western British Isles began to be collectively referred to as Celts, or Kelts. The term itself is misleading, inaccurate and wildly generalistic, but it is fascinating how firmly it has stuck. It is a term which masks the different and important histories of a great number of kin-groups and kingdoms which grew-up in the non-English parts of Britain in the centuries after the departure of the Romans. The abandonment of the word 'Celt' in British historical discourse is long overdue.

There would be another generation of histories of England in the eighteenth and nineteenth centuries, some expounding a Whig view, others a decidedly imperialistic one. These we will turn to shortly. But for now, we should examine the issue that so raised the hackles of William L'Isle: the battle for the continuing study of the Old English language.

6

THE END OF AN ERA

THE BATTLE FOR LANGUAGE

When Abraham Wheelock, the pioneering lecturer in British and Saxon Antiquities died in 1653, Cambridge had no replacement for him. With some agitation from Ussher, some of the money which had supported the post went towards William Somner's Old English dictionary. Somner (1606-69), very much a royalist during the Civil War, was also the registrar to the ecclesiastical court at Canterbury. He published in 1659 his *Dictionarium Saxonico-Latino-Anglicum* which he had been working on for some years. He had in fact been helping others with their own dictionaries including that of Edward D'Ewes (1602-50). D'Ewes, who had not always seen eye to eye with Sir Henry Spelman, had a part to play in Somner's *Dictionarium*. The work was based partly on Somner and on Nowell and included a version of Ælfric's *Grammar*, and was published not in Cambridge, but in Oxford. A century had passed since Nowell's *Vocabularium*. Now the aspiring Old English language scholar had at his fingertips both a grammar and a dictionary, the tools of the trade.

If Cambridge had won the race to appoint the first lecturer in something approaching Anglo-Saxon studies, then Oxford would become the new centre of gravity. As we have observed, Oxford was already in love with King Alfred. But the work which scholars such as Francis Junius (*c.*1590-1677) undertook had effects which lasted centuries. Junius, who left his collections with the Bodleian Library, and who is considered to be the 'father of Germanic philology', had a humanist classical education in the

Netherlands. In 1621 he came to the household of Thomas Howard, the earl of Arundel, whom he served as a librarian for 30 years. He had a keen eye for cultural history and became an authority on the historical criticism of art before becoming attracted to the similarities between the Dutch and the English languages which led him to look deeply into the history of these languages to find a common ancestor.

Working both in the Netherlands and in London and Oxford, Junius was an exhaustive word list compiler and transcriber of texts. By 1648 he was assisting D'Ewes with his dictionary and soon he was another of the notable visitors to the Cottonian library where he made many of his transcripts including a copy of the metrical version of King Alfred's translation of Boethius' *De Consolatione philosophiae*. Junius was very interested in Old English poetry and has been credited with being the first to spot its metrical structures, even if he did sometimes transcribe them in a prose format.[1]

In around 1651 Junius had received a manuscript from Ussher which contained within it a series of Old English biblical poems including *Genesis, Exodus, Daniel, Christ and Satan*. The identity of the original compilers of the verses are still argued over today, with Canterbury, Malmesbury and Winchester each staking a claim. But the point is that the resulting *Cædmon* published by Junius at Amsterdam in 1655 was the first to use the special Anglo-Saxon types which Junius bequeathed to Oxford on his death. In 1665 Junius published at Dordrecht an annotated edition of the Gothic and Anglo-Saxon Gospels, working closely with Thomas Marshall (1621-85), the future rector of Lincoln College, who was also resident in the Netherlands. Junius lived out his final years in Oxford and following his death in 1677, the next few decades were to be very productive among the Oxford Anglo-Saxon scholars as a result of his legacy. Edmund Gibson's *Chronicum Saxonicum* of 1692 and Christopher Rawlinson's edition of *Boethius* of 1698 both used Junius' types and were based partly on his work.

In 1679 an Anglo-Saxon lectureship was created at Oxford at Queen's College. Its first post holder, William Nicholson (1655-1727), left after just two years to pursue an ecclesiastical career but remained a close supporter of Old English projects thereafter. His successor, appointed in 1698 was Edward Thwaites (1667-1711) who numbered among his contributions to

Anglo-Saxon studies an edition of the Old English *Heptateuch* produced in the same year.[2] By the following year Thwaites had attracted a good number of students. He is known to have complained that he had to teach them on limited resources:

> We want Saxon lexicons. I have fifteen young students and but one Somner for them all.

The answer to Thwaites's problem came from his colleague Thomas Benson, who produced a *Vocabularium Anglo-Saxonicum*, an epitome of Somner's larger dictionary, designed to meet the needs of an expanding school of Anglo-Saxon literature. Meanwhile, John Fell (1625-86), in a bid to give the University Press some new impetus, started a project on an Anglo-Saxon grammar which was eventually taken over by George Hickes (1642-1715), a man who seems to have courted controversy, but whom was not without his admirers.

Hickes, was appointed dean of Worcester in 1683 but had taken a dangerous personal political decision after the 'Glorious Revolution' of 1688. He had refused to pledge the oath of allegiance to William and Mary paying a heavy social price for it. Quite how he managed to deliver such a huge volume of important historical work and continue to collaborate with Thwaites, Humfrey Wanley (1672-1726) and others, is anyone's guess. Hickes even spent the summer of 1695 in hiding at Shottesbrook with Francis Cherry, where he assumed a disguise and changed his name to Dr Smith. Whilst he brought the consternation of many of his countrymen upon him, his self-inflicted ostracisation did at least give him time enough to turn to what was clearly a passion. He published in 1689 his *Institutiones grammaticæ Anglo-Saxonicæ, et Moeso-Gothicæ* which used the Junian types to good effect and included within it a brief catalogue of Anglo-Saxon manuscripts.

Between 1703-1705 Hickes wrote a huge Latin volume entitled *Linguarum Vettarum Septentrionalium Thesaurus Grammatico-Criticus et Archaeologicus* which contained a chapter 'On the Usefulness of Northern Literature'. To Hickes, the Anglo-Saxon, Viking and Celtic worlds were all part of a colourful north European diaspora which he felt that his peers should learn from; and many of them did. Hickes's *Linguarum* was borrowed by Thwaites in his 1711 *Grammatica Anglo-Saxonica*, the first book of Old English grammar. Hickes worked closely with Humfrey Wanley. Between them, working from 1703-05 Hickes and Wanley produced an impressive thesaurus in the form of *Antiquæ Literaturæ Septentrionalis Libri Duo* that was so complete as to virtually bring the study of the Old English language to a halt. It contained in its first part Hickes's *Linguarum* and in its second Wanley's *Librorium Vettarum Septentrionalium, qui in Angliæ biblioth. extant, catalogus historico-criticus.*

Wanley, a former draper's apprentice, is an interesting and seminal figure in Anglo-Saxon studies. His passion for ancient languages led him to depart from his chosen trade and venture south in the same year that Hickes had gone into hiding. But Hickes would later say of Wanley that his skills in manuscript studies and in the identification of ancient hands were second to none, either ancient or modern. One of his many contributions to the field is that he developed the notion of dating hands in undated manuscripts using the benchmarks of those in dated charters as a point of reference.

Wanley, having established himself at University College, became an assistant at the Bodleian Library and produced a series of facsimiles of ancient manuscripts which became known as his *Book of Specimens*. Later, when he moved to London, he became the librarian for Robert Harley (1661-1724), the speaker of the House of Commons. Wanley was one of three others who were appointed to report upon the condition of the Cottonian library in 1703 just a few years before its disastrous destruction. Also, at around this time he was also working on a catalogue of the Harleian manuscripts. But it is for his catalogue of ancient northern books, which included descriptions of Cottonian items now lost, that he won lasting admiration and it is this which he and Hickes included in the second part of *Antiquæ Literaturæ*.

In just the first 20 years of the eighteenth century these scholars were responsible for producing 12 books which were published containing within their pages genuine Anglo-Saxon material of substance. This compares to the mere handful (although important) produced in the closing decades of the previous century. But if we are to believe the evidence we have at hand, the world of Anglo-Saxon studies, particularly on the matter of language, was about to go through its first real lull. One story above all others will serve to demonstrate the difficulties that people were beginning to face, that of the Elstobs, whose passions were easily as great as their contemporaries.

'LIGHT AND FLUTTERING WITS'

Having nothing else to do, I have some thought of publishing a set of Saxon Homilies....

Elizabeth Elstob to Ralph Thorseby.

Hickes's influence spread rapidly. Amongst those who were captured by the spirit he imbued were William Elstob (1673-1715) and his sister Elizabeth (1683-1756).[3] Theirs is a story worth the telling, for it demonstrates above anything else what some scholars went through in their efforts to light a passion.

William Elstob entered Queen's College, Oxford, in 1691 and later became a fellow of University College in 1696 where he stayed until 1703. Wanley remarked of his character that he was 'an honest gentleman'. His scholarly activities in the world of Anglo-Saxon studies were limited in the first instance to his contributions to other projects undertaken at both University College and Queen's, where he had also studied. These were mainly Latin translations including work on Andrew Fontaine's essay on Anglo-Saxon coins. But after Thwaites had dropped his project of preparing Alfred's translation of *Orosius*, Elstob found himself with something he could make his own. Unfortunately, the work was not published until 1773 when Daines Barrington printed it at his own expense. For the Elstobs, expense was the predominate problem throughout their careers, but their achievement is all the more remarkable for it. A title page and two leaves of the *Orosius* were in fact printed in 1699. But in 1703 William moved to London to become minister of St Swithin's and St Mary Bothaw, where his sister joined him as a housekeeper. It would prove to be a difficult time for them.

Elizabeth was born on 28 September 1683 in Newcastle Upon Tyne, daughter of Ralph, a merchant who died when she was just five years old. Not only was Elizabeth passionately devoted to the revival of interest in the Old English language, but this 'Saxon Nymph' as she was called, rightfully holds the accolade, along with Mary Astell, of one of England's first feminists. William had taught her Greek, Latin, Old English and other Germanic languages and from their new base in London they set about editing and transcribing a number of ancient manuscripts, sometimes even with the help of their 10-year-old serving boy James Smith. But Elizabeth complained in a letter to Ralph Thoresby in March 1709 that:

> [William] has many things to do, if he had leisure and encouragement; King Alfred's Orosius, he had ready for the press and a great many materials towards the Saxon laws, and a promise of more ... and being a University College Man, would willingly publish all that King Alfred did.[4]

William was indeed working on that set of laws. He had wanted to re-edit Lambarde's set of 1568 laws which had been revised by Wheelock in 1644. He proposed to add further Anglo-Saxon laws, annotations, an introduction, prefaces and a glossary as well as an index. By 1712 it was actually ready for press, but William hit a familiar stumbling block. He lacked the support for the project both financially and morally. His sister would suffer similarly, but with what seems to have been an additional insult to her sex.[5]

Elizabeth had been no less busy at this time. She had just published *An English-Saxon Homily on the Birthday of St Gregory,* one of Ælfric's homilies. No sooner was it circulating among subscribers than Elizabeth began to work on a major project of both sets of Ælfric's Catholic homilies. Although it was never printed, it was in fact the only edition of the homilies until 1844 when Benjamin Thorpe published his edition. Elizabeth had borrowed two Cottonian manuscripts from the British Library and by February 1710 she was busy transcribing them. Two years later she had a manuscript ready and took it to the Oxford Press. Hickes, her great supporter, had written to Dr Charlett, Master of University College, and had said of the manuscript that it was 'the most correct I ever saw or read' and that it would 'be of great advantage to the Church of England against the papists'. And yet this and other recommendations for publication appear to have fallen upon deaf ears.

This set-back for Elizabeth had what would seem to be sexism at its root. And it may have catalysed an already deeply held conviction. In July 1713 an essay had been published written to her uncle Charles Elstob canon of Canterbury Cathedral entitled *Some testimonies of learned men in Favour of the intended edition of the Saxon Homilies*. Supportive quotations were included from the pens of none less than Hickes, Wanley, L'Isle, Leland, Ussher, and Wheelock. But most importantly a defence was made against the perceived inappropriateness that a woman should have been the author of the work.[6]

There was more misfortune to come for Elizabeth when she decided to seek royal patronage for the project. She applied to the Lord High Treasurer (Harley) in order to secure the queen's bounty, but this met with no success initially. In stepped George Hickes with a powerful reminder that Elizabeth (who seems to have forgotten about it) had given a gift of a copy of *Textus Roffensis* to the Harleian Library. Now some support gathered in the form George Smallwood, the queen's almoner and bishop of Bristol. In June 1713, the queen agreed to grant the bounty with Harley's consent, but very soon Harley was dismissed on charges of corruption and in early August the queen died. As if this was not enough bad luck, the threats against the non-juring bishops who had refused to recognise King William re-surfaced and as we might recall, Hickes was one of them.

However, in early 1715 Oxford did manage to issue a proposal and a two-page specimen of the edition. Again Elizabeth was confounded, this time by the death of her brother William, who had been ill for some time. By the end of the year Hickes was gone too. The homilies only ever got as far as a 32-page proof.

But Elizabeth, despite the traumatic events of 1715 was both inspired and inspirational. She produced a vernacular version of Hickes's *Thesaurus*. It even attracted the admiration of Thomas Jefferson across the Atlantic, himself a noted Anglo-Saxonist. The title was quite specific: *The Rudiments of Grammar for the English-Saxon Tongue First Given in English with an Apology for the Study of Northern Antiquities.*

Elstob's inspiration, other than that of her guardian Hickes, apparently came from one of her lady friends who was keen to learn Old English. She had smarted at Jonathan Swift's savage remarks written in 1712 about the Old English tongue. Swift, following Nash and Dekker's lead had published *A Proposal for Correcting, Improving and Ascertaining the English Tongue* in which he said that the old language was too monosyllabic and could do with some Latinisation to improve it further. He had gone as far as to insult scholars such as George Hickes as 'laborious men of low genius'. This was too much for Elizabeth. She responded in quite a different way than her contemporaries who preferred to wear their political colours very clearly on show. Elstob was an intellectual. She was convinced that Swift was ignorant of the origins of the English language and should not have been attempting to legislate on it, so she set about dismantling him and his associates in her *Apology*. It was harsh but fair treatment. Whilst Elizabeth acknowledged that there was room for improvement in contemporary English, she saw the source of this coming from a study of Old English and not from Latin and she rounded upon these classicists implying that they were merely being fashionable and had small intellects to boot. These 'light and fluttering wits', as she called them, were arrogant.

In her preface, which was addressed to Hickes, Elstob praises her mentor and explains why she set about the work:

> Indeed, I might well have spared myſelf the labour of Such an Attempt, after the elaborate Work of your rich and learned *TheSaurus*, and the ingenious Compendium of it by Mr *Thwaites*; but conſidering the pleaſure I myſelf had reaped from the Knowledge I have gained from this Original of our Mother Tongue, and the others of my own sex, might be capable of the Same ſatisfaction I reſolv'd to give them the Rudiments of that language in an Engliſh Dreß. However, not till I had communicated to you my Deſign for your Advice, and had receiv'd your repeated Exhortation, and Encouragement to the undertaking ...
>
> ... I have given moſt, if not all the *Grammatical* Terms in true old *Saxon*, from Ælfrick's *Translation* of Priſcian to ſhew the Polite Men of our Age, that the language of our Forefathers is neither so barren nor barbarous as they affirm, with equal Ignorance and Boldneß. These Gentlemen's ill Treatment of our Mother

Tongue has led me into a ſtyle not ſo agreeable to the Mildness or our Sex, or the usual manner of my Behaviour … but the love and Honour of one's Countrey, hath in all Ages been acknowledged such a virtue, as hath admitted of a Zeal even somewhat extravagant.

Elstob could not understand why those who spoke proudly of their country could seek to enhance the English language 'by divesting it of the Ornaments of Antiquity, or separating it from the Saxon Root, whose Branches were so copious and numerous.' Elstob went on to decry the ignorance of Swift and his circle, whilst trying to point out to them that the simplicity of the ancient language was its virtue. The want of knowing the 'Northern Tongues' as she called them, had occasioned an unkind prejudice towards them. Although Elstob did not betray her political loyalties at a sensitive time, she did expand on some of her more emotive reasons for studying the language and culture of her forefathers. In response to the general criticism of Germanic languages as harsh, she said:

I never cou'd find myself shocked with the Harshness of those Languages, which grates so much in the Ears of those that never heard them. I never perceived in the Consonants any Hardness, but such as was necessary to afford Strength, like Bones in a human Body, which yield it Firmness and Support. So that the worst that can be said on this occasion of our Forefathers is, that they spoke as they fought, like Men.

Elizabeth Elstob's debts however, had mounted since the death of William. She had inherited her brother's financial burden and she seems to have taken the decision to more or less disappear for a while. She left most of her books and manuscripts with a neighbour and when she came back to retrieve them the neighbour had vanished along with the material. She never saw them again.

In 1735, George Ballard, a ladies' stay maker from Chipping Campden and a keen antiquarian and Anglo-Saxonist was advised by a Sarah Chapone to contact a village school teacher in Evesham known to her as Frances Smith. But Chapone knew her by another name, that of Elizabeth Elstob.

There began a relationship between Chapone, Ballard and Elstob which set Elizabeth on a course out of total obscurity and into the light of the early feminist movement. She spent her last days as a governess to the children of the Duchess of Portland, the daughter of William Harley in whose house she died in 1756 at the age of 73, a remarkable, but by no means unique woman.

The story of the Elstobs and the difficulties they both faced in having their work published and circulated has been taken by some people to be the signal of the first great lull in the Anglo-Saxon revival which was by now nearly two centuries old. Indeed, there does seem to have been a quiet period following the deaths of Hickes and Wanley and whilst Elizabeth Elstob was living out an entirely new kind of life, something happened which might have been symbolic of the end of an era. There was a disastrous fire at the Cottonian Library.

Although a great deal of work had already been carried out transcribing and listing the contents of the library, the losses were difficult to bear. Here is an account published in the *Gentleman's Magazine* in December 1731:

> A Fire broke out in the House of Mr *Bently*, adjoining to the King's School near *Westminster Abbey*, which burnt down that part of the House that contained the King's and *Cottonian* Libraries: almost all the printed Books were consumed and part of the Manuscripts. Amongst the latter, those which Dr *Bentley* had been collecting for his *Greek Testament*, for these last ten Years, valued at 2000£.

But despite this disaster, it was not the end of Anglo-Saxon studies. One character still had a hold over the English mind. They simply could not put him down. It is time to look again at the fate of Alfred the Great in the next phase of the Anglo-Saxon adventure.

7

IN THE AGE OF EMPIRE

ALFRED GATHERS PACE

The turn of the seventeenth and eighteenth centuries saw the beginnings of a new interest in 'Alfredism', made all the more possible by the discovery of the Alfred Jewel found in 1693 at North Pemberton in Somerset during drainage digging. In 1703 Hickes successfully explained the extraordinary piece as an æstel, or 'pointer' in his *Thesaurus*, like the one described by Asser. The item eventually found its way into the Ashmolean where it is still is today. Around about the same time as the discovery and examination of the Alfred Jewel, an archaeological excavation was taking place. In 1700, Lord Weymouth, one of the four Lords who had gone to Holland in 1688 to invite William of Orange to take the throne, excavated at Athelney Island and found timbers of what he took to be Alfred's 'domicile'. So firm was the assertion of Weymouth that a staff cut from one of the timbers was even exhibited in the Bodleian until 1780.

So, physical evidence of Alfred's reign was now being appended to that provided by the pen. But it was the arrival of a new German monarchy into England in the form of George I (1714-27) in the early eighteenth century that required some sort of cultural justification in the minds of many leading politicians. Set against the background of the Act of Union of 1707 a unifying figure was needed to bring a more wholly 'British' identity into the argument. Alfred had begun a new journey. The Whigs in particular were keen to follow a line which portrayed the ancient Anglo-Saxon monarchy as patriotic kings. But where lay the origins for a curious notion that Anglo-Saxon government had been constitutional and based on assemblies of freemen, a sort of liberal democracy? The struggles between king and parliament of the previous century had clearly demonstrated that common lawyers perceived the English parliament to have a very ancient root to it. Strangely enough, it was in a classical piece of writing from which the inspiration was drawn. The idea gained some intellectual acceptance through the reading of Tacitus amongst the educated gentry. Here, in the *Germania,* could be discerned the outline of a Germanic eutopia, an independent community of free self-ruling warriors. The notion that the cousins of these tribes of the German forests brought a similar style of governance to England at the turn of the fifth and sixth centuries has remained more or less intact ever since. It was a view which even found acceptance on the other side of the Atlantic. But for the rest of the century in England both Whig and Tory alike would take what they could from the plentiful material provided by the growing legend of Alfred. As far as the Hanoverians were concerned at least, their association with the ancient Saxons was not allowed to go uncelebrated. Samuel Gale had urged the new monarchy to base itself in Winchester just like its ancient counterparts had done. Moreover, in 1722, Edmund Gibson, the bishop of London, dedicated a revised edition of his translation of Camden's *Britannia* to King George I thus:

> Not only our histories, but our language, our laws, our customs, our names of persons and names of places do all abundantly testify, that the greatest part of your majesty's subjects here are of Saxon original. And if we enquire from where our Saxon ancestors came, we shall find, that it was from your majesty's Dominions on Germany.

Whilst Anglo-Saxon scholarship did continue after its heyday in the two or three decades surrounding the turn of the century, particularly in the form of David Wilkins's edition of a corpus of Anglo-Saxon Legislation in 1721, John and George Smith's *Bede* (1722) and Francis Wise's *Asser* (1722), a star rose upon whose shoulders were laid the burden of living up to the contemporary and increasingly popular image of King Alfred as the mirror of ancient princes. The upshot of this was that for the first time people had a real role model for this notion of an ideal Anglo-Saxon king, but it would all end a little too prematurely for the subject of everyone's admiration.

Prince Frederick (1707-51) was the son of George II (1727-60) and Caroline. He was also the father of George III (1760-1820). His arrival in England in 1728 came just a year after his father's accession to the throne, but by the following year he was invested as the Prince of Wales. The prince received his first poetic instruction from the pen of Sir Richard Blackmore (c.1654-1729). Blackmore had until recently used the Arthurian myth as a way of drumming a unity of purpose in support of the Hanoverian monarchy, but he switched in 1723 to the increasingly popular Alfred. The date is significant. Prince Frederick was not yet living in England, yet he had to read Blackmore's poem along with its dedication from his continental home. The prince was clearly being intellectually prepared for his forthcoming role. *Alfred, an Epick Poem* borrowed heavily from Walker's edition of Spelman's *Life* and contained within its dedication to the prince a description of Alfred as 'A prince sprung from the ancient Saxon race of your own native land.'

Whilst Oxford in the 1720s was embroiled in the continuing debate over the origins of the university and Alfred's connections with it, others around the country were beginning to see the potential of Alfred as an adornment to their grand architectural plans. As early as 1721 Lord Bathurst, encouraged by a literacy circle which included Alexander Pope, was planting a beautiful rural retreat in the English Forest Style. He built a wooden picnic shelter in the grounds of Cirencester Park. It was an odd affair which went through two names before being called *Alfred's Hall*. It was hailed as 'the first of all castellated follies … a true sham'. The building went through several phases of rebuilding and extension in stone and received a Tudor-style makeover at the expense of a demolished sixteenth-century building in 1732. Previously known as *The Wood House* and *King Arthur's Castle*, this grand Gothic building in Oakley wood seems only to have acquired its Alfredian association after it was pointed out to Lord Bathurst that this was where the king had stayed before the battle at Edgington in 878. More to the point, however, Alfred was winning and Arthur was losing. The greatest figure in British history was no longer a Briton, but a Saxon.

A little later, when Viscount Cobham, an opponent of Sir Robert Walpole, was creating his grand *Temple of British Worthies* at his home in Stowe in 1733, he commissioned painter and architect William Kent to include a bust of

King Alfred in a row of 16 heads. The temple is a spectacular monument. It is semi-circular in shape and set with sixteen busts in two complementing arcs of eight. On the left side are the figures representing men of letters such as Alexander Pope, Sir Thomas Gresham, Inigo Jones and John Milton, among others. On the right side are depicted those famous for their military and political actions such as King Alfred, the Black Prince, Queen Elizabeth I, Sir Walter Raleigh and Sir Francis Drake. Eight of the worthies had been made by Jan Michiel Rysbrack (1694-1770) in the 1720s and then Peter Scheermakers (1691-1781) provided sculptures for the rest of the niches which included that of Alfred closely modelled on an engraving which first appeared in de Rapin Thoyras's *History*, a grand work which we will shortly examine. A central pyramid was set with a bust of Mercury who was supposed to lead the worthies to the Elysian Fields, the name given to the whole of Stowe's carefully designed wooded valley landscape, fed by an artificial river Styx.

The temple has been called an ideological building. It seems that Cobham and Kent's choices of personage for the niches were politically motivated. Cobham had been dismissed from Queen Anne's army and was one of a number of Whigs who opposed Walpole's ministry. Queen Anne's omission from the temple may be no surprise. Cobham was not alone in being an opponent of the Whigs whilst still promoting his own vision of Alfred. Both Samuel Johnson and Doctor Johnson took similar views.

The Gardens at Stowe accommodated along with the *Temple of British Worthies* and the *Temples of Ancient and Modern Virtue* a number of other iconographical schemes of sculpture, mainly on a classical theme and related to love and sexuality. Cobham also installed some statues of the pagan Saxon gods having apparently been inspired so to do by Richard Verstagen's *Restitution of Decayed Intelligence in Antiquities* (1605). The *Restitution*, with its Germanic origins leanings, appealed to Viscount Cobham, who asked Rysbrack to produce the sculptures to populate a Saxon temple, but sadly the sculptures are long since dispersed.

Then in 1735 Caroline, the princess of Wales, asked the same sculptor to carve a statue of Alfred for William Kent's Octagon pavilion at Carlton House on the fringe of St James's Park. Once again, Alfred was accompanied by fellow 'action hero' Edward, the Black Prince.

The 1730s saw a great deal of public debate on the origins of the White Horse Hill figure at Uffington. The claims were that it was an Alfredian design. We can now, of course, consider the convincing proof that it was in fact a much older creation, dating back to end of the Bronze Age, but the debate at the time kept Alfred in the hearts and minds of the people, particularly those in that particular area of Berkshire. The Uffington White Horse fiasco is important in that it shows once again how Alfred could be used by people for their own petty political objectives. Francis Wise, the man whose version of Asser had impressed at Oxford, published a pamphlet in 1738. Wise was keen to become the first librarian of the Radcliffe and thought he would do himself no harm at all by suggesting that the White Horse had been carved on the instruction of Alfred to celebrate his victory over the Danes at the nearby battle of Ashdown in 871. His pamphlet was entitled *A Letter to Dr Mead Concerning Some Antiquities in Berkshire.* Mead was a patriot sympathiser with some links to Prince Frederick, so Wise considered his audience to be most influential. The horse, he argued, represented Alfred's banner. It just so happened that there was a white horse on the arms of the House of Brunswick too. It all provoked a spectacular and unforgiving brawl. An anonymous publication probably written by William Asplin, a pretender to the same job as Wise, attacked the suggestions made about the horse and rightly drew an artistic parallel for the design with those on the reverse side of many of the coins of the British Iron Age. This repost was entitled *The Impertinence and Imposture of Modern Antiquities Displayed...* and it attracted a defence not from Wise in the first instance, but from a Richard North who wrote *An Answer to a Scandalous Libel* in 1741 to be followed by Wise's own thoughts the following year. But as well as demonstrating the use of Alfred in such a squabble the upshot of all this fuss was that the people of Berkshire began genuinely to believe that the White Horse was Alfred's. They went further too and identified other features of the landscape with the king including a sarsen block known as the Blowing Stone from which it is said Alfred summoned his troops. The legend of Alfred was gathering pace.

Prince Frederick, now a great patron of the arts, commissioned a play to be performed in the grounds of Clivedon, Buckinghamshire, which became something of a talking point – *Alfred: a Masque* was performed on 1 August 1740 partly as a celebration of Princess Augusta's birthday. In it, the great king of the Anglo-Saxons is compared to the great and the good of the centuries which came after him, particularly Edward III, Queen Elizabeth and William III. The literary endeavours of James Thomson, a man who loathed royal tyranny, and David Mallet were encouraged by music by Thomas Arne. The play has had a lasting effect on British popular culture, for it included Arne's strident and uplifting *Rule Britannia* which manifests itself in the form of a 'grand ode in the honour of Great Britain'. The great success of the play is borne out by its transformation into a major production, largely rewritten by Mallet, first performed in Drury Lane in 1751 where the lead role of Alfred was played by none other than David Garrick, the greatest actor of his age. That year also marked the death of Frederick. Had he lived, he might have completed a grand architectural scheme at his residence in Kew which was to include a reconstruction of Mount Parnassus incorporating nine busts of great worthies in which Alfred was to be set alongside key figures from the ancient world, but unfortunately, the idea did not materialise. We will never know how the fortunes of King Alfred might have fared if Prince Frederick had lived on.

Other schemes, however, have left a lasting impression still visible in the English landscape today. In 1762 Henry Hoare (1705-80), an eminent banker whose estate at Stourhead in Wiltshire was but a stone's throw from Egbert's Stone where Alfred had rallied a beleaguered army in 878, conceived an idea to build a gigantic redbrick tower and named it *King Alfred's Tower*. Known to his family as 'the magnificent', Hoare commissioned Henry Flitcroft, a Palladian-influenced architect to build the tower. It still stands to a height of 160ft, commanding imposing views of Alfred's kingdom. The tower was built to celebrate the ending of the seven years war against France and the accession of George III, but being deliberately placed near Egbert's Stone, it was also on the ancient boundaries of the counties of Somerset, Dorset and Wiltshire and the tower had one corner of its triangular footprint in each county. In the summer of 1764, Hoare wrote to his daughter Susanna with the following words:

> I have one more scheme which will crown or top it all. As I was reading Voltaire's *L'Histoire Générale* lately, in his character of Alfred the Great he says, Je ne sais'il y a jamais eu sur la terre un homme plus digne des respects da la posterité qu'Alfred

le Grand, qui rendit ces services à sa patrie. Out of gratitude to him I propose ... to erect a Tower on Kingsettle Hill where he set up his standard after he came out of concealment in the Isle of Athelney near Taunton, and the Earl of Devon had worsted the Danes ... I intend to build it on the plan of Sn Mark's Tower at Venice, 100 foot to the room which the staircase will lead to and 4 arches to look out in the 4 sides to the prospect all round.

And in April 1770, when the structure had reached just 15ft in height, Hoare said 'I hope it will be finished in as happy times to this Isle as Alfred finished his Life of Glory in then I shall depart in peace.'

The building was finally finished in 1772 and was completed at an estimated cost of between £5000-6000. It stands on a green sandstone plinth about 1m above ground level and is constructed of over 1.2 million red bricks forming walls 2ft 9in thick, the walls being set in the Flemish Bond style. Evidently there was no use of scaffolding throughout the project: the workmen simply sat on top of the structure as it rose. Modern visitors to the monument are frequently surprised to discover that the tower is completely hollow inside, having only a 205-step spiral staircase to lead the visitor on an exhausting climb to a viewing gallery which rewards them with views over three counties for miles around.

The last word on the tower must go to the inscription which Hoare had placed beneath a remarkable statue of the king:

ALFRED THE GREAT AD 879 on this Summit
Erected his Standard
Against Danish Invaders
To him We owe The Origin of Juries
The Establishment of a Militia
The Creation of a Naval Force
ALFRED The Light of a Benighted Age
Was a Philosopher and a Christian
The Father of his People
The Founder of the English
MONARCHY and LIBERTY

Hoare was not the only one who saw in Alfred an opportunity to spend his money on something extravagant. Until relatively recently, on a hill just outside of Leeds, there was an extraordinary structure perhaps symbolising in its dilapidated state the romanticism and passion which has often surrounded the legend of Alfred. Jeremiah Dixon (1726-82) of (Chapel) Allerton and Gledhow, once the High Sheriff of the county, built a fantastic Gothic castle from the designs of John Carr (1723-1807) on Tunnel How Hill overlooking the town. It was known as *King Alfred's Castle* and surviving pictures of it in the years before its destruction in 1946 show a typical Gothic revival building. Dixon, a wealthy merchant, had clearly done well and after buying Gledhow estate had apparently lived the life of a country squire. His passion for Alfred resulted in this grand construction in 1769 at the highest point outside the town in Meanwood, a romantic setting if ever there was one. Once again, in the inscription on the wall of this grand folly which was recorded before the collapse of the twentieth century, the message was clear:

To the Memory of

Alfred the Great

The Wise, the Pious and Magnanimous

The Friend of

Science, Virtue, Law and Liberty

This Monument Jeremiah Dixon of Allerton

Gledhow caused to be erected.

AD MDCCLXIX

Meanwhile, back in Oxford, the passion for Alfredian commemoration continued unabated. In 1771 Viscount Folkestone gave a marble bust of the king to Oxford which was based on the Rysbrack one from Stourhead. In a later development in 1776 Sir Roger Newdigate MP and a group of associates commissioned an extravagant architectural fireplace for the dining hall at University College. Carved by Hayward and designed by Henry Keene, it was a Gothic masterpiece. The jambs and the canopy were modelled on the fourteenth-century Westminster Abbey tomb of Aymer de Valence, but there was also a profile bust of King Alfred in the central roundel.

As the relationship between Britain and France deteriorated and the grim prospect of a French invasion reared its head in the 1790s a bizarre series of patriotic plays were put on in London which portrayed Alfred as the great defender of a beleaguered and righteous nation against the invading foreigner. In these performances, the Danes were thinly disguised as the French and in 1798 *A Grand Historical Ballet of Action (Entirely New)* was performed at Sadler's Wells complete with the now familiar borrowed ending from the 1740 Masque.

Curiously, the French were not as anti-Alfred as one might expect. After the Treaty of Amiens (1802), when the two warring nations experienced a lull in hostilities, the Anglo-Saxons had a brief spell of fame on the French stage in the form of a three-act melodrama based on the story of Egbert, Alfred's father, portraying him as the first king of a united England, a theme widely accepted by English scholars of a former generation. Similarly, books began to appear about Alfred in Germany and in 1820 at La Scala in Milan, Alfred became the subject of an opera. The father of the kingdom of the Anglo-Saxons had once again achieved the status that he and his grandsons had held in their own time, that of the international celebrity.

SOME INFLUENTIAL HISTORIES

This nation exhibits the conversion of ferocious pirates, into a highly civilised, informed and generous people – in a word, into ourselves.

Sharon Turner. *The History of the Anglo-Saxons* (1799-1805). Vol II xi-xii

Between 1726-31 the first English edition of Paul de Rapin Thoyras's (1661-1725)[1] *The History of England, as well Ecclesiastical as Civil* was published in 15 Volumes, its French counterpart being already in circulation in eight volumes. Translated by Nicholas Tindal and dedicated to the Right Hon. Thomas Lord Howard, Baron of Effingham, *The History of England* was a very popular book and went through several editions spanning the first half of the century. The Huguenot de Rapin Thoyras was born at Castres in Languedoc in 1661 and had come to England with his family in 1686. He had been a soldier for a number of armies, but went to Ireland with the English and during the taking of Limerick was shot in the shoulder and never seemed to fully recover from the injury. He did retain enough energy however, to write a colossal piece of work. His *History* is a lengthy though entertaining read. Of particular interest is his treatment of the native Britons whom he describes as backward in their manners and living in little more than mud huts and his annihilation of the Brut myth in a chapter entitled *The Fabulous Origins of the Britons* is full of invective against the famous old story.

De Rapin Thoyras's love affair with English history was based around the constitutional argument and it was sometimes more of a struggle for him than it should have been. According to the preface in the English translation of his giant work the author 'wanted to be informed of the original of the English Constitution' and so set about studying the Anglo-Saxons, but found it a 'disagreeable and discouraging task'. It seems de Rapin Thoyras was aware that there had been a historical argument for the beginnings of the English Constitution being in the pre-Conquest period, but seems to have enjoyed delving into it a great deal less than his immediate predecessors.

This notwithstanding, Rapin (as he is often called) was most influential. In 1729 John Lockman (1698-1771) published his *A New History of England by Question and Answer Extracted From the Most Celebrated English Histories, Particularly M. Rapin de Thoyras*. Though based largely on Rapin, it was aimed at a much younger audience and became enormously successful seeing at least 25 editions taking it well into the nineteenth century. But Rapin's was not the only history available at around this time. There was William Guthrie's *General History of England* of 1744-51 and the best-selling *Complete History of England* by Tobias Smollet (1721-71) of 1757-58.

Nothing could challenge Rapin's place at the top of these histories of England until the position was admirably assumed by David Hume's (1711-76) *The History of England from the Invasion of Julius Caesar to the Revolution in 1688* (1759-62), published initially in six volumes. Hume's work is not as entertaining a read as Rapin's and it tends towards dryness for the modern reader. He did, however, profess some discernable admiration for Alfred although generally speaking Hume's vision of the Norman contribution to English history was more positive than many of his contemporaries. Between them Rapin and Hume had sparked something of an obsession for early English history and there followed a number of books in the later half of the eighteenth century on the subject, some a great deal more reliable than others. The popularity of these works, such as Thomas Mortimer's *A New History of England* (1764-66), published in three volumes and dedicated to Queen Charlotte, was improved upon by the adding of a visual dimension to the subject. Samuel Wale's illustrations in Mortimer's book were of an exquisite quality and concentrated on some of the more famous moments of Anglo-Saxon history such as Alfred creating the shires and King Edwy's infamous confrontation with St Dunstan over the small matter of a celebrated ménage à trois. But Mortimer's work, while of value for its beautiful production and solid scholarship is also of note in that it reveals what he thought of one of his contemporaries. In a section where Mortimer is accounting for the Cornish campaigns of King Egbert in the ninth century[2] he lambasts Rapin for his inaccuracy over the dates of these campaigns saying:

> Had the French historian given himself the smallest trouble to enquire into this matter, he would have found that it cost the Saxon conqueror no less that thirteen or fourteen years of bloody conflict to vanquish these glorious assentors of their native liberty.

There was a great proliferation of books around this time, all of which pretended to be something of great import, some of which were influenced by the work of those above. Authors such as William Montague, Temple Sidney and William Russel took advantage of the format of serial publication and generated a great number of subscribers between them through the 1770s as did G.F. Raymond with his *A New, Universal and Impartial History of England* (London 1777-90). And so it went on in a similar vein to the turn of the century and beyond. But, once again, not everyone had a sympathetic view of the Anglo-Saxons. James MacPherson, the controversial Scottish poet and author published in 1771 his *Introduction to the History of Great Britain and Ireland* which whilst being famous for its anti-Irish stance also contained the most overt Anglophobia of the time. MacPherson generated great heat in his denunciation of the 'barbaric' Saxons and their role in British history, but his views on the matter were neither widely held nor greatly regarded.

Working from the British Museum Joseph Strutt (1749-1802) produced three large illustrated works from 1773 to 1779. Strutt's first offering, *The Regal and Ecclesiastical Antiquities of England* (1773) contained representations of all the English monarchs since Edward the Confessor, so had little course to refer to the Anglo-Saxons, but his second work *Horda Angel-Cynnan; or A Compleat View of the Manners, Customs, Arms, Habits, &c. of the Inhabitants of England, from the Arrival of the Saxons, till the Reign of Henry the Eighth* (1774-76) included pictures of Anglo-Saxons in various forms of contemporary dress, which although crude in nature were nonetheless surprisingly accurate. Strutt, who firmly believed that the Saxons formed the basis of the English nation, produced a third work which represented the culmination of his studies and was entitled *The Chronicle of England; or, A Compleat History, Civil, Military and Ecclesiastical, of the Ancient Britons and Saxons, from the Landing of Julius Ceasar in Britain, to the Norman Conquest, with a Compleat View of the Manners, Customs, Arts, habits &c., of those People* (1779). It featured improved engravings on his earlier efforts. Remarkably different from Strutt's visual contribution to the recollection of the Anglo-Saxons was the work of one of the most influential figures ever to produce material on the era. Sharon Turner (1768-1847) brought Anglo-Saxon history to a wider audience than ever before with a contribution that was cited time and time again throughout the early nineteenth century. Born in London, he became a solicitor until he decided that he was too drawn by the attraction of ancient literature to continue with his profession. Turner is responsible for a notable translation of *Beowulf*, but by far his most important work was *A History of the Anglo-Saxons* (1799-1805). It was written in a lofty style emulating Gibbon, but was very well researched and became accessible to a lot of people. The book went through many editions and was read well into the Victorian age. Turner, an obvious patriot and never one to mince his words, set his stall out early in his preface to volume I (viii):

May not the progress of the human mind from barbarism to knowledge be
viewed in epitome in the hiſtory of every nation which has undergone this happy
progreſſ? It is the Author's intention, in this third part of his Work, to exhibit the
gradual advances of the Anglo-Saxon intellect; to diſplay the ſavage pirate ſlowly
ameliorating into civilised, moral and scientific man … but this attempt will be
peculiarly difficult; much illusion of conjecture muſt be guarded against; many
little traits muſt be collected, without which the picture cannot be completed,
and conſequently, some time must elapse before the performance can venture to
approach the public eye.

Many of the things about Anglo-Saxon England which the Victorians came
to accept as historical facts have their roots in Turner. For example, Turner
lauds the achievements of Alfred, whilst castigating Æthelred in a manner
that many scholars copied in the years to come. Poor Æthelred, who was
'only fit for a cloyster' receives perhaps the most damning account of his
reign any historian has ever written. Here are a few examples which serve
to demonstrate the style of Turner and the strength of his invective:

> The reign of Ethelred is a ſubject displeasing to narrate. Indignation, at the most
> helpleſſ puſillaniminty, kindles every moment. In the preceding reigns, from
> Alfred to Edgar, we have beheld the rife, and the full meridian of the Anglo-
> Saxon glory. The English spirit was never agitated by danger, but it acted to
> triumph. By their exertions a rich and powerful nation had been created which
> might have continued to predominate in Europe with increasing honour and
> great national felicity.

> Vol III, Chapter XII. p196

There is page after page of this historical assassination, but perhaps the best of all
of the invectives is the one in which Turner more or less gives up the ghost:

> Misery and folly are ſometimes ſo multiplied, that they mock the descriptive
> powers of language. The condition of England, in this man's reign, cannot for this
> reason, be adequately painted.

Notwithstanding the attack upon a king for letting the side down, the rest of the volumes are exhaustively and carefully researched. There were appendices on language, coinage, laws and land, on manners, government and constitution, on poetry (in which Turner excels himself as an expert on *Beowulf*), literature and the arts. There is little doubt as to the affiliation of Sharon Turner. He took a very Germanist view of early English history. David Hume, for example, had emphasised the Norman French influence upon the English language, but Turner saw it as still essentially a Germanic tongue. In revealing his love affair with the Saxons, he is quite explicit in what he says:

> Our language, our government, and our laws display our Gothic ancestors in every part. They live, not merely in our annals and traditions, but in our civil institutions and perpetual discourse.

> Vol I 188–89

Turner bemoaned the fate of Anglo-Saxon antiquities as he rather erroneously saw it. He stated that the British public had turned their back on the period:

> It has been the fashion with some to under-value the history of our original ancestors. Wit which trembles at labour, and genius which pants to create, have committed the Saxon annals to contemptuous neglect.

> Preface to Vol II, page x

If it had been the case that other scholars had glossed over the Anglo-Saxon period with what Turner described as 'inattentive rapidity', Turner himself would do a lot to rectify it. For him 'the Anglo-Saxons were a people whom philofophy may contemplate with instruction and pleasure, whatever the fate of the prefent effort to pourtray them.' (Ibid xiv).

But Turner was ultimately successful. In his 1820 preface to the third edition, he was able to reflect a little on his success, expressing some admiration for the increasing interest in the subject since he first sat down to write. Indeed, his work won him admiration in America. In 1841 a review of his history was published with high praise in the *North American Review* (53) in which the reviewer sought to lay claim to Alfred and Edward the Confessor on behalf of the American people. The famous bond of the Anglo-Saxon peoples both sides of the Atlantic, which we shall shortly examine, had strengthened.

And yet the recollection of Anglo-Saxon England was not always so eloquently delivered as it was in Rapin, Hume or Turner. There were some publications which were not as influential as others, but remain important for the way in which their authors chose to approach the subject. In 1812 Thomas John Dibdin (1771-1841) wrote a notable piece of nonsense entitled *A Metrical History of England; or recollections in Rhyme, of Some of the Most Prominent features in Our National Chronology, form the Landing of Julius Caesar, to the commencement of the Regency*. Dedicated to George and Joseph Ranking with a sycophantic preface, the whole thing was written in verse from start to finish and it makes for difficult and painful reading. The first part, in which the Anglo-Saxons make their entrance, is forebodingly entitled *From the Aborigines to the end of the Heptarchy* and the tone does not improve throughout the work, despite the claim in the preface that the historical notes which accompany each section were thoroughly researched. It is worth including a fragment here, since it serves to demonstrate that whilst scholars were at work writing some best-selling material, there lay on the shelves of the parlour windows of middle class households a lighter version of English history:

> The truth demands, yet we record with pain,
> How brief the honours of this short lived reign.
> Crowns take some value from a nation's voice,
> And HAROLD was, 'tis said, the PEOPLE'S choice:
> HAROLD, (the son of GODWIN) who proclaim'd
> That he by EDWARD was successor named;
> WILLIAM DUKE OF NORMANDY, declares,
> The same pretence, and these two self-named Heirs,

Alike, rejecting each other's word,

Refer decision to sharpest sword;

Mean time, as oft the muse of hist'ry sings,

The subjects suffer for contending kings.

On a more discerning note, Joseph Rickman (1776-1841) made a groundbreaking and largely successful attempt in 1817 to appreciate an aspect of Anglo-Saxon material culture which had been given short shrift by Turner. Turner had very little to say in a positive light on the subject of Anglo-Saxon art and architecture, but Rickman's *An Attempt to Discriminate the Styles of Architecture in England from the Conquest to the Reformation* included one of the first ever essays on the subject of the architecture of the pre-Conquest period. It was a subject which would pick up speed in the twentieth century, but remains important in this context for the early date of its publication.

During the early 1830s, Palgrave's (1788-1861) *The Rise and Progress of the English Commonwealth* was an influential book and incorporated a chapter on the Anglo-Saxon era. His work was complemented by the cartographic publications in 1833 of G.W. Collen, particularly *Britannia Saxonica*, which was essentially a map of Britain during the height of the heptarchy, which the author here called an 'Octarchy'. But it is in the early Victorian period where we find the next stage in the influential publishing of matters Anglo-Saxon in England, in particular the work of a well-known member of a thespian family. J.M. Kemble, whose stance did a lot to augment the work of Turner, was an influential figure in Anglo-Saxon studies. But before we examine his contribution, we need to look across the Atlantic and assess a phenomenon which amounts to the greatest success the Anglo-Saxons ever had beyond the shores of England. They went far.

AMERICA AND THE MYTH OF RACE

The Language and Literature of the Anglo-Saxons must ever be a subject of lively and enduring interest to the descendants of that race, wherever scattered abroad over the many peopled globe....The original fountain of our laws flowed in this dialect. The light of Christianity first shone on the British island through its medium.[3]

In 1775, the Committee for the 2nd Continental Congress appointed a naval committee who chose to buy five fighting vessels for the fledgling American fleet. Present at the meeting were John Adams and Benjamin Franklin. Adams later recalled they had named one of the ships *Alfred* 'in honor of the founder of the greatest navy that ever existed'.[4] The ship, a 24-gun frigate built in Philadelphia the previous year had formerly gone by the name of *The Black Prince*. Of course, the navy which *Alfred* was to be pitted against was in fact the navy which most scholars agreed was the brainchild of the Old English monarch himself, but this did not seem to bother the Americans. There is good reason why it should not have done. As we search for the basic tenets of American Anglo-Saxonism, we shall find that relations with the mother country worked on a number of levels and owed a great deal to contemporary and sometimes convenient political visions of the shared Anglo-Saxon past.

At first glance, there might seem to be something of a paradox in the idea of the Americans adopting Anglo-Saxonism as a device to bolster their newly found cultural identity at the end of the eighteenth century. At the dawn of the new nation, American patriots would seem to have been faced with the problem of how to square the following circle: their recent ancestors had left one country, settled on another land thousands of miles away, fought wars of independence against the mother country, and won themselves a new nation. Nobody had told them what it should look like, sound like or feel like. Now they had to design a cultural template for it and they chose to delve deep into an historic era which they thought had resembled their own pioneering migration period namely, the Anglo-Saxon era.

To some, the story of early America had overwhelming similarities with the great *Adventus Saxonum* of the fifth and sixth centuries. Despite the subsequent intrusion of racial and overtly religious motivations in the adoption of Anglo-Saxonism by leading American politicians and religious figures, it was a constantly repeated theme in the writings of the American scholars of the day and profoundly affected the approaches of both Thomas Jefferson (President 1801-09) and Benjamin Franklin. In fact, Jefferson even went as far as mentioning the direct parallel in a letter to George III in 1774. But for Franklin, his version of the theme was quite extreme. In 1773 Franklin argued in his *Edict by the King of Prussia*,[5] that if Americans were to be subject to the king of England, then the English in turn ought to owe allegiance to the German king on account of a similar history of settlement and migration. There also seems to have been a vital similarity in the way in which both historical groups viewed the notion of territory and expansion. It was an 'elastic' concept for the early Anglo-Saxons in Britain and so it would be for the Americans. When the American felt restricted in his expansionist tendencies by the British, he sought to defend himself by comparing his own style of land acquisition and tenure to that of the Anglo-Saxons, suggesting also that the feudal impositions of a post-Conquest monarch should have no bearing on American territorial ambitions. History would prove it to be a winning position.

Arguments have raged for some time over the original ethnic make-up of early 'white' America and which of the many cultural groups in a massive land was the most dominant. But as far as the inexorable rise of American Anglo-Saxonism is concerned, the various groups of seventeenth-century settlers whose influences are thought to have been the most significant in this regard have been identified as the Puritans of New England, the Quakers of the middle Atlantic, the southern English cavaliers of the Coastal South and the Anglo-Scottish Presbyterians of the Appalachian hinterland.[6]

Perhaps the most influential of these groups who traced their origins back to the motherland was the community in New England. Here, some ideas were held to be true which continued to dominate later American nationalist thinking. There was a clear Puritan sense of what has been described as both 'election and mission' in New England, the land here being often compared to Canaan or described openly as a promised land. This sense, the rise of Boston as a major centre of communication and the industrious work of religious figures between 1725–50 across the Eastern half of the country who took their ideas on the road and acted as something of an early news-and-views service to remote settlements, gave rise to the notion of Protestant America.

But there were other aspects of the picture to be painted before American Anglo-Saxonism could be fully viewed. The revolution provided the canvas. It was a war which divided Whig and Tory in Britain and in America. In the end, a Whig vision prevailed, but inevitably, the story is complex. Encouraged by some Whig writers in Britain such as Edmund Burke and James Fox, Thomas Jefferson and George Washington knew that independence was their only choice. But it is to Jefferson, the father of American Anglo-Saxonism, to whom we must turn.

Using the language of Hickes and Elstob, Jefferson had proposed a chair at the college of William and Mary for 'the ancient languages and literature of the north'. Jefferson had made the connection that such a chair would help to promote what he thought were obvious links between the history, laws and customs of his country and old England. In fact, Jefferson had written to an English Whig radical, John Cartwright (whose works were popular in America) and told him that he 'hoped Virginia would divide its counties into wards of six miles square, for these would answer to the hundreds of your Saxon Alfred'. Jefferson borrowed heavily from the Whig ideal of history: the view that the common law and government by parliamentary consensus had their roots in some sort of utopian Anglo-Saxon past appealed to him. He seemed to feel that this was at variance with the Tory view of the shared Anglo-Saxon experience, which if not entirely accurate, met with wide agreement. Cartwright was told by Jefferson in 1824 that:

> it has ever appeared to me, that the difference between the Whig and the Tory of England is, that the Whig deduces his rights from the Anglo-Saxon source, and the Tory from the Norman.

What he meant by this was that he supposed the Tory view to have adopted the notion that since Magna Carta in 1215, there had been a gradual encroachment on the power of the king by the commons. Jefferson also took the view that the Ancient Constitution, an Anglo-Saxon beast, had been cruelly violated by Norman aggression and here there was a way to solve the apparent paradox. The Normans from the American viewpoint became associated with aspects of tyranny and despotism, whereas the Anglo-Saxons, like their modern-day Whig champions were lovers of liberty and equality. Although such freedoms never really existed in the

Anglo-Saxon world, the model was a workable and powerful one with wide appeal. It brought a centuries-old argument onto a new stage in a new land. The Anglo-Saxons had done it again: a successful second *adventus*.

The symbolism of the Anglo-American *adventus* pervaded the highest levels of the new bureaucracy. In 1776 a committee sat at which Jefferson was present to deliberate on the design of the Great Seal of the new country. Jefferson, according to Adams, had made the suggestion that it should carry an inscription reading:

> The children of Israel in the wilderness, led by a cloud by day and a pillar of fire
> by night; and on the other side, Hengist and Horsa, the Saxon Chiefs from whom
> we claim the honor of being descended and whose political principals and form
> of government we have assumed.[7]

There was no less zeal in the American approach to philology. Jefferson was successful in getting the University of Virginia to include Old English in its series of language courses by 1825 and he shared with others a genuine belief that in the study of the language a person could easier understand the common law. Other American universities would not be quite so quick to adopt the language, but Virginia's experience is at least an example that the subject was being taken seriously.

Philology was one thing. Romantic sentimentalism with a nod in the direction of the notion of the Anglo-Saxon as a 'noble savage' was another. And then there was the myth of race, with all that has come to mean. The racial aspect of Anglo-Saxonism surfaced again in Victorian England, but here in America it was used quite overtly as a tool for ethnogenesis, a form of cultural legitimisation.

Henry Wadsworth Longfellow (1807-82), who sat on the romantic side of the fence, became Smith Professor at Harvard University in 1835. His ancient language studies took him all over Europe, especially the Germanic north. In 1838 he wrote an article for the *North American Review* which appraised the Englishman Joseph Bosworth's *Dictionary* and works from other eminent Anglo-Saxonists including one J.M. Kemble whose own contributions would become seminal. Longfellow, who found agreement from others in his ideas, was quick to make the link as Jefferson had done before him between the study of Old English and its moral benefits in the contemporary world. He even went as far as suggesting that it would mitigate against the influences of foreign fashion. For Longfellow, the American dream was an Alfredian invention, something purely Anglo-Saxon. Quoting the monarch, he draws the parallel between the Declaration of Independence and the views of the king: 'God has made all men equally noble in their original nature. True nobility is in the mind.'[8]

But this is about as far as Longfellow takes the argument. He prefers to slip into the romanticising of the nature of the Anglo-Saxon as a player in a Gothic masterpiece – rude, honest and simple. It is a view which would have chimed with the dominant Christian groups in America, but just to ram the point home and make the Anglo-Saxon a true American, he is compared to the very native Americans whom he thought shared a similar noble heritage and love of things natural.[9] They even shared the same sorts of names, he said. Names such as 'Noble Wolf' were like the Saxon Æthelwulf, and other Saxon names were like 'our' Indian names.

But was there a link between language and race? Could philology and ethnology be lumped together in the same study framework? Louis F. Klipstein thought so. In 1849 Klipstein published in New York his *Analecta Anglo-Saxonica. Selections, in Prose and Verse, from the Anglo-Saxon Literature; with an Introductory Ethnological Essay, and Notes, Critical and Explanatory* in two volumes. It was reasonably popular, being reprinted in 1856 and issued as a new edition in 1871. Klipstein has often been accused of being a commercial failure and indeed is supposed to have ended his life as a drunk in Charleston, but there was clearly an audience for this material. The introductory essay is almost a hundred pages long and draws heavily on the links between the study of the language and race. It makes uncomfortable reading for the modern scholar. He traces the Germanic tribes back to a cradle of civilisation in India and then outlines their inexorable march westwards from there. Not only were these ancient peoples the real Anglo-Saxons, they were the real Americans. The New Englander he states is the classic Anglo-Saxon, having a love of migration among other things. On it goes in a vein that will no doubt sound familiar to a modern reader.

Moreover, it is given liberal sprinklings of the more overtly Germanic terms of Goth and Teuton, which for Klipstein were both interchangeable and synonymous with the term Anglo-Saxon.

In fact, this whole notion of Gothicism was used as an argument in America against the Romanism which it was assumed the Norman Conquest represented. It was a convenient way of justifying on cultural and philological grounds the true nature of Englishness. The Roman influence on Anglo-Saxon language and culture was something which was a bolt-on extra, so to speak. The Germanic bedrock was represented by the Saxon and not the Norman, and so forth.

The last word on Klipstein must go to his reviewer, who no doubt firmly believed every word he wrote:

> The United States, beginning with the English Stock, and grafting upon it scions from every other European nation, grows every-day stronger with a power of progress no human mind can measure.[10]

We cannot be too harsh with our own judgements on these opinions. Klipstein could not have seen what was going to happen in Europe in the following century, cannot have imagined how much these words would still hurt in the twenty-first century. He, like many others, truly believed in the Anglo-Saxon myth, and difficult as it is to bear, the racial aspect of it loomed large in his mind. As far as our story is concerned, however, where do we next look for the Anglo-Saxons? Had race completely taken over the argument? The answer to that question lies in the old country in the delightful though sometimes rather odd creative celebrations of England's founders served up through the various forms of popular culture. For the moment, race is left aside. The Anglo-Saxons for some time back in England had been literally stepping into the limelight, appearing in a wildly disparate set of material, sometimes with amusing consequences.

8

CENTRE STAGE

THE ANGLO-SAXONS CONQUER POPULAR CULTURE

The Anglo-Saxons had been the focus of a good deal of creative attention before they reached their apogee in the nineteenth century. John Milton's *commonplace book* of around 1634, for example, reveals a deeper interest in Anglo-Saxon history in terms of its appeal to the imaginative mind than we might have expected. Among the themes he thought might offer the dramatist some interest were a selection of episodes from the reign of Æthelred II. These included the grisly massacre of the Danes on St Brice's Day in Oxford, King Swein's siege of London and the intriguing sedition of the English Ealdorman Eadric Streona, a man whose turncoat politics has given him a poor reputation among patriotic scholars for centuries. In Milton's list these three Æthelredian topics were accompanied by the inevitable Alfredian ones. Alfred disguised as a minstrel in the Danish camp makes an appearance as does the general story of his life which Milton supposed would lend itself admirably to the genre of the 'historicall poem'.

The darkest episode of Athelstan's reign where the king has his brother Edwin murdered at sea seems also to have appealed to Milton perhaps for the strength of the repent that the king subsequently was forced to show. Moreover, Harold and William's little struggle at Hastings is also mentioned along with the suggestion that the work might begin with the appearance of the ghost of the slain Alfred the Atheling, Edward the Confessor's brother who had allegedly been murdered by Godwin, Harold's father.

The dramatic story of Edmund Ironside, which in the form of an anonymous play of around this time may already have been known to Milton, is also given some interesting treatment in the *commonplace book*, where the themes of his defeat of the Danes at Brentford followed by his personal combat with King Cnut are given thought alongside his proposed murder at the hands of Eadric Streona at the behest of Cnut. The marriage of Cnut's daughter Gunhild to Henry III, the Holy Roman Emperor, also seems to have appealed to Milton as did the relationship between Edward the Confessor and his wife Edith, daughter of Godwin. Milton reveals the potential of the Anglo-Saxons to satisfy an appetite for drama, but would they live up to it?[1]

Plays

As it would turn out, it would not be John Milton who gave these themes a popular airing. Thomas Middleton (1580-1627) had already had a good crack at an Anglo-Saxon subject with his 1619-20 *Hengist – King of Kent or The Mayor of Quinborough*. The work included an amusing announcement to King Vortigern from a gentleman:

> GENTLEMAN: Send peace to all your royal thoughts, my lord; A fleet of valiant Saxons newly landed Offer the truth of all their service to you.
> VORTIGER [sic]: Saxons! My wishes! Let 'em have free entrance And plenteous welcomes from all hearts that love us; They never could come happier.

After the restoration of the monarchy, the theatres reopened in England and among the countless dramas and comedies were numbered some plays which picked up on a theme Milton had highlighted as having dramatic potential. This was the story of the marriage of King Edgar to Ælfthryth the widow of Æthelwold of East Anglia, the king's foster brother. Æthelwold had been instructed to woo Ælfthryth on behalf of the king and most of the ingredients for a farcical piece of romantic moral drama then ensued. The theme was eagerly and frequently returned to over the years. First, there was Edward Ravenscroft's *King Edgar and Alfreda* a tragicomedy of 1677 written apparently about 10 years earlier. Then, as we have observed, it appeared again in Thomas Rymer's *Edgar or the English Monarch*, an excruciating rhymed verse play which seems never to have been staged much to the annoyance of its author. At Drury Lane in 1709 Aaron Hill's *Elfrid or the Fair Inconstant* was performed. It had taken a little more than a week to write, and it was later revised as a more comprehensive offering in a play entitled simply *Athelwold* (1732). A dramatic poem of 1752 by William Mason called *Elfrida* also covered the same subject and was adapted for the stage, coming across to its audience as something of a Greek Tragedy. Later still, the subject seemed to continue to have some appeal. In 1843 William Henry Smith (1808-72) saw a performance of his play *Athelwold* which was published three years later. Then in 1893 Amélie Rives, a minor novelist, wrote another *Athelwold*. The theme returned once again in 1927 with Edna St Vincent Millay's *The King's Henchmen*. So, Æthelwold's tale has been particularly well attended. But what of the others?

John Browne had written his play *Athelstan, a Tragedy* in 1756. *Athelstan* is not a particularly memorable work in terms of its contribution to English literature, but this play 'As is acted at the Theatre Royal, Drury Lane' starred none other than David Garrick the leading actor of his age as Athelstan, the 'Duke of Mercia'. The character at the centre of this drama was not the historical king of England, however, but bore his name nonetheless. In its epilogue there is a revealing passage penned apparently by Garrick himself and spoken by a Mrs Cibber, which went thus:

... Shakespear *read* French! *roars out a surly* cit:
When Shakespear *wrote, our Valour match'd our* wit:
Had Britons *then been fops, Queen* Bess *had hang'd* 'em;
Those Days, they never read *the French – they bang'd* 'em.

The real King Athelstan, now a largely forgotten hero of Anglo-Saxon England, would receive further treatment as the years went by. A dramatic chronicle by George Darley entitled *Ethelston, or the Battle of Brunanburh* was published in 1841. Later, Tennyson's *The Battle of Brunanburh* was published in 1880 to wide critical acclaim. Sadly, no popular dramatist has looked upon Darley's 'sleeping hero' with sympathy for some considerable time.

Edmund Ironside, much as Milton had suggested, provided plenty of licence. An anonymous Elizabethan play, sometimes attributed on stylistic grounds to none other than Shakespeare was performed around 1590 and entitled *Edmund Ironside – A true Chronicle History called War hath made all friends*. Here, Eadric Streona gets up to his old tricks again, deceiving both sides in the great struggles of 1016. In Act IV.1.110 the scoundrel is unmasked by a certain Ælfric, very much to Eadric's annoyance:

EDRICUS [sic]: Traitor? Remember this: malice hath a perfect memory.

Our anonymous playwright, it seems, was a perfect judge of character. Much later, in 1791, Ironside made another starring appearance in *Edmund, Surnamed Ironside*, a play by Jane West, who was mainly a novelist. Once again, little has been done since on a life packed with material.

In 1724 George Jeffrey published his *Edwin – A tragedy*, which focussed on the drama of the life of the ancient king of Deira, but it was a young king with a similar name, King Edwy, who proved to be a runaway favourite. We may recall the dubious morality of the young tenth-century King Edwy, who dallied longer than he should have done with two noble ladies on the night of his coronation feast much to the consternation of St Dunstan. The theme of Dunstan and his moral outrage featured in a number of plays. Thomas Warwick published in 1784 his *Edwy*, then, in 1788 Frances Burney wrote *Edwy and Elgiva* which was revised until it was performed in London in 1795. On and on the juggernaut rolled with Thomas Sedwick Whalley's *Edwy and Edilda* of 1800, Charles Jared Ingersol's *Edwy and Elgiva* of 1801 and Henry Taylor's 1842 offering of *Edwin the Fair*. Interestingly, in none of these plays does St Dunstan get sympathetic treatment for prizing apart the lovers.

What more can we say about Alfred's appeal to the creative mind than we have already said? The answer is, of course, much more. Plays abounded: *Alfred or the Magic Banner* by John O'Keefe was published in 1796. Here, O'Keefe, who also had a penchant for the story of Lady Godiva, has Alfred decreeing trial by jury towards the end of the play. His work also inspired Isaac Pocock's musical drama *Alfred the Great or the Enchanted Standard* of 1827. Then there was James Sheridan Knowles's *Alfred the Great or the Patriot King* of 1831 and after this, *Alfred, a Patriotic Play* from the pen of Martin K. Tupper. In fact, it would seem that Alfred is the one Saxon nobody can keep their hands off.

One interesting contribution to the dramatic memory of the Anglo-Saxons comes in the form of Ann Yearsley's *Earl Goodwin*, which she began in 1789 and which was staged in Bristol in 1791. Here, the father of King Harold is portrayed as a statesman in the Whig mould, pitting himself against the strength of the monarchy in the form of Edward the Confessor. As for the son of Godwin, Harold turns up in Richard Cumberland's *The Battle of Hastings* (1777) and the ill-fated king even lent himself to the imagination of Tennyson in his play *Harold* (1876) which includes an interesting and perhaps historically accurate argument which took place between the king and a monk called Hugh Margot just before the battle of Hastings:

MARGOT: Hear me again – for the last time. Arise,

Scatter thy people home, descend the hill,

Lay hands of full allegiance in thy Lord's

And crave his mercy, for the Holy Father

Hath given this realm of England to the Norman.

HAROLD: Then for the last time, monk, I ask again

When had the Lateran and the Holy Father

To do with England's choice of her own king?

ACT V, scene I

There would be plenty of drama left in the Anglo-Saxons in the years which followed. However, the effects of the First World War on the English perspective on the subject of Germanism somewhat blunted the edge of the creative imagination. Before this unhappy phenomenon occurred, however, the Anglo-Saxons were everywhere painting a huge picture in the minds of their descendants.

Paintings and fine art

From the late eighteenth century the world of the Anglo-Saxons began to capture the imagination of fine artists working in a variety of media, by far the most popular of which was the large-scale historical painting. So, what were the themes which so enraptured those who chose to *visually* represent the story of the Anglo-Saxons? Drawing their inspiration from the histories of the eighteenth century it seems that the most popular themes from Anglo-Saxon history were as follows. Vortigern and his struggles with the Saxons and his love affair with Rowena; Alfred the Great at Athelney Island and his encounter there with a pilgrim with whom he shared his last piece of bread (who turned out to be St Cuthbert); King Edgar's moral character; Edward the Martyr's famous murder at the hands of the courtiers of Æthelred; King Cnut turning back the tide; various themes related to Edward the Confessor's life; some occasional aspects of the power and reign of Athelstan and a time-honoured favourite of the Augustinian conversion of the Saxons to Christianity. Perhaps it of significance that the received view of Anglo-Saxon history was by now firmly rooted in the West Saxon school. Few of the themes above can be said to fall within the exclusive remit of Mercian, Northumbrian or East Anglian popular histories and apart from the obvious story of the conversion, what is there of Kent?

From the time of the Society of Arts competition in the 1760s which offered a premium for 'original historical pictures' from British or Irish history 'containing not less than three figures as large as life' the rollercoaster of fine art depictions of Anglo-Saxon history was unleashed. Andrea Casali (1705-84) did well with his *The story of Gunhilda* (1760) depicting the tale of Cnut's daughter and her marriage to the German Emperor and later at the Society of Arts/Free Society in 1763 Robert Edge Pine (1730-88) went one better and scooped the first premium with *Canute reproving his courtiers for their impious flattery*. The second premium was won by one of Pine's pupils John Hamilton Mortimer (1740-79) for his *Edward the Confessor Spoiling his Mother at Winchester*. Mason Chamberlain the Elder (*c.*1727-87) followed up the following year with *King Alfred in a cottage: large as Life*.

The foundation of the Royal Academy in 1768 helped the cause further. Angelica Kauffmann (1741-1807) displayed a pair of paintings, one entitled *Vortigern, king of Britain, enamoured with Rowena, at the banquet of Hengist, the Saxon general* (1770) and the other *The Interview of King Edgar with Elfrida, after her marriage to Athelwold* (1771). These were among the first pictures on an Anglo-Saxon subject to be exhibited at the Royal Academy and the Edgar theme would be returned to by William Hamilton in 1774. Other themes which excited the imagination were the stories of the death of Harold in 1066 and the romance of Hereward the Wake, the resistance fighter against the Normans.

King Alfred was by now a runaway success in the minds of the public and it is perhaps only natural that he should have been reflected in the grand artworks of the day. But there had been a curious impostor. M. Baculard d'Arnaud, a French historian had written about King Alfred in his 1783 *Délassements de l'homme sensible ou anecdotes diverses* and perhaps influenced by a painting and or engraving by Benjamin West (1738-1820) had muddled his Alfreds. He had picked up on a story prevalent in Leicestershire that a certain Alfred III, the Duke of Mercia who may have been active in the eighth century, once visited the residence of Lord d'Albanac where he took a shine to one of his daughters. There are two things wrong with all this. First of all, d'Arnaud transferred this tale (familiar to the dukes of Rutland) to the wrong Alfred, and secondly, it is a highly dubious story about a very doubtful figure of history. Nevertheless, the impostor, in his proper guise, appeared in West's 1778 offering at the Royal Academy in a painting commissioned by the duke of Rutland entitled *William de Albanac presents his three daughters to Alfred III, King of Mercia*. West, whose background was in Pennsylvania, rose to become the historical painter to King George III and his *Alfred the Great Divides his Loaf with a Pilgrim* (the grand scale version of which was presented at the Royal Academy in 1779) represents a return to safer historical ground. It was presented the next year to the Worshipful Company of Stationers and Newspaper Makers by the publisher Boydell and was later engraved and published along with many others.

But it was not just the history painter to the king who got in on the act. William Blake (1757-1827) also had a portfolio of Anglo-Saxon themes to speak of, even if they were only drawings. In 1780 he chose Earl Godwin's famous demise at a banquet and showed the event as a sort of divine punishment for Godwin's murder or complicity in it of Alfred the Atheling, but he never finished the drawing. As well as *The death of Earl Goodwin*, Blake also drew *St Augustine converting Ethelbert of Kent*. Other themes, including

Alfred and the cakes may have been intended for a small book of the 1790s which Blake seems to have been working on entitled *The History of England, a small book of Engravings*, but it does not survive, although a 1790s watercolour on the subject of *Queen Emma's ordeal* may have been intended to be part of it.

It is to the ambition of Robert Bowyer (*c.*1758–1834) that we owe the grandest effort of all. Bowyer had planned a magnificent edition of Hume's *History*. For this he wanted to start a grand scheme which involved the commissioning of a number of artists who would paint chosen scenes from the history which would then be turned into engravings and published in the new work. Bowyer was, of course, a great fan of historical painting. By 1793 he had some works hanging on permanent display in his 'Historic Gallery' on Pall Mall. Ten of the paintings dealt with themes from Anglo-Saxon England including one by Richard Westall on the subject of a young Alfred meeting Pope Leo. The grand project of Hume's magnificent edition was underway and between 1793 and 1806, available for subscribers only, individual parts with attendant engravings were issued. The whole massive work could be bound if the acquirer wished, into five or even 10 volumes, the engravings being optional as a separate volume or integral with the work. It was beautiful. It was magnificent. It was a catastrophic failure. It was just too sumptuous for words. Notwithstanding the commercial failure of the venture, Bowyer received a great deal of sympathy from commentators at the time. Recording the fact that Bowyer had been given the power by an act of parliament to dispose of his material to raise funds, the correspondent for the *Gentleman's Magazine* in 1806 had this to say:

> The fame of the various and splendid works which so pre-eminently characterise the Historic Gallery in Pall Mall are too generally well known to require a minute detail. It is sufficient therefore that its great collection of paintings are executed entirely by members of the Royal Academy from events of the highest interest in the British Annals.

He goes on to state that Hume's *History* had been 'the most superb publication, without exception in Europe' and then tells of Bowyer's misfortune:

In the attainment and on the execution of these various and great works Mr Bowyer expended above 100,000l. A series of unpropitious times and circumstances respecting the Fine Arts, having rendered the disposal of the above splendid collection expedient, Parliament have passed an Act, in order to enable Mr Bowyer to effect such a disposal by a lottery as any other mode would obviously be attended with a most heavy loss on that fortune he so meritoriously devoted to the noble object of bringing the arts of Painting, Drawing and Engraving to such perfection as to prove an honour and ornament to the genius of his country.[2]

The 22,000 tickets that were issued at three guineas each with the attraction of 1451 'capital prizes' went some way to restoring Bowyer's losses and despite the failure of Bowyer's project, the story does at least demonstrate the power of the early history of England to inspire people to choose the highest possible of art forms in which to represent it.

At around the time that Bowyer was contemplating his sorrows, in commemoration of Alfred's most celebrated encounter Sir David Wilkie (1785-1841) painted *Alfred Reprimanded by the Neatheard's Wife* in 1806, which was later engraved by James Mitchell in 1828. The march of the Anglo-Saxons in a visual form simply would not cease.

One by one they came until what had been a trickle turned into a flood. The notion of the Anglo-Saxons as the true forefathers of the contemporary English had finally come to rest in the minds of the nation. There was William Dyce's *St Dunstan Separating Edwy and Elgiva* (1839), Richard Dadd's *Alfred the Great reflecting on the Misfortunes of his Country* (1840) and *Elgiva, the Queen of Edwy, in Banishment* (1840). Dyce's *Baptism of St Ethelbert* (1846) was part of the decoration of the south wall of the House of Lords. John Everett Millais contributed with a haunting composition simply entitled *Elgiva* (1847) and probably in the next year he was followed by Alfred Stevens with *King Alfred and his Mother*. In 1852 Daniel Maclise painted his giant *Alfred the Saxon King Disguised as a Minstrel in the Tent of Guthrum the Dane,* now in the Laing Art Gallery Newcastle Upon Tyne. But perhaps the most significant paintings on Anglo-Saxon themes of this era were hung in the new Houses of Parliament.

There was much gnashing of teeth over the entries to the competition to decorate the new Houses of Parliament. The place had burnt to the ground in October 1834, both houses being consigned to the ashes. From 1841 Sir Charles Barry's building at the palace of Westminster was being erected and a select committee was soon appointed to ponder the internal decorations. In 1842 the first competitions were held for the cartoons which would be the springboard for the designs of the frescoes for the walls. Any subject from British history could be chosen as well as themes from Spenser, Shakespeare and Milton. Of the 20 Anglo-Saxon subjects hanging on the walls of Westminster Hall 11 were based on the conversion of the English to Christianity and a great deal of the others were Alfredian. King Harold, Edward the Martyr and King Cnut brought up the rear. Charles West Cope's (1811-90) *The first trial by jury* won a prize of £300 and a £200 prize went to John Callcott Horsley (1817-1903) for his *St Augustine preaching to Ethelbert and Bertha*. A second competition was announced in 1843 and held the following year. The rules were more or less the same as before but this time sculptures were added to the mix and Alfred made three appearances in the round as a result. As far as the Anglo-Saxons are concerned, the chosen themes were the same as before, including one picture by John Martin on the theme of Cnut. The third competition was held in 1844 for frescoes for six arched recesses in the House of Lords and here the subject of the baptism of King Ethelbert of Kent made an appearance. But it was with the fourth competition that the big oil paintings came along. This competition took a little while to get together. It was first announced in 1844 and was subsequently re-announced in 1845 and 1846 for 1847.

Nine prizes were to be offered for oil paintings on any subject within religion, history or poetry; £500, £300 and £200 were the prize categories. The winning paintings would be hung around the Palace of Westminster. In 1847 the competition was held in Westminster Hall and included 123 paintings. Some entrants attracted more criticism than others. For example, F.S. Archer's *Alfred the Great with the Book of Common Law* was castigated as a 'tame, spiritless specimen of vulgarity'. Based directly on a lamentation over the dead body of Christ, Frederick Richard Pickersgill supplied to the competition *The Burial of Harold* (1847). It drew considerable comment.

People had seen this episode so many times before, that *Punch* was moved to comment that it hoped:

> British artists would leave off finding his body any more, which they have been doing, in every exhibition, for these fifty years.

The other painting on an Anglo-Saxon theme which still adorns the wall of Westminster Hall was painted by G.F. Watts in the same year. *Alfred inciting the English to resist the Danes* is a monumental piece of work packed with meaning. We are fortunate enough to be led through it, detail by detail by the artist who wrote to a Miss Duff Gordon about the work in December 1846. He said the painting was 'dedicated to patriotism and posterity' and when describing Alfred he said 'I have endeavoured to give him as much energy, dignity, and expression as possible, without exaggeration.'

The painting was one of only three to win a prize of £500. But even this tremendous and quintessentially Victorian effort at reshaping the past does not go the whole way. The Anglo-Saxons in the form of King Alfred had made a number of appearances around Westminster during the competitions, but by far the most impressive and symbolic sculpture was made by William Theed at the suggestion of Queen Victoria. The sculpture, now in the Royal Collection of Victoria and Albert dressed as Anglo-Saxons at once captures the Germanism of the monarchy, whilst suggesting to its audience something which was already being widely acknowledged: the English were the Anglo-Saxons.[3]

Portraits and engravings

The influential histories of the eighteenth century had been the vehicle for the arrival on the scene of a visual and more accessible form of Anglo-Saxon history. This came initially in the form of engraved portraits featured in the earliest versions of Rapin's *History*. They included King Egbert, King Alfred and King Cnut. Later, in Tindall's translated edition of Rapin, the earlier portraits were replaced by new depictions by George Vertue who had illustrated Wise's edition of Asser[4] Alfred was now complete with accompanying spears, swords, harp, scrolls and a captured Viking standard. Another of Vertue's portraits would show William the Conqueror symbolically holding Britannia in chains. During the 1760s and 1770s engravings by Charles Grignion, and others, of drawings by Samuel Wale (1721-86) depicting themes from Anglo-Saxon history were published in a number of the popular histories we have already mentioned. Similarly, a series of illustrations appeared by Hamilton and Edwards in the 1770s and 1780s.

Notwithstanding the continued tensions between England and France, the Saxons continued to be presented more or less for their own sake as well. There was a great interest in the golden age of the tenth century in particular, with Edward the Elder, King Edgar, King Edwy and their attendant courtroom dramas being recalled in both literary and fine art form.

Literature

These visual representations of the great figures and events in Anglo-Saxon history were accompanied by countless poems and books, some of dubious quality, but they reflected a deeply held Victorian philosophy. People were becoming convinced that they were the direct inheritors of the Anglo-Saxon way. A society ruled by a monarchy and yet with a democratically elected government – the ultimate Anglo-Saxon compromise. A nation of committees and democratic consensus not without its figureheads and heroes, even if some of them ultimately failed in their own contemporary struggles.

As far as the Victorian child was concerned there was the phenomenally successful *Little Arthur's History of England* (1835) written by Maria, Lady Callcott. Its inclusion here allows us to bridge the gap between popular instruction and the romantic novel based on Anglo-Saxon themes which were now very much on the march. First published in 1835 in two octodecimo volumes, this trip through every period of England's history went through 70 editions in its first hundred years. The preface was dedicated 'to mothers' and its tone is set in a friendly and helpful way directed to the attentive child of the title. It starts with the immortal notion that 'A very long time ago, Britain was so full of trees that there was very little room for houses.' But the Anglo-Saxons are given a great deal of coverage in eight different chapters allowing little Arthur to learn much of the salient features of the era, and the sweeping generalisations are perhaps understandable:

> Everything seemed to be going well with the Britons and the Romans, when a great misfortune happened which I must tell you about ... by little and little the Saxons and the Angles drove the natives out of almost all Britain.

That said, in the chapter on Edward the Confessor, little Arthur learns something which might well have stood him in good stead had he chosen to pursue Anglo-Saxon history later in life:

> I do not think the English would have allowed Duke William to be king so easily, if he had not told them that Edward the Confessor had promised that he should be king and persuaded them that Prince Edgar Atheling, who, as I told you, ought to have been king after Edward, was too silly ever to govern the kingdom well.[5]

For adults, the genre of the historical novel was getting to grips with the Anglo-Saxons. Sir Walter Scott's *Ivanhoe* (1819) gave popular access to the notion of the oppressed Anglo-Saxon, disinherited yet proud.[6] After *Ivanhoe*, there was Edward Bulwer Lytton's *Harold, the Last of the Saxon Kings* of 1848, which contains in its title only a half-truth. Later still, there was Charles Kingsley's *Hereward the Wake* of 1866. It was an era that is still the dream of the modern Anglo-Saxonist. Unlike the previous centuries which were certainly populated by earnest scholars and historically minded politicians, here in the Victorian age, there was a consensus on all sides of the political divide. Alfred had appealed to the old Whig and Tory alike, the Anglo-Saxons as a whole to the monarchist and the flag bearer for the common man. Small wonder then, that so many themes from Anglo-Saxon history were portrayed by such a wide variety of artists and hung in such a wide variety of public and private places.

Running alongside the popular commemoration of the Anglo-Saxons in the form of the great history paintings and small engravings was another, perhaps more subtle, genre, that of the historical novel. This was an era when the facts as presented in fiction were blurred with reality to the extent that it is probable that the creative work was taken more or less as gospel. It seems this was the case with *Ivanhoe*. Set in the twelfth century during a time of continuing strife between Saxon and Norman, the opening chapter of this famous masterpiece involved a discussion between the Saxon Gyrth, a swineherd, and Wamba, a servant, on the consequences and effects of the Norman Conquest on the language and society of the English. It became a stance which saw the Normans as enslavers of the English and polluters of their language and it was difficult to dislodge from the popular mind, for much the same thing was being said in academic circles.

In 1844 Charles Macfarlane published his *Camp of Refuge*, a work set around the time of the Norman Conquest, but within a few years Bulwer-Lytton's *Harold, the Last of the Saxon Kings* would set the tone. In the preface to his first edition the story is given a comparative treatment with the Trojan wars. Bulwer-Lytton saw the whole struggle between William and Harold as something of a Homeric epic and indeed the whole tone of the novel smacks of being inspired by *The Iliad*. But it is for its sympathetic portrayal of Harold as the flag bearer for an English national character that the work was most influential. Here is what Bulwer-Lytton had to say of his main character in his dedicatory epistle to the Right Hon. C.T. D'eyncourt, M.P:

> In the character of Harold – while I have carefully examined and weighed the scanty evidences of its distinguishing attributes which are yet preserved to us – and, in spite of no unnatural partiality, have not concealed what appear to me its deficiencies, and still less the great error of the life it illustrates,– I have attempted, somewhat and slightly, to shadow out the ideal of the pure Saxon character, such as it was then, with its large qualities undeveloped, but marked already by patient endurance, love of justice, and freedom – the manly sense of duty rather than the chivalric sentiment of honour – and that indestructible element of practical purpose and courageous will, which, defying all conquest, and steadfast in all peril, was ordained to achieve so vast an influence over the destinies of the world.

But just before *Harold* had come out, there had been something of great significance in the interpretation of the Anglo-Saxons published by Benjamin Disraeli (1804-81). Disraeli, an accomplished novelist, whose fame would have been secure had he not had such an illustrious political career wrote *Sybil, or the two Nations* in 1846. It was an attempt to show that the class divide in England and the subsequent poverty of the lower classes was not just a Whig observation. The Norman descendants are of course the rich ones, and the Saxons the poor. The novel went a long way towards consolidating the myth of class by converting it into a national historical myth with clear-cut boundaries, but again it stuck in the minds of its readers. There was an attempt here also to portray the history of England as one long continuous tale, with each new group adding to the achievements of the other:

> o! England, glorious and ancient realm, the fortunes of thy polity are indeed strange! The wisdom of the Saxons, Norman valour, the state-craft of the Tudors, the national sympathies of the Stuarts, the spirit of the latter Guelphs struggling against their enslaved sovereignty,– these are the high qualities, that for a thousand years have secured thy national developement.

Whilst these novels were shaping opinion of England's past, there were continuing contributions from the pens of poets. Wordsworth had 22 chronological sonnets on Anglo-Saxon themes published in 1822, but something less profound, though still amusing, was given to us by another poet. Similar to the way in which the subject was approached by Dibdin, but using exclusively the form of sonnets, there appeared in 1854 a book of *Sonnets on Anglo-Saxon History* by Ann Hawkshaw (1813-85). Certain subjects, it seems attracted the romantic minds of the Victorian poet. The whole of the Anglo-Saxon period from the original settlement of the migrants to the Norman Conquest was covered by Hawkshaw. Unlike Dibdin's affected metrical assault on modern sensibilities, Hawkshaw's sonnets are still quite readable today. Hawkshaw seems to have had a fascination with druidism in the early Saxon period, placing a sonnet in this section of her book where strictly speaking, no druid had a right to appear. But what is more revealing than the inclusion of a famous old subject for the romantic mind is the fact that the book contains eight sonnets on the subject of the role of St Dunstan in Old English history, beating the number of sonnets given to Alfred by three. Perhaps surprisingly, the number of sonnets celebrating Earl Godwin and his struggles with Edward the Confessor, also match those given to Alfred. The last but one sonnet which is one of a number which close the book, makes some questionable assumptions, but does at least show how the Victorian mind was grasping the meaning of the Norman Conquest in popular culture and from what we have said so far, there should be no surprise to hear it:

CONQUERED, but unsubdued in spirit still,
The sullen Saxon tilled the Norman's field,
Chained down to earth he still refused to yield,
The conqueror's foot could never crush his will;
With a slave's heart he might his tasks fulfil,
But no slave's heart was his, and daily toil
Wound not around his soul a deadening coil,
Its higher hopes and faculties to kill.
And so the conquerors had to yield at last,
E'en to the conquered language, laws and name;
And as their sons in freedom grow, that past
Is looked upon with reverence, not with shame,
And hearts that beat beyond the Atlantic tide,
Turn to that far-off time with love and pride.

Yet the novels continued to come. Sometimes they were written by authors with worthy credentials indeed. Charles Kingsley, chair of modern history at Cambridge had a special penchant for the tale of Hereward the Wake and penned a novel on the subject which was widely read. The attraction of the struggle of the conquered English against their masters was lost on no one. In his prelude to *Hereward the Wake, Last of the English* (1866), Kingsley at once captures the general feeling at large at the time. Hereward's story was like so many others of later medieval history in that it was a fight for liberty and justice. The Englishman simply could not lose:

When the men of Wessex, the once conquering race of Britain, fell at Hastings once and for all, and struck no second blow, then the men of the Danelagh disdained to yield to the Norman invader. For seven long years they held their own, not knowing, like true Englishmen, when they were beaten; and fought on desperate, till there were none left to fight. Their bones lay white on every island in the fens; their corpses rotted on gallows beneath every Norman keep; their few survivors crawled into monasteries, with eyes picked out, or hands and feet cut off, or took to the wild wood as strong outlaws, like their successors and representatives, Robin Hood, Scarlet, and John, Adam Bell, and Clym of the Cleugh, and William of Cloudeslee. But they never really bent their necks to the Norman yoke; they kept alive in their hearts that proud spirit of personal independence, which they brought with them from the moors of Denmark and the dales of Norway; and they kept alive, too, though in abeyance for a while, those free institutions which were without a doubt the germs of our British liberty.

And so it seems that the Anglo-Saxons not only had conquered popular culture in the period from the middle of the eighteenth to the late nineteenth centuries, but had more or less reversed the Norman Conquest to boot. The 1880s and 1890s saw more literary endeavours, particularly in the field of juvenile novels such as the *Chronicle of Aescendune* by A.D. Crake and Emma Leslie's *Gytha's Message*, but by now the Anglo-Saxons were almost home and dry. There was one, however, who saw the whole triumphant re-working of English history as something to be lampooned. For William Makepeace Thackeray it had all gone just a little too far. In his *Miss Tickletoby's lectures on English History* (published in Punch in the 1880s) the burlesque character of Miss Tickletoby gets almost everything wrong in her talks, including a mix-up of dates, people and places, but still has enough conviction to state to her audience how angry she felt that 'Beggarly, murderous Frenchmen should have beaten our honest English in the way they did.'

Thackeray's humour notwithstanding, the Saxons were clearly in the driving seat. But before we examine the arguments of those responsible for something of a Norman fight-back, there is much to explore in the world of the Victorian Anglo-Saxon and his greatest figure deserves particular attention.

KEMBLE AND HIS AUDIENCE

John Mitchell Kemble (1807–57) was a man of many facets. He was the son of Charles Kemble, the actor, and was the elder brother of the actress Fanny Kemble, whose life outlasted her brother's. Educated at first at a school in Clapham run by Charles Richardson, who used some of his boys to help him compile a *Dictionary of the English Language,* Kemble may have become interested in philology at an early stage in his life. After this, he attended the King Edward VI Free Grammar School of Bury St Edmunds. By the time he went to Trinity College, Cambridge, on the 26 June 1824, Kemble was already developing an interest in philosophy. His approach was not the norm, and he was an energetic talker on political and historical subjects. He would prefer metaphysics to mathematics and Anglo-Saxon to Latin, it is said. It all led his famous sister to question whether his passions might even injure his health. Fanny was certainly clear that his labours would not necessarily be rewarded with the degree he so craved.

But John Kemble was one of those unstoppable characters. At Trinity he soon became a member of an elite and secretive debating club founded in 1820 by George Tomlinson known as the *Cambridge Apostles* and sometimes called the *Cambridge Conversazione Society*. Kemble performed admirably for this stage and he was also known for his frequent contributions to the Union Society. His papers to the *Cambridge Apostles* were apparently long remembered. The group would discuss a subject of their choice every Saturday night and there were no limits to or censorship of the subject matter. Kemble's own contributions do not survive in full though it is recalled that he had once said 'the world is one great thought and I am thinking it.'[7]

Quite what gave Kemble his remarkably lofty attitude is not known. It was sometimes remarked of the Kembles that they somehow seemed to be imbued with a degree of arrogance. Certainly, it was an attitude which betrayed a deeply held conviction of superiority, but it led to observations such as that made by Thackeray's daughter, Anne:

> The Kembles strike one somehow as a race apart. They seem divided from the rest of us by more dominant natures, by more expressive ways and looks; one is

reminded of those deities who once visited the earth in the guise of shepherds, as wanderers clad in lion skins, as nurses and huntresses, not as Kembles only.[8]

By 1828, Kemble was an Anglican priest. Having upset his Cambridge examiners with his strongly held views, he went to Germany during his vacation in 1829 with Charles Barton. It was a watershed for him. He had gone there ostensibly to pursue his study of German philosophy at Munich. His intellectual interest switched soon after this trip from philosophy to philology, and it is around this time that Kemble became well acquainted with the work of Jacob Grimm (1785-1863), whose own philological law regarding sound change in the Germanic branches of the Indo-European languages became widely accepted. Here in Germany, where Kemble would get much of his subsequent inspiration, he realised that a country was finding itself. The scholars there were thorough, studied widely and their diligence impressed him. There was an awakening interest in the Germanic and non-classical past in Germany as an expression of national identity. Germanism was its root and Kemble took it to about as far as it was possible to take it. He would later write that the Germanisation of England was a phenomenon attributable not to the traditional fifth and sixth centuries but something which he perceived stretched back to the days of the Germanic elements of the late Roman armies of Britain. The notion of Germanism continued to gather steam in England when the great Victorian Saxonist Benjamin Thorpe translated Happenberg's 1834 work *A History of England Under the Anglo-Saxon Kings*, in 1846, but it is to Kemble's own efforts that we must now turn.

Kemble returned to England. Then, after a brief adventure as a revolutionary in Spain in 1830-31 when he got involved in a plot to overthrow the despotic regime of King Ferdinand VII, he came back once again. His decision to return to his love of philology may well have been dictated by the moral dilemma surrounding his widely observed dalliance with a 16-year-old Spanish girl named Francisa. A career in the Church would now surely prove to be a difficult prospect. And so to Trinity College he returned. For the next two years he spent much time in the Trinity and Corpus Christi libraries familiarising himself with the Old English manuscripts, occasionally visiting the British Museum to complement his studies. After contributing some material to the *Foreign Quarterly Review* and *The Philological Museum* he began work on his edition of *Beowulf* which was published in 1833. In this work, Kemble paid tribute to Grimm, whom he described as a '... tribute of admiration and respect from perhaps the first Englishman who has adopted and acted upon his views.'

Kemble busied himself with lecture tours on the subject of the history of the English language but found himself performing in front of smaller audiences each time, for which Kemble was not entirely blameless.[9] In 1834, Kemble gave a good review of Thorpe's *Analecta Anglo-Saxonica* in the *Gentleman's Magazine*. Here, he vented his feelings about the poor quality of English researchers when compared with their German and Danish counterparts, likening their lack of discipline to that of a schoolboy and suggested the punishment be the same. The targets of the attacks were the previous incumbents of the Rawlinson chair of Anglo-Saxon at Oxford: only three of the nine had ever published anything by 1834. But the attack led to a rear guard action and did Kemble no favours in the long run, especially after the chair in question was reconstituted by Joseph Bosworth in 1858. Kemble's arrogance, as well as his talent, was now widely acknowledged.

Kemble spent much of 1834 trying to consolidate his German connections and in this he was successful enough to win himself a wife. After correspondence earlier in the year, he visited Jacob Grimm in August and met Natalie Auguste, daughter of Johann Amadeus Wendt, Professor of Philosophy at Göttingen. Shortly before his marriage, Kemble found a role as editor of the *British and Foreign Review*, a position he kept until 1844. It was a journal that took a pro-European view and its message was clearly that the intellectual life of Englishmen would be greatly enhanced by cross-channel cooperation as opposed to some sort of splendid isolation, a subject with which Kemble was personally familiar. But his political editorship aside, Kemble had time to preside over the English Historical Society and also continued to produce his Anglo-Saxon works. He laboured on his translation of *Beowulf* which was published in 1837 and between 1839-48 he published a six-volume edition of Anglo-Saxon charters, the most comprehensive resource of charters of its kind entitled *Codex Diplomaticus Ævi Saxonici*. Before he embarked on his greatest of all works, *The Saxons in England*, in 1849, Kemble managed to produce two other works of note: an edition of the legend of St Andrew in the Vercelli book (1843) and an edition of *Salomon and Saturn (1848)*.

By 1844 Kemble's fortunes had waned after a spell as a theatre censor and the collapse of the *British and Foreign Review*. He had parted company with his wife and by 1849 was living in relative discomfort with his children in a cottage in Hertfordshire.

But it is for his *Saxons in England, a History of the English Commonwealth till the Period of the Norman Conquest*, that Kemble attracted great fame. Published in the same year as he narrowly failed to obtain the chair of modern history at Cambridge, Kemble poured his patriotism into the work as any reader of the opening dedication could not fail to observe:

TO

THE QUEEN'S MOST EXCELLENT MAJESTY,

THIS HISTORY

OF THE PRINCIPLES WHICH HAVE GIVEN HER EMPIRE

ITS PREEMINENCE

AMONG THE NATIONS OF EUROPE

IS

WITH HER GRACIOUS PERMISSION

INSCRIBED BY

THE MOST HUMBLE AND DEVOTED

OF HER SERVANTS.

Kemble's *The Saxons in England* was a hard-hitting piece of work. The subject, he said was a very 'grave and solemn one'. Throughout Europe Kemble said thrones were tottering 'and the deep foundations of society were convulsed' and yet the present queen sat on her throne in a degree of security made possible for her by the attitudes and institutions of her Anglo-Saxon forebears.

Shot and shell sweep the streets of capitals which have long been pointed out as the chosen abodes of order....Yet the exalted Lady who wields the sceptre of these realms sits safe upon her throne, and fearless in the holy circle of her domestic happiness, secure in the affections of a people whose institutions have given to them all the blessings of an equal law. Those institutions they have inherited from a period so distant as to excite our admiration.

For Kemble, the Victorian age had managed to unite the twin Anglo-Saxon attitudes of complete obedience to the law with the greatest amount of personal freedom.

We have a share in the past and the past yet works in us; nor can a patriotic citizen better serve his country than by devoting his energies and his time to record that which is great and glorious in her history, for the admiration and instruction of her neighbours.

The book is another gigantic effort. It called into question much of what had gone before. Kemble even attacked the narrative interpretations of Bede and the *Anglo-Saxon Chronicle* as presented by both Turner and Happenberg. It was clear to Kemble that he wanted the history books rewritten:

I confess that the more I examine this question, the more completely I am convinced that the received accounts of our migrations, our subsequent fortunes, and ultimate settlement are devoid of historical truth in every detail.

Kemble was convinced that the received wisdom was based on only a poor understanding of a very few sources and he was in a good position to know that there were many other relatively untouched sources to be interpreted:

[the sources are] a confused mass of traditions borrowed from the most heterogeneous sources, compacted rudely and with little ingenuity, and in which the smallest possible amount of historical truth is involved in a great deal of fable.

Kemble moved to Hanover in 1849-50. He was still there in 1854. He had become interested in the material aspects of Germanic culture and was a surprisingly good archaeologist for his time. He excavated the burial mounds on Lüneburg Heath and the surrounding area and was adept at spotting ploughed-out remains, something of an intuitive skill without the aid of modern technology. He gave a series of lectures at the newly opened Royal Museum at Hanover on his discoveries. On his return to England in 1855 he published some papers in *Fraser's Magazine, Archaeologia* (in which he published a paper of early English runes) and the *Archaeological Journal* and had found a publisher for his German excavations which was to be a volume entitled *Horae Ferales*. However, when *Horae Ferales or Studies in the Archaeology of Northern Nations* was completed by Dr R.G. Latham in 1863 after Kemble's death it was not the work Kemble had envisaged.

Kemble's fortunes had revived by the time he left for Dublin in 1857 to address the Royal Irish Academy. But on 26 March, his poor health caught up with him and he died of pneumonia. He had had a remarkable life and was clearly a tremendous contributor to the field of Anglo-Saxon studies. His work on *Beowulf* published in 1833 and 1837 was of great influence, as were his comprehensive collection of charters which included newly discovered material. In fact, Kemble was always aware of these new discoveries and still wished to publish updated versions right up to the time of his death. The task, however, fell to W. de Gray Birch of the British Museum who took the collection up to the year 975. By recognising the growing power of archaeology in the search for the Anglo-Saxons, Kemble showed himself to be the first truly all-round Anglo-Saxonist of the modern age. We shall follow the fortunes of those who wielded the spade and the trowel as we now move into an era when Anglo-Saxonism acquired several new and occasionally sinister dimensions to it.[10]

THE VICTORIAN ANGLO-SAXONS

What were the attributes which make up an Anglo-Saxon? According to the Victorian scholar, the answer was as follows. A love of freedom and a hatred of anarchic disorder coupled with a respect for the law. This at least represented the political disposition of an Anglo-Saxon. As for personal attributes, these were most important of all: to be able to exhibit restraint, self control, rational thinking and have a healthy distrust for enthusiasm. Yes, anyone who embodied all of these things was an ideal Anglo-Saxon.

One wonders how many of these attributes no longer apply to a modern English man or woman, but it is important to realise that these views at the time were widely and firmly held and that they were preached as much by the leading lights of academia as by anyone else. That is not to say that there is anything inherently wrong in holding these views, but the gulf between the ideal and the reality was as wide then as it surely is now. Vestiges of the Victorian notion of the Anglo-Saxon still survive in England, though we must turn now to examine not only how the notion grew but how the historians of the age drove the machinery of the Anglo-Saxon revival forward.

There was a growing tendency in Victorian England to view the Anglo-Saxons not so much in the pure Germanistic way that Kemble had, but to see them as an insular variation on a theme. This was particularly true of the Oxford School who rose to prominence in the second half of the century. Here in England, the Germanic hordes had got it right. They had set up a Germanic Utopia which even their homeland had failed to match. Kemble's direct love affair with Germany was considered with suspicion. The Anglo-Saxons needed a divorce from Germany if their Englishness was to be expressed coherently to a modern and confident audience.

As early as 1807, long before Kemble had really got going, but at about the same time as Turner was writing his greatest work, the Revd James Ingram gave his inaugural lecture as professor of Anglo-Saxon at Oxford. Here, he directly appealed for Anglo-Saxon studies to be based purely on patriotic grounds. But mere patriotism was not everything in this mysterious world of global Anglo-Saxonism. The race issue came again to the fore. This time, perhaps predictably, the connection was with America, but this particular piece was written by a *Times* columnist on the eightieth anniversary of the American Declaration of Independence on 8 July 1856. It is a jaw-dropping demonstration of the inner workings of the supremely confident mind of the Victorian Anglo-Saxonist:

Anglo-Saxons must surely be wanting to themselves if they make no bond of communion of their common birth and parentage. We Englishmen, then, see in the American energy, industry, and indomitable spirit the tokens of the Anglo-Saxon blood, and we feel proud of our race. The sight inspires cheerful and animated prophecy, and we see in this master race a powerful and dominant agent in the future history of the world. We see that this race has a destiny, that it does not seem to die out after it has done some great acts, as other races have done, but to possess an inexhaustible life; that it spreads, and covers the earth, and that wherever it goes, it conquers nature, establishes law, and imparts the blessings of peace, order, and civil liberty. Doubtless it is for no nation or race to boast, for the 'jealous divinity' of even Pagan religion punished the boaster. Indeed, the boaster punishes himself, and soon falls in the natural order of things, for this reason – that the boasting spirit is an idle one. The Monarch who looked from his wall and said 'Is not this great Babylon that I have built?' was a true boaster; he thought he had done enough; he was satisfied with his work, and he abandoned himself to the repose of a perfect self-complacency, unruffled by action. But the Anglo-Saxon is industrious, and genuine industry does not boast, because it has not time, and because industrious spirit looks to the future; the boastful one to the past.

The transatlantic bond, then, was still a strong one. In academic circles in England, the influence of the Oxford School reached its peak in the 1860s and 1870s amid a celebration of English nationalism. The key players of this School were Edwin Guest; William Stubbs (1829-1901); J.R. Green (1837-83) and E.A. Freeman (1823-92), whose *The History of the Norman Conquest of England, its Causes and its Results* (six volumes 1867-69) was and still is the greatest work ever produced on the subject despite its patriotic pitfalls. Their brand of Anglo-Saxonism lay firmly rooted in Bede and the *Anglo-Saxon Chronicle* and it has taken scholars of a more recent generation an almighty effort to shift the focus.

Somewhat less entertaining, although it could be seen these days as amusing, were the assertions of some historians that the original Saxon invasions had been nothing less than an annihilating slaughter. Green, for example, in his *Short History of the English People* (1874), vehemently subscribed to this long-held view, but was also keen to point out the insular variation on Germanic culture was by far the most worthy: 'The new England ... was the one purely German nation that rose upon the wreck of Rome.' (9:11). The Stubbsian view was no less laudatory of the Teutonic influence, claiming in his *The Constitutional History of England* (1880) that early Anglo-Saxon political institutions were 'The most purely German that any branch of the German race has preserved.'

The racial element to the argument had begun to appear in the 1860s. It was not entirely the case that the argument belonged to the contemporary Christian intellectual fraternity, either. Race, it seemed, was a word to be liberally used by anyone with an agenda. In 1864 a lecture was published in a pamphlet entitled *A Lecture on the Israelitish Origin of the Anglo-Saxons*. Here, some extraordinary claims were made. On comparing the Anglo-Saxon invasion of Britain with the arrival of the Israelites into Canaan, the author states 'There is little or no mixture with conquered race, as is universally the case when other than Teutonic race form colonies.'

The author is adamant that the Anglo-Saxons are in fact the children of one of the lost tribes of Israel. And, on the origin of the word *Saxon*, the author demonstrates what can be done if we dismiss our opponents and push the boat out:

> We suppose it derived from Isaac, whose name, as we learn from Amos.Vii 9 16. the Israelites, shortly before their captivity, had assumed to represent their nation. It was usual to contract the commencement of the name when combining it with another word and in familiar conversation, and thus Saxon means Son of Isaac. But we need not the aid of Etymology on this subject.[11]

This curious lecture demonstrates to us a number of aspects of the Anglo-Saxon adventure through history up to this point in the 1860s. How inextricable they are from the world of religion, whether it is pagan, Christian or Jewish, how the more overt usage of race has overtaken language in the arguments of all parties and also how and why people clearly wanted to claim the Anglo-Saxons as their own. The power and impact of the Anglo-Saxons on a contemporary mind would never reach quite such dizzy heights again.

And so the racial arguments continued throughout the nineteenth century, sometimes with amusing results. L.O. Pike in 1866 wrote a book entitled *The English and their Origin*. It is a work shot through with spurious ethnological assumptions which does not in fact take the turn one might expect of a Victorian scholar of this period. Here is a seemingly significant part of the preface:

> I suppose no one will deny that if any literary task is worth undertaking an Englishman may consider all time well spent which is spent in attempting to ascertain what are the bodily and mental features possessed by the majority of Englishmen, to what sources those features are to be traced, and how far they resemble or differ from the marked features of other nations.

One might have expected a rant in the support of the Teutonic master race to have followed this forthright announcement, but Pike's observations, flawed as they were, led him to conclude that Germanism had little to do with it after all. Adopting a joint ethnological and philological approach which included the examination of hair colour and stature, Pike cooked up a theory which said that the characteristics of Englishmen, especially those of a strong will, energy and athleticism were in fact pre-Teutonic in origin.

The approach manifested itself in the form of the comparison of cultural and physical traits of contemporary English people as observed by writers who published their work in respectable journals of the day. Their observations seem to us today to be nothing short of outrageous, although we have to understand that even at their time of writing they were considered a little controversial. Two examples will serve to show the passion which the subject aroused.

G. Allen wrote in the *Fortnightly Review* of 1880 a paper entitled *Are We Englishmen?* In it, he made a number of observations. He viewed the blurring of the British and English identities as a Tudor influence brought about by the necessity to demonstrate unity in the country, a phenomenon subsequently strengthened by the Act of Union. This blurring, he argued '... led the whole world to talk of England as if it were in reality Wales.'

Allen acknowledged that Freeman and Green had been most influential in educating people as to the Teutonic nature of England's institutions, and went as far as saying that the nation was indeed Teutonic in form if not in matter, but he raised the point that the contemporary population was surely basically native and not Germanic in stock:

> While in language, laws, customs and government we are preponderantly or entirely English, yet in blood we are preponderantly, if not overwhelmingly Kymric or Gaelic.

Allen cited contemporary Jamaica as an example of this phenomenon, stating that were it not for the obvious physical differences between the natives and their masters a casual observer might think that the Jamaican was an Englishman. He then launches into an attack on what he sees as a racial argument gone too far. The Anglo-Saxons must be taken down a peg or two, since their dominant view seems to be taking over the argument. In a side swipe at those who argued for Germanic blood pumping through the hearts of all Englishmen, Allen noted that 'Silly Suffolk' was the conventional phrase given to the most Teutonic county in Britain. But he ended his paper on a more serious note:

> A fair recognition of the strength of the Keltic element in England itself – an element which, as I believe, has done much to differentiate our national character from that of the slow and ponderous continental Teutons – may help to break down this unhappy prejudice of race.

It was an interesting rebuttal to the prevailing wind of opinion on the matter and some useful comparisons to other cultures were made, although the approach was scarcely scientific. But when people tried to justify their theories on the racial aspect of the Anglo-Saxon influence in Britain by using some form of scientific analysis, their results seem to the modern reader to be vaguely absurd. Nuggets of information, much of it spurious, are seized and used to reinforce stereotypes long adhered to by the authors of the research. A classic example of this sort of nonsense, which must rank as essential reading by way of a warning to any modern student of the Anglo-Saxon legacy is J. Foster Palmer's 1885 rant published in no less a journal than that of the Royal Historical Society entitled *The Saxon Invasion and its Influence on our Character as a Race.*

Palmer saw the early Dark Ages in England in purely black and white terms. It was a struggle between two different races, the Celt and the Saxon. Like Allen, he acknowledged that there was much native blood flowing through the veins of a modern Englishman, and also like Allen, he provided a foreign example, in this case that of China, to show how a race remains essentially the same in blood stock despite numerous conquests. But Palmer's discourse on the physical characteristics of the British races and the behavioural traits thereof bring a tear to the modern eye.

The nation, Palmer concludes, is made up of three basic types: the Iberian (or prehistoric) stock, the Celtic stock and, of course, that of the Saxons. The Iberian influence is to be observed more often the further down the social scale one travels. Their features are said to include a short, stocky appearance and dark, curly hair. Similarly the Celts are short but muscular whilst the Saxons are the tallest of the lot. The Danish and Norman invasions of Britain are dismissed as having little or no influence over the gene pool. Some small amount of evidence is tabulated to show that there are different skull sizes in groups over the country, but it is all far from convincing. And then from nowhere in particular, except from the mind of the author comes this:

> Of our mental qualities we appear to derive from the Saxon our practical common sense, our business capacity, our power of adapting ourselves to circumstances, and what we may call in general terms, the faculty of colonisation.

Artistic and literary achievements are the province of the Celts who are praised for such contributions, but who also bring us mendacity and licentiousness. But there is apparently a drawback in the character of the Saxon. He is prone to alcoholism. Palmer considered this potentially divisive trait for a while and then leaped to the defence. Citing a *British Medical Journal* article of 1883[12] he explained a cultural tendency towards alcohol usage as a benefit: 'The alcohol bred races of the world, being almost invariably physically, morally and intellectually superior to those among whom abstinence is the rule.' After all, says Palmer 'The Tasmanians, the lowest of them all drank nothing but water.' Predictably, the American Indians were brought into the argument, it being suggested their intolerance for alcohol was part of their downfall.

Let us stay a little longer with Palmer, if we can possibly bear it, for it serves to prove a point. The superiority of the Saxon can be manifested in a love of truth he says. This is necessary for the observance of scientific matters. The fellows of the Royal Society he notes, without providing the evidence, are 'two inches taller than the average Englishman'.

And it is to the mind of the modern Englishman that the Anglo-Saxon has given the most:

> [The Saxons'] mental activity, acting on the contemplative Britons brought about
> that combination of thought and action which has made the England of today,
> and from which has been evolved that comprehensive English intellect of which
> Shakespeare is the type.

It is difficult to say which aspect of the Victorian legacy is greater. Is it the great march of scholarship culminating in the huge volumes of democracy-loving scholars such as Freeman whose work is still required reading to this very day, or is it this pervasive and niggling notion that the Anglo-Saxons were somehow a superior race who have imbued the modern Englishman with worthy characteristics? Even after the horrors of the Second World War, this latter notion, whilst no longer in its zenith, would not quite go away, and it is arguable that it still has not.

But we should end on a Victorian piece which demonstrates that despite the great heights to which the Anglo-Saxons had risen, there was at least one man prepared to attack them mercilessly. The Scottish born Thomas Carlyle (1795-1881) wrote a monumental work *Frederick the Great (1858-65)* in 21 volumes which received mixed reviews. The assault on the Anglo-Saxons occurred in Volume IV.3 and contained a view not widely accepted although it was indeed delivered with passion. It is included here because it is a fine example of how to construct an argument on a platform of ignorance:

England itself, in foolish quarters of England, still howls and execrates lamentably over its William Conqueror, and rigorous line of Normans and Plantagenets; but without them, if you will consider well, what had it ever been? A gluttonous race of Jutes and Angles, capable of no grand combinations; lumbering about in pot-bellied equanimity; not dreaming of heroic toil and silence and endurance, such as leads to the high places of this Universe, and the golden mountain-tops where dwell the Spirits of the Dawn. Their very ballot-boxes and suffrages, what they call their 'Liberty,' if these mean 'Liberty,' and are such a road to Heaven, Anglo-Saxon high-road thither,- could never have been possible for them on such terms. How could they? Nothing but collision, intolerable interpressure (as of men not perpendicular), and consequent battle often supervening, could have been appointed those undrilled Anglo-Saxons; their pot-bellied equanimity itself continuing liable to perpetual interruptions, as in the Heptarchy time. An enlightened Public does not reflect on these things at present; but will again, by and by. Looking with human eyes over the England that now is, and over the America and the Australia, from pole to pole; and then listening to the Constitutional litanies of Dryasaust, and his lamentations on the old Norman and Plantagenet Kings, and his recognition of departed merit and causes of effects,- the mind of man is struck dumb!

Carlyle's invective notwithstanding. The Anglo-Saxons were firmly ensconced in English hearts and the general public loved it.

STATUES AND CELEBRATIONS

Alfred is the most perfect character in history.... No other man on record has ever so thoroughly united all the virtues both of the ruler and of the private man ... there is no other name in history to compare with his.

E.A. Freeman. *The History of the Norman Conquest of England* (1867-69). Vol I p53-5

Such was the sentiment not just of Freeman, Alfred's champion, but of a great many other Victorians. As the Victorian era wore on the fame of Alfred in England did not recede. But, if we are to believe the words of those who organised it, the great millenary celebration of Alfred's birth held at Wantage in 1849 did not quite attract the highest calibre of guests as the organisers wished. Unstoppable though he might seem, Alfred it seemed had just a little way to go yet before his apotheosis. The celebrations at Wantage had been the idea of J.L. Brereton, proprietor of a rather short-lived journal called *The Anglo-Saxon*. Martin Tupper, a frequent contributor to the journal complained in Volume I of 1849 that he had had little or no response from the great and the good when he attempted to entice them to the event. The mayor of London had refused the Guildhall as a venue for the banquet claiming an outbreak of cholera as an excuse and so they had to do the whole thing back at Wantage. This disappointment notwithstanding, a remarkable event was held on 25 October 1849 to which around 10,000 people were attracted including local members of the landed gentry. Despite claims of poor organisation, the celebrations did produce some lasting results after a fashion. The Rev. J.A Giles, vicar of Bampton was a self-confessed Alfred fan and he had written A *Life and Times* of the king in the previous year. After the event, he produced *The Jubilee Edition of the Complete Works of King Alfred the Great* (1851) in two volumes.

But what of the dynasty of Alfred? It is important to remember when considering these public celebrations of Anglo-Saxon history, that it was not always Alfred at the heart of it. For as long as anyone could remember, there had been a mounting block in the Market Place in Kingston Upon Thames. This was the 'town of kings', that famous place in Surrey, the lauded town of the coronations of seven Anglo-Saxon kings, all the issue of Alfred the Great. First, there had been Edward the Elder in 900, then perhaps most famously of all, his first son Athelstan in 924 around whom something of a cult was built in Kingston by seven times mayor W.E. St Lawrence Finny. Then came Athelstan's brother Edmund in 939 and after his passing in 946 his brother Eadred took the throne. Then, in 956 the young and unfortunate Edwy inherited the crown of the kingdom. King Edgar (959-75) was not thought to have been crowned at Kingston, but his successors Edward the Martyr (975-79) and Æthelred II (979-1016) were. And so the 'Seven Saxons' as they came to be known received a grand makeover and re-launch in 1850. The monument erected that year was built around the rediscovered mounting block made of sarsen. It has never been proved that this was the stone upon which England was founded, but it is hard to explain its long acknowledged presence in a renowned royal tun. The coronation stone, as it stands today is still set within its Victorian railings, designed with seven corners, each tipped with a 'Saxon' spear. There are no hints that the celebrations were dogged in the same way as the Wantage ones two years earlier. The town was fascinated by its Saxon heritage and publicly linked the whole spectacle to the presiding queen, the descendant of Kingston's own kings.

The disappointment at Wantage in 1849 did not seem to bother anyone there. The town would soon receive a fine statue of Alfred. It was the work of Robert Loyd Lindsay, Conservative MP for Berkshire and later Lord Wantage. He commissioned a statue of Alfred from Count Gleichen which was unveiled before the eyes of the Prince and Princess of Wales in 1877. The inscription is suitably triumphant:

> Alfred found learning dead, and he restored it; education neglected, and he
> revived it; the laws powerless, and he gave them force; the Church debased, and
> he raised it; the land ravaged by a fearful enemy, from which he delivered it.
> Alfred's name will live as long as mankind shall respect the past.

Alfred could not and would not lie down. There were even calls for him to be celebrated as England's patron saint around the turn of the century. But it was at the millenary celebrations of the king's death in 1901 at Winchester that the pageant was at its most magnificent. Behind this was Frederic Harrison, vice-president of the Royal Historical Society. He had something of a track record in centenary celebrations having been involved in those of the Domesday Book in 1886 and the Armada in 1888, so the struggles of Wantage past were less likely to occur. Also, Harrison was well connected in Liberal circles. A national committee was set up in 1898 and it declared its intentions to commemorate 'the king to whom this Empire owes so much'. Coming on the back of Queen Victoria's Diamond Jubilee celebrations of 1897 and also coinciding with the Boer War, the celebrations would have a nationalistic tone to them. Many British politicians and the American ambassador were there in Winchester for the celebrations. Much of the money (£5000) needed to purchase the great statue of Alfred had actually been raised in America. Alfred Bowker, mayor of Winchester and secretary to the committee had managed to make sure Winchester was the chosen venue for the event. Hamo Thorneycroft's statue of Alfred in the Broadway at Winchester was unveiled by Lord Rosebery, the former prime minister. Alfred simply could not be raised any higher.

Alfred's daughter Æthelflead, the 'Lady' of the Mercians found her own way into the affections of the townsfolk of Tamworth. In 1913 a millenary celebration was held to commemorate the anniversary of the founding of the town by this redoubtable warrior leader. 'Queen Ethelfleda', who had campaigned in the saddle against the Vikings of the north and who had looked after her special charge, the young Atheling Athelstan, was also thought to have founded the site of Tamworth Castle. The town held Æthelflead in high regard for it was she who wrested back control of Tamworth from the Danes in 913, but they also had great affection for her nephew Athelstan. So, in July 1913 a whole week of celebrations were announced that included a pageant complete with actors playing roles from the lives of the Anglo-Saxon characters, and more lastingly, the unveiling of a magnificent statue erected near the Holloway Lodge of the castle. The statue was designed by local stonemason Henry Charles Mitchell and shows the Lady of the Mercians with sword in her hand caressing her little nephew encouraging him to help her guard the fortress which rises behind them. Athelstan gazes up at her thoughtfully and lovingly. The sculpture is a moving one and has a sentimentality to it that few memorials to any Anglo-Saxon figures possess. But the whole affair was very parochial. The statue was carved by Edward George Branwell, a former student at the Tamworth Arts classes and a City and Guilds of the London Art School. There had been a grand procession through the town before the arrival at the scene of the unveiling. This honour was carried out by Earl Ferrers, a descendant of one of the great families who once lived in the castle and those present at the unveiling were almost exclusively local dignitaries who included the mayor, town clerk, mace bearer and the custodian of the castle. Although there were 11 visiting mayors from towns across the north and central midlands, there was no former prime minister, no national leader or member of the royal family.

After the unveiling of the statue a procession led by the Tamworth Branch of the Territorial Force with attendant bugle band was followed by a parade of ex-servicemen, postmen, Ambulance Corps, fire brigade and VIP guests to the town's Assembly Rooms for a public luncheon. Here Earl Ferrers did his best. He proclaimed that the Lady would stand in the town for truth and right and for patience and perseverance, energy, patriotism and courage. These were the things, he said, which had made Tamworth what it was. The Revd William Macgregor followed up with a similar sentiment and a eulogy on the subject of her charge the boy Athelstan and he too claimed the statue would show the world what Tamworth could do. But war was coming. The country's mind was on other things.

The First and Second World Wars would go someway towards denting Alfred's superstar status and the reputation of his line. The twin themes of Germanism and racial propaganda made people in England a little wary. The great wealth of material that had been churned out on Alfred up to the turn of the century became a mere trickle. But as we will observe, Alfred still seems to occupy the popular hearts and minds to this day. It is perhaps not insignificant that at the last night of the proms each year the most raucous and patriotic of all the tunes played is that of *Rule Britannia*, which as we have observed, has its root in a masque of 1740.

So we must leave the fading memory of the great figures of Saxon England as the men and women who attended these great local pageants went off to prepare for war, and turn the clock back to look at the ways in which the spade and not the pen contributed to the revival of the Anglo-Saxons.

9

UNEARTHING THE ANGLO-SAXONS

A MATERIAL INTEREST

To be technically accurate, the interest in the physical remains of the Anglo-Saxons goes back a long way before the days of Leland and the itinerant antiquarians of the sixteenth and seventeenth centuries. We might recall William of Malmesbury's touching description of the chapel of Alfred at Athelney Island imbued with so much Christian symbolism at a time of deep crisis. We are also told by Roger of Wendover in the thirteenth century that excavations were undertaken at burial mounds in Redbourne in Hertfordshire during the twelfth century by monks who were looking for the bones of St Amphibalus.[1]

Later, in the seventeenth century, Sir Thomas Browne had found some 40-50 cremation urns in a field near Old Walsingham which although he believed them to be of Roman date, a common mistake at the time, he published a description of his findings in *Hydriotaphia, or Urn Buriall, or, A Discourse of the Sephulchrall Urnes lately found in Norfolk* (1658). But, as people began more and more to stumble across what soon became a vast and rich resource for Anglo-Saxon antiquaries and archaeologists in the form of early migration period pagan cemeteries, there were some chance finds which helped spark the interest of people in the Anglo-Saxons. Many of these chance finds may well have come from early period graves themselves, such as weaponry, beads and other personal adornment, but the discovery of the Alfred Jewel in 1693 could hardly have come at a better time when we consider the growing reputation of Alfred at Oxford.

But Thomas Wright, writing in 1852 at a time when Anglo-Saxon archaeology can truly be described as having taken-off, made the observation that most of the Anglo-Saxon material culture from the *early* period in England came from the pagan graves of the many hundreds of cemeteries. In this, he was quite right. And yet at the time of his writing, even after the spades of more than a handful of pioneers had revealed grave after grave, he could say:

> The largest and most important collections of Anglo-Saxon antiquities are those of Lord Londesborough, Dr. Fausett of Heppington near Canterbury, and Mr W.H. Rolfe of Sandwich, all taken from barrows in Kent. Smaller private collections are found in different parts of England and a few articles belonging to this class are met with in most local museums; but there is as yet no public collection of early Anglo-Saxon remains of any importance.[2]

The Anglo-Saxon cemeteries of the pagan era in England are an extraordinary resource. The settlers who came to the shores of Britannia in the fifth and sixth centuries have left us not only with a vast array of material culture enabling archaeologists to determine cultural complexities within different groups; the nature of trade and exchange; the rituals surrounding death, burial, warrior status and kin-group organisation, but they have also left us with themselves, their very remains. And from these bones people have, as we have seen, attempted to deduce a great many things.

But who were the pioneers who had brought the physical remains to the attention of a wide audience? The answer lies in the stories of two men of Kent. The Anglo-Saxon cemeteries of Kent are among the largest and richest in terms of material culture in the country. It is not difficult to imagine in the eighteenth century a person walking past a sandy quarry to see the evidence of his ancestors literally seeping out of the ground before his eyes. And, in the days of the pioneers, this is precisely what happened. Sometimes people were attracted by the great burial mounds which littered the landscape too. The Revd Bryan Faussett (1720-76), for a time curate of Kingston, had seen an early antiquarian investigation at Charlton Down in 1730 as a young boy.

He must have gained his lifelong interest from this experience. Although he would return to Charlton Down on at least two other occasions Faussett's first excavation appears to have been at Tremworth Down near Crundale, followed by extensive work at Gilton, Ash, in 1759. Here, ancient skeletal remains were revealed by the processes of sand extraction. Some locals had found it expedient to investigate the contents of the graves by burrowing in from the side of the sand banks and cliffs creating a patchwork of miniature 'ovens'. Faussett quickly saw the sense in excavating from the top down to reveal the graves in a more scientific manner, but at the same time was quite capable of getting through up to 50 such graves in a few days and at Gilton the following year he did just that.[3] But it seems, like others, Faussett was not entirely sure what he was looking at. Some of the remains of the people he discovered he thought to be either 'Romanised Britons' or 'Britons Romanised'. These inaccurate interpretations notwithstanding, modern scholars are blessed with his painstaking accounts and descriptions surviving in the form of Charles Roach Smith's 1856 publication of Faussett's manuscript material entitled *Inventorium Sephulcrale*.

In 1762 Faussett became a fellow of the Society of Antiquaries. Between 1767 and 1773 he opened over 300 graves along the Canterbury to Dover road which wound along the Downs near Kingston. And it is for his discovery of the Kingston brooch on the Barham Downs in 1771 that Faussett remains famous to this day. The circular brooch is a classic piece of early Anglo-Saxon workmanship incorporating a gold framework of cells set with garnet, blue glass and shell. The brooch is on display at Liverpool Museum, having arrived there with much of the Faussett Collection after the British Museum had refused to purchase it in 1853. It would seem that whilst the people of England were busily preparing their celebrations of ancient Saxon kings at Wantage and Kingston Upon Thames in the years around 1850, the world of officialdom was still a little slow in seizing the opportunity to buy for the nation its very own treasures. This failure of the British Museum to purchase the Faussett material after the death of Faussett's grandson in 1853 met with the great consternation of Charles Roach Smith who drew a not unreasonable comparison between the museum's willingness to gather the icons of other countries at the expense of the English.

The Revd James Douglas (1753-1819), the author of *Nenia Britannica, Or a Sepulchral History of Great Britain, from the earliest period to its general conversion to Christianity* (originally issued in 12 parts between 1786 and 1793), was another man of Kent, who was also a surveyor and keen antiquary. He had less trouble than Faussett in reaching a firm conclusion about the identity of the people in his graves. Working slightly later than Faussett, he published his material of excavations undertaken between 1779 and 1793 and explained the rationale behind his conclusion that his bodies were those of the Saxons. The cemeteries, he argued, were always close to villages with Saxon names and in an early observation on their distribution he pointed out that they were strewn only over the areas of the country that the Anglo-Saxons were supposed to have conquered. Douglas was, in fact, well ahead of his time. His scientific approach to Anglo-Saxon archaeology was largely ignored for at least two generations. He had concentrated on relative dating using numismatics as a guide and he had looked at soil composition and the usefulness of crop marks in identifying graves. All of this would be returned to in a later age of scientific investigation, but Douglas remains one of the great unsung heroes of English archaeology.

Kemble, of whom we have already heard, was one of the few Anglo-Saxonists who successfully crossed the trowel with the pen. The significance of his contribution to the material culture of the period lay in his meticulous observations of artefact types, particularly in the discipline of pottery. His conclusions that there were great similarities between the 'English' and 'German' material were influential in changing the views of both German antiquaries (many of whom thought that much of the material on their doorstep was of Slavic origins) and the English. He published his work on the subject in *On Mortuary urns found at Stade-on-the-Elbe, and other parts of North Germany, now in the museum of the Historical Society of Hanover* (1856). The similarities between these mortuary urns, were in fact, enough for Kemble to have expressed the two cultures as identical, separated as it were, by just a stretch of water.

Despite Charles Roach Smith and Thomas Wright's earnest efforts, not everyone in the nineteenth century was as scrupulous as Faussett, Douglas and Kemble had been. There was a great deal of wanton destruction of archaeological sites across the country at a time of expanding transport systems and developing urbanisation. Roach Smith and Wright were so concerned about this threat to the nation's buried heritage that they founded in 1843 the British Archaeological Association which was energetic in its opposition to the inertia of antiquarian movements to do anything about the large-scale destruction taking place. At its Canterbury Congress in the following year an audience of over 200 people were able to visit the opening of eight barrows at nearby Breach Down where excavations had been presided over by Lord Conyngham, the president of the Association. Delegates were also treated to the display of the Faussett collection, this being a full 10 years or so before its departure to Liverpool.

John Yonge Akerman made a great contribution to Anglo-Saxon archaeology when he published in 1847 *An Archaeological Index to the Remains of Antiquity in the Celtic, Romano-British and Anglo-Saxon Periods*, allowing others to see the bigger picture. The excavations continued. In 1852, William Wylie published another landmark excavation entitled *The Fairford Graves*. In his preface to this beautifully illustrated account of this Gloucestershire discovery he sets out his motives in language which has a familiar ring to it:

> In these matters we are all contributing our quota to the mass of information respecting the early manners and customs of the Teutonic race, which is slowly but surely accumulating, gathered by the unthanked toils of the archaeologist from the various settlements of their numerous tribes throughout Europe. The subject is not merely interesting to us alone as a national one, but intimately concerns all who claim to belong to the great and noble Teutonic family.

As time went on, and as archaeology became more of science as the noble antiquary faded, a new set of people were able to make great strides in chronologies, typologies and in associating what they excavated with the historical record. Data was piling up thick and fast by the turn of the century and archaeologists were able to assess the continental provenance of the Germanic settlers through pottery typologies, look at distribution maps of artefacts and cemeteries and examine the social organisations represented by variations in the burial rite in the various cemeteries. Names which predominated in the study of the Anglo-Saxons in the first half of the twentieth century had these ideas as their main focus. E. T. Leeds of the Ashmolean Museum published some groundbreaking material on a variety of topics and Nils Åberg became the leader in typologically assessing early Saxon art styles. J.N.L. Myres assessed pottery in relation to the spread of early Saxon settlement. Other famous names of the next generation who tried to explain through archaeology the tangled complexity of the possible political status of the early Anglo-Saxons included Mortimer Wheeler, Vera Evison and Sonia Chadwick Hawkes. By the middle of the twentieth century Anglo-Saxon archaeology was, as it still is today, a vibrant and widely published discipline within archaeology as a whole, with new ideas in interpretation being offered with great frequency. There are many more names from the huge list of modern professional archaeologists one could mention for their contributions to the science in the twentieth century, but there is one piece of work by an amateur that was undertaken on the eve of the Second World War which took everyone's breath away.

THE MAN IN THE MASK

Few people who have come to Anglo-Saxon studies in the decades since the Second World War can deny the influence upon them of the dramatic events which unfolded alongside the Deben Estuary in 1939. It was an extraordinary revelation set within a place of competing ideologies. Here, at Sutton Hoo, history and archaeology met in a spectacular union which raised almost as many questions as it answered about life, death and the nature of royal power in early Anglo-Saxon England. Nor has the intense interest in Sutton Hoo died down over the last few years.

Perhaps the most surprising of all the aspects of the discovery by Basil Brown of the great ship burial beneath Mound I (complete by good fortune with funerary chamber and attendant equipment) was the realisation that two worlds had collided here in the seventh century to the point where the line of fusion between them was barely discernible. Archaeologists and historians have been aware for some time of the notion of the differences between an ideal and a reality. Take for example, how an Anglo-Saxon king rules his people. His ideal is expressed symbolically at his coronation with symbols of power held aloft and promises of good rule publicly made. But the reality of wielding that power would involve a grim prosecution of the king's family interests and the military execution of his policy and so forth. But here, above a heathy and wooded Suffolk slope rested a man who was buried with overwhelming physical evidence that an ideal and a reality were one and the same.

But another clash is evident at Sutton Hoo: that of the Christian and the pagan. It is generally thought that the man buried there was Raedwald, the king of East Anglia. Raedwald had been a Bretwalda, the most powerful of all the kings in the early Saxon kingdoms. The time of the king's burial in around AD 625 was a time of transition in England from the pagan faith to the Christian. Rather than being uncomfortably at odds with one another, the two traditions seem to have been curiously familiar bedfellows. Put simply, if England was to produce an archaeological treasure from the Anglo-Saxon era, it could hardly have come from a more fascinating episode.

One wonders what J.M. Kemble would have made of Sutton Hoo. He, like others of his time, would surely have been fascinated by the Germanic nature of the royalty. He would have been keen to to exercise his own mastery of the trowel alongside Basil Brown. But the honour would not fall to him. Nor would it fall to E.T. Leeds, or any of the other eminent Anglo-Saxon archaeologists in the first instance at least. Instead, in a rather old fashioned arrangement, the discovery was made by Basil Brown at the behest of Mrs Edith Pretty. It was the most famous triumph of the amateur trowel there has ever been in England. Brown, who knew the soils well around Suffolk, had been recommended to Pretty by the local museum at Ipswich. He undertook the excavation of three smaller mounds at the Sutton Hoo cemetery in 1938 discovering a small boat burial and a number of artefacts which were important in their own right. But in the early summer of 1939 he returned to make an attempt on Mound 1, the largest mound in the cemetery which had been a favourite of Mrs Pretty's for some time. The ensuing discovery of the great ship burial has been much published. In short, as Brown worked his way towards the burial chamber and realised it was undisturbed, it became clear to both him and officials from Ipswich Museum that professional help was needed. This was going to be a find of international importance. Charles Phillips, W.F. Grimes, Stuart Piggott and O.G.S. Crawford, all big names in their day, came to work alongside Brown who took something of a back seat for the rest of the excavations.

But why were the effects of the discovery so profound? What did the discovery of Sutton Hoo actually mean? Certainly there was the ship itself to assess. At 90ft, this was a long and somewhat beamy vessel which was rowed by 40 oarsmen and steered by a steering paddle lashed to the hull. She showed signs of repair, so it can be assumed that she was an operational vessel. More to the point someone held enough power even after he had died to coerce hundreds of men to drag the ship up the side of an extremely steep valley. The presence of the very ship herself is testimony to the nature of the power. Nor did the burial chamber disappoint. An iron cauldron with a fine wrought iron chain arrangement showed us how tall a Wooden Saxon Hall might have been, the helmet showed through its shape and decoration how Germanic kings based part of their power symbolism on a mixture of their own mythology and late Roman military equipment. The purse lid, shoulder clasps, buckles and drinking horns demonstrated once again the exquisite techniques of the Anglo-Saxon jeweller. The great silver Anastatius dish represented a cherished item from the east. The Coptic bowls also showed us the extent of the Dark Age trading networks. The native British hanging bowl showed cultural contact with other insular communities. The Mediterranean silverware and Christian spoons showed the meaning of religion to the buried man. Then there was the weaponry and armour. The sword was one of the finest examples of its kind, beautifully pattern welded, ever found in any cemetery of the period in England or on the continent. A huge decorated shield of fine construction was unlike anything from any of the other warrior burials of the early Saxon cemeteries. The Merovingian coins revealed not only the state of development or otherwise of Anglo-Saxon coinage at this time, but their number (37, plus 3 blanks) almost certainly indicates a form of payment for the oarsmen to row the king to safety in the afterlife. And finally the symbols of power, one of which has stayed with the monarchy from that day to this: the 'sceptre' with its whetstone and the curious iron stand which has yet to have a rational explanation assigned to it.

It is little wonder that the place has been returned to over the years. Between 1965-71 a team from the British Museum excavated at the site to answer some of the questions posed by the 1939 work and this material was written up by Rupert Bruce-Mitford. Again from 1983, using every type of investigative technology he could employ, Martin Carver of the University of York came to the site and undertook a series of excavations eventually resulting in the book *Sutton Hoo: Burial Ground of Kings?*

And all this in England. Today, the visitor to the National Trust site has plenty to see and plenty to do including a structured walk around the cemetery and the chance to see some fine material on display in the visitor centre, including a magnificent reconstruction of the burial chamber and replicas of all its artefacts. There is no doubt about it. The impact of archaeology on our understanding of the Anglo-Saxons has been immense. The impact of Sutton Hoo on our imagination has been bigger still.

10

THE MODERN AGE

CONTINUING TENSIONS

There were still some historians who were embarrassed enough about the Norman Conquest to more or less brush over it. Lord Macaulay, writing in 1895 in the first part of his *History of England From the Accession of James II,* went as far as suggesting that:

> During the century and a half which followed the Conquest, there is, to speak strictly, no English history. The French Kings of England rose, indeed, to an eminence which was the wonder and dread of all neighbouring nations. They conquered Ireland. They received the homage of Scotland. By their valour, by their policy, by their fortunate matrimonial alliances, they became far more popular on the Continent than their liege lords the Kings of France.

But it would not last. A growing tide of opinion was expressing itself in favour of the impact of the Norman on English history. Towards the end of the nineteenth century some new giants emerged on the scene and they were not all of the mind of their predecessors. In fact, the twentieth century sees the beginning of something of a Norman counter-strike with some very accomplished and detailed research being conducted on feudal tenures and the impact of post-Conquest developments on the notion of the English state. Among the champions of the new order was F.W. Maitland (1850-1906). Maitland, whose background was in the history of law, produced an influential work entitled *Domesday Book and Beyond* in

1897 which placed the stress on the Norman legal contribution. Then there was J.H. Round (1854-1928). Round's pioneering work on Anglo-Norman governmental and social structures can hardly be doubted, but what he did to the reputation of the foremost Anglo-Saxon scholar of the previous generation was as close to a character assassination as one could get. E.A. Freeman, the leading light of the Victorian era, whose *History of the Norman Conquest* was still being widely read in Round's day, received nothing less than a torrent of abuse from the feudal scholar in *Feudal England* (1895), so much so that it bears repeating and laying out in the same way that Round did. Freeman's works, Round said, were 'still surrounded by a false glamour and that one must further expose his grave liability to error'. Moreover, 'just as his bias against the Roman Church led Mr Froude to vindicate Henry [VIII] in order to justify the breach with Rome, so Mr Freeman's passion for democracy made him an advocate on behalf of Harold.'

In fact, it was here on the battlefield of Hastings that Round had much to say about Freeman. He berated the grand old man for a number of inconsistencies, some of which were true and others not so true, but it was clear to a wide readership that a new age was dawning. The Normans would have their say. Feudalism and its impact were now being stressed. Just a glance at the index of J.H Round's *Feudal England* reveals a deliberately catalogued assault on the work of Freeman: 'his contemptuous criticism' is listed along with 'when himself in error'; 'his "facts"'; 'underrates feudal influence'; 'confuses individuals'; 'his pedantry'; 'misconstrues his Latin'; 'his guesses'; 'imagines facts'; 'his confused views'; 'his special weakness'; 'his dramatic tendency'; 'evades difficulties'; 'misunderstands tactics'; 'his Domesday errors and confusion'; 'distorts feudalism'; and finally 'necessity of criticising his work'. There was no doubt about it. The Saxons had a new, or rather a very old enemy to face once again.

But the Anglo-Saxons had been around for a long time and were made of sterner stuff. H.M. Chadwick (1870-1947) in his *Studies on Anglo-Saxon Institutions* (1905) set the record straight with an in-depth analysis of the arrangement of Anglo-Saxon social and political organisations, whilst C. Oman's (1860-1946) offering of 1910 entitled *England Before the Norman Conquest* was influential until it was eclipsed by the work of Sir Frank

Stenton (1880-1967). Stenton, who turned from pro-Norman observer to become one of the twentieth century's greatest Saxon scholars produced what has become something of a bible for students of the period, namely the Oxford History of England Series publication *Anglo-Saxon England* (first published in 1943).

Stenton was ably accompanied by Dorothy Whitelock (1901-82) and between them they stressed the importance of the Anglo-Saxon achievement against a continuing murmur from other scholars that they might have over-reacted in favour of the Germanic argument. By the middle of the twentieth century (and still today) the academic arguments were as healthy and robust as one might expect them to be. But what of modern popular culture? How would the Anglo-Saxons fare in the modern age now that the vision of the Victorian idealist had faded?

THE SILVER SCREEN

The twentieth century has provided one form of popular culture by which the successes of many things are measured. The motion picture has occasionally ventured into the world of the Anglo-Saxons with some amusing and revealing results. It must be said that Hollywood has seen greater gain in the Arthurian legends. Moreover, we should accept that the appeal of the Viking sagas has outweighed the contribution to the silver screen of the Anglo-Saxons. But there have been films based in these Ancient British or Scandinavian themes where the Anglo-Saxons have made an oblique appearance. One such film was the infamous *The Vikings* (1958) directed by Richard Fleischer and starring Tony Curtis, Kirk Douglas and Janet Leigh, complete with visible vaccination scars on a Viking arm, gold wristwatches and a ludicrous plot led by a Scandinavian with a Brooklyn accent. Janet Leigh played the part of the Anglo-Saxon princess over whom so much Viking blood was being spilt as the throne of Northumbria became free for the taking. This was a tale of pure fiction so far removed from anything remotely helpful to a modern observer that it was then, and still is now, excruciating to watch.

As far as the fictitious storylines are concerned, the Saxons often seem to get themselves wrapped up in their long-running struggle of post-Conquest England against their Norman masters. Henry Hathaway's *The Black Rose* (1950) which starred Tyrone Power and Orson Welles saw a young Saxon nobleman forced to run away from oppression in Norman England. He took with him his faithful retainer and his long bow. They travelled together to China and embroiled themselves in the struggles at the court of Kublai Khan. The post-Conquest struggle for justice theme is of course picked up again in Richard Thorpe's *Ivanhoe* (1952) based on Sir Walter Scott's novel. Here, the dispute between Richard and John sharply divides a community between Richard's Saxon supporters and the Norman followers of John. It is a theme which surfaces again and again and in its most recent form was central to the plot of Kevin Reynolds's *Robin Hood, Prince of Thieves* (1991) starring Kevin Costner in the lead role.

But when we consider what the Anglo-Saxon era has to offer the modern film director, it is nothing short of a tragedy that more has not been made of it all. The story of Harold's rise to power and his fall at Hastings, the tale of Hereward the Wake, the titanic military struggles of King Athelstan, the martyrdom of the young Edward, the bravery of Edmund Ironside, the battle between Godwin and the crown – all of these are perfect material. And yet when we trawl through the movie listings we find just two characters who have won over the director's mind. In 1955 Arthur Lubin directed *Lady Godiva of Coventry* starring Maureen O'Hara, a film based around the famous story of Godiva, the wife of Earl Leofric, who took a nude ride on horseback through the Mercian town in order to protest at taxes. But here again, before their time even, the Normans are brought into the plot to spice up the dramatic antagonism between Saxon and Norman.

But one man has made it through. There is no surprise that it is Alfred the Great. And Clive Donner's 1969 film of the same title has become something of a cult classic for many. David Hemmings and Michael York spar against each other as Alfred and Guthrum in an orgy of well-orchestrated battle scenes and appropriate gore. Alfred wants to be a priest at a time when the Kingdom of East Anglia is falling to pieces under the onslaught of the Danes and Wessex seems to be the invader's next target. Alfred's Queen

Aelhswith scampers through the woods barefoot (after all, she is only a queen) and switches sides after being assaulted by her own husband in an unnecessary revelation of the character's dark side. Nevertheless, Alfred pulls himself together and in one golden moment he discovers an ancient book on how to drill an army into a perfect fighting machine. From his fastness in the marches he rallies the remnants of his kingdom bringing the story to its inevitable and successful conclusion. But this is all we have. Alfred, the subject of a thousand heated debates in centuries gone by, the man who has been given the various accolades of being the father of the common law, the founder of an English kingdom, restorer of the Church, instigator of trial by jury and defender of the people was reduced in 1969 to two hours and two minutes of character assassination and mediocrity.

But it is not all so bad. The extraordinary absence of the Anglo-Saxons from the big screen save for the few hackneyed clichés outlined above has been more than offset by the great wealth of English documentary histories and archaeological investigations shown on the small screen. Here also, Old English literature has even made a breakthrough in the most delightful of ways. Yuri Kulakov's *Beowulf* (1998) was an animated film for TV of the famous story starring the voices of Joseph Fiennes and Derek Jacobi and it visually transported the viewer to the exact world which the original poet had set the story in. But it is with the TV documentaries that the Anglo-Saxons have stayed in the limelight. For nearly three decades Michael Wood has been influencing the public hearts and minds on the matter since his groundbreaking series of the early 1980s. *In Search of the Dark Ages* traced the historical and archaeological evidence for the reigns of Offa, Alfred and Athelstan. In modern times programmes such as *Time Team* (who excavated Alfred's church at Athelney in 1998) and *Meet the Ancestors* have taken the mantle, whilst also promoting the science of archaeology in general to a wide and seemingly insatiable audience.

Perhaps it is only a matter of time before the Anglo-Saxons make a realistic and dramatic appearance on the silver screen. If it happens, it would be pleasing to see it occur without ludicrously anachronistic body armour, without the centuries old struggle between Celt, Saxon and Norman, but with the gripping tale of the struggle for unification of a country.

TOLKIEN, ROHAN AND THE SAXONS

How does one define J.R.R. Tolkien's (1892-1973) impact on the popular conception of the Anglo-Saxons? Both directly and indirectly, it has been huge. Tolkien, professor of Anglo-Saxon language at Oxford between 1925 and 1945, was an expert in English language and literature and a close friend of C.S. Lewis with whom he attended *The Inklings*, an Oxford-based literary discussion group which met at The Eagle and Child public house in Oxford on Thursday nights. Tolkien is of course famous for his spectacularly successful *The Hobbit* (1937) and *The Lord of the Rings* (1954-55) trilogy, but counts among his contribution numerous academic articles on the linguistic, philological and cultural aspects of the development of English language and literature. The initial academic hostility to the idea of Tolkien's fiction as great works of literature has been utterly swamped by the popular adulation of his work in both its literary form and its cinematic adaptations.

For the purposes of the present volume, it is the nature of Tolkien's approach to the idea or 'feeling' of an Anglo-Saxon culture in his work which is of significance. Traditionally, many people have observed that the culture represented by the Rohirrim, the horse-loving men of the Mark, in *The Two Towers*, the middle book of *The Lord of the Rings* trilogy, had its fictional roots firmly based in the reality of an Anglo-Saxon past. Indeed, the 2002 movie directed by Peter Jackson prompted critics and reviewers to recall the association. John J. Miller, America's *National Review National Political Reporter* said in that year that:

> Speaking of Rohan, the movie reminded me of one book critic's comment that Rohan culture is essentially the culture of Tolkien's beloved Anglo Saxons, with a dash of Plains Indians tossed in. Jackson makes his Riders of Rohan look like they'd be equally at home alongside Beowulf or Crazy Horse. The major difference between them and the Anglo Saxons is that Rohan is also a horse culture. When Aragorn, Legolas, and Gimli encounter the Rohirrim, spear-toting riders circle and surround them, like a scene from the Old West.[1]

But of course, there is more to it than that. There is a smack of the Sarmatian cavalry to the Rohirrim, too. We should be particularly careful when we assign only one inspiration to the author for the kingdom of Rohan. However, the similarity with Old English in Tolkien's choice of language for this ancient tribe of Men is overwhelming. Tolkien, the author of a famous 1936 paper entitled *Beowulf: the Monsters and the Critics* seems to have really let himself go with the literary culture of the Rohirrim. There are echoes of *Beowulf* everywhere. Legolas says of Meduseld, King Théoden's Golden Hall, 'The light of it shines far over the land'. This is a direct lift from line 311 of the famous Anglo-Saxon poem. The language they speak in Rohan is so strikingly similar to Old English, that we are even told that it is a speech 'sundered from their northern kin'. Their poetry too is constructed along similar lines as the following example will demonstrate. When Aragorn, Gandalf, Legolas and Gimli come across 'The King of the Golden Hall' in the chapter of the same name, they pass through several burial mounds, an experience so moving it prompts Aragorn to sing to himself an ancient poem in the language of Rohan which he then translates into the Common Speech:

Where now the horse and the rider? Where is the horn that was blowing?
Where is the helm and the hauberk, and the bright hair flowing?
Where is the hand on the harpstring, and the red fire glowing?
Where is the spring and the harvest and the tall corn growing?
They have passed like rain on the mountain. Like a wind in the meadow;
The days have gone down in the West behind the hills into shadow.
Who shall gather the smoke of the dead wood burning,
Or behold the flowing years from the Sea returning?

Compare this melancholic piece of wordsmithery with the following passage from the real Anglo-Saxon poem *The Wanderer:*

Where is the horse now, where the hero gone?
Where is the bounteous lord, and where the benches
For feasting? Where are all the joys of hall?
Alas for the bright cup, the armoured warrior,
The glory of the prince. That time is over.
Passed into the night as it had never been.
Stands now memorial to that dear band
The splendid lofty wall, adorned with shapes
Of serpents; but the strong blood-greedy spear
And mighty destiny removed the heroes,
And storms now strike against these stony slopes.

So, the language element of the Rohirrim culture clearly has much to owe to Tolkien's Anglo-Saxon studies, but what of the other similarities? Tolkien was keen to play these down, but it is the case that the men were tall and fair with blue eyes and looked more or less like we should expect an Anglo-Saxon to look. Jackson's portrayal of them in the motion picture however, gives more width to the interpretation, a width Tolkien might have enjoyed had he seen it. Here, the horsemen have classic Sarmatian helms, some with horse tail plumes and cheek pieces based around the late Roman cavalry helmet types suggesting that Jackson, if not Tolkien, was borrowing from a wider pool of cultures than just the Anglo-Saxons. But there is something intriguing in the back-story of the Rohirrim. They were the lords of the Mark, the fighters at the frontier. A people landlocked, holding the fort against others from all sides. It all chimes rather nicely with the real history and disposition of Anglo-Saxon Mercia, Tolkien's favourite kingdom. Another aspect of the story which seems to recall the Anglo-Saxon era in suspicious detail is the predicament of Rohan's King Théoden who, when the fellowship discover him, is possessed by the spirit of Saruman and evilly counselled by the intriguing Wormtongue. The correlation between this scenario and that of an embattled Æthelred II and the rise to power of his quickly promoted Mercian ealdorman Eadric Streona whose capability for deceit was legendary, is another overwhelming aspect of the tale of Rohan and it must have been an episode of Anglo-Saxon history well known to Tolkien.

In reality, cultures similar in essence to the Rohirrim existed all over early medieval Europe and throughout the contemporary northern world. Tolkien was familiar with all of them, their histories and their literature. What we have with the Rohirrim is an early medieval culture given an Anglo-Saxon language and an Anglo-Saxon gloss. Tolkien's well-documented cautions to his audience not to take too specifically the associations with Anglo-Saxons seem to be perfectly well founded. In his Appendix F in *The Lord of the Rings*, where he speaks of the modernisation of the forms and spellings of place-names and personal names used in his descriptions of Rohan he says:

> The Mannish languages that were related to the Westron should, it seemed to me, be turned into forms related to English. The language of Rohan I have accordingly made to resemble ancient English, since it was related both (more distantly) to the Common Speech, and (very closely) to the former tongue of the northern Hobbits, and was in comparison with the Westron archaic ...
>
> This linguistic procedure does not imply that the Rohirrim closely resembled the ancient English otherwise, in culture or art, in weapons or in modes of warfare, except in a general way due to their circumstances: a simpler and more primitive people living in contact with a higher and more venerable culture, and occupying lands that had once been part of its domain.[2]

Notwithstanding the resemblance of the Rohirrim story to that of the exiled Anglo-Saxons who fetched up on the shores of the Black Sea, there is, in essence, something about the whole *The Lord of the Rings* trilogy which speaks loudly for the Anglo-Saxons and appeals to the minds of the readers. The Anglo-Saxons must surely remain as the most obvious historical cultural identifier employed by Tolkien in his work. To deny the influence of *The Lord of the Rings* upon modern popular culture would be myopic, and by a legitimate extension, to deny the influence upon Tolkien of the Anglo-Saxons would seem churlish. It is through this once lambasted and derided piece of literature that the Anglo-Saxons live on today. One wonders quite how comfortable Tolkien would have been with the monsters and the critics he has created.

THE MODERN VIEW?

So, notwithstanding the rather meagre coverage of the Anglo-Saxons in the genre of modern film, what does the country really think of them? In 2002 the BBC launched a nationwide vote on national television and over the Internet to establish the top 100 Britons of all time. The project was not without its controversy since two of the chosen were in fact Irish nationals, but for our purposes the project was interesting. An Anglo-Saxon made it into the top 20. Let us examine the list:

1. Sir Winston Churchill (1874-1965), Prime Minister during the Second World War
2. Isambard Kingdom Brunel (1806-59), engineer.
3. Diana, Princess of Wales (1961-97), first wife of HRH Charles, Prince of Wales (1981-96)
4. Charles Darwin (1809-82), author of *The Origin of Species*
5. William Shakespeare (1564-1616), poet and playwright
6. Sir Isaac Newton, physicist
7. Queen Elizabeth I of England, monarch
8. John Lennon (1940-80), of The Beatles, musician
9. Horatio Nelson, 1st Viscount Nelson, naval commander
10. Oliver Cromwell, Lord Protector
11. Sir Ernest Shackleton, polar explorer
12. Captain James Cook, explorer
13. Robert Baden-Powell, 1st Baron Baden-Powell, founder of the Boy Scouts
14. Alfred the Great, King of Wessex, king of the Anglo-Saxons
15. Arthur Wellesley, 1st Duke of Wellington, military commander and statesman
16. Margaret Thatcher, Prime Minister
17. Michael Crawford, actor
18. Queen Victoria, monarch
19. Sir Paul McCartney, of The Beatles, musician
20. Sir Alexander Fleming, pharmaceutical innovator

It is a peculiar list with a number of surprises, not least of which is Michael Crawford's outranking of Queen Victoria, but there is another much more interesting fact. Alfred the Great, the one Anglo-Saxon in the list, predates the earliest of all the other candidates by a colossal 664 years. Alfred narrowly missed the top 10. Such a position in the top 10 would have qualified him for having an episode of the subsequent documentary TV series dedicated solely to him and championed no doubt by an enthusiastic celebrity. It is a spectacular tale of survival for one of England's greatest ever figures. In years to come some of the more eccentric and contemporary candidates on this list will simply disappear, although it is hard to see how Winston Churchill could or should ever be dislodged. But would even Churchill's memory last 1106 years after his death?

The list was interesting for a number of other reasons. Throughout this volume we have looked not only at the changing fortunes of the memory of the Anglo-Saxons, but also at the effects of the support given to the historical peoples in what could perhaps be described as opposing camps. The 'Celts' or, for want of a better term the 'indigenous British' have fought running battles with the Saxons for centuries for the hearts and minds of the readers of history books. The Normans too, the great thorn in the side of the Anglo-Saxons, have frequently turned the minds of historians in their favour. But where were these great enemies of the Anglo-Saxons in this colossal survey? Well, William the Conqueror, for so long heralded by some to have been the greatest monarch of English history, was nowhere to be seen. And, galloping in on her chariot at number 35 in the list was Boudica, the famous British Queen whose argument with Rome became legendary. This noble warrior queen fetched-up a full 16 places above King Arthur in the list, a figure whom we might have expected to be in the top 10. But these two ancient British characters are not like Alfred. Their memory is tarnished by the spectacular warping their legends have received since earliest times.

What are the reasons for the success of King Alfred? The modern notion of Alfred and that of the Anglo-Saxons in general owes much to the efforts we have outlined above, particularly to the vestiges of the notions we have been handed by the Victorians. But the point is that all along the road, the bending and the twisting has more or less stayed outside of the spectacular, legendary and heroic. With the Anglo-Saxons we have real characters and tangible achievements. This is why their memory is still so strong.

CONCLUSION

There are, of course, a great many characters in Anglo-Saxon history with which people can have their fun. Leaving aside the more frivolous aspects of the material covered here, it should be clear that the Anglo-Saxons over the centuries have often been used for very serious motives indeed, being thrust into the heart of political, religious and constitutional debates which were literally dividing the country. The Anglo-Saxon period is really one that has lasted to this very day. It is clear that the Anglo-Saxons have had their opponents, both before 1066 and afterwards. The adventure of the Anglo-Saxons as told in *The Anglo-Saxons: the Verdict of History* should suffice to prove that they have always been something more than a mere passing interest to the people of the English-speaking world.

Let us briefly compare the authenticity of the Anglo-Saxons to their erstwhile competitors, the Ancient British. Whilst it is true to say that no one in Britain ever called themselves a 'Celt' before 1700,[3] the same sort of thing cannot be said of the Anglo-Saxons in respect of their own self-identification. The word 'Celt' is, in fact, an invention of the eighteenth century. It was a convenient phrase which lumped a great many colourful native British polities and cultures into one amorphous group. It became a cultural identifier for the non-English parts of Britain after the Act of Union in 1707. Nobody in the west of Britain during the early medieval period ever called themselves a Celt. For the Anglo-Saxons, the story is completely different. The Alfredian vision of a united kingdom of Wessex and Mercia styled itself at the time as 'the kingdom of the Anglo-Saxons'. Later, it would become 'the kingdom of the English' with grand pretensions to accrue power across the whole of the British Isles. The Anglo-Saxons had a name for themselves and they used it widely.

If we recall the nodal points along this great journey we will find there is nothing really mythological, anachronistic, fantastical or false about the Anglo-Saxons. Even the most partisan champions of the Anglo-Saxons in our story such as the Leveller John Lilburne have had good or at least pertinent reasons to employ them in their struggles.

We have established that an exiled group of English people, who called themselves precisely that, had taken their cultural identity with them after the Norman Conquest and supplanted it in a new and strange land to great effect for several centuries. We have examined how in England under the Normans Anglo-Saxon cultural identity was far from destroyed. In fact, it is fair to say that in many cases, the Normans celebrated the memory almost as heartily as the English if the writings of the twelfth-century historians are anything to go by. They were searching for an identity they knew the Anglo-Saxons already had.

The great kings of Anglo-Saxon England were clearly not lost to posterity. Alfred is and always will be a more believable figure than Arthur. This is because he is a perfectly real character. The administrative, political and military achievements of Alfred's son and grandsons will always represent the rock upon which England was founded. An army of scholars, whatever their motives, have said the same thing throughout history and they are right.

We have seen too, how the medieval mind stretched back into the Anglo-Saxon past, not just because of fond memories of ancient kings, but for the very contemporary necessity of proving the legitimacy of medieval religious institutions and other political arguments surrounding rights and privileges. Slowly, as the enquiring minds of itinerant medieval historians gave ground to the first antiquaries, we have shown where the Anglo-Saxons played a part by literally popping out of the landscape to greet the new observer. Then there was Ælfric, the Anglo-Saxon abbot of Eynsham. Had he not insisted on the usefulness of the vernacular in his teachings, it is hard to see where Queen Elizabeth's *Ecclesia Anglicana* could have found its mandate. Archbishop Wulfstan, whose role as a senior government advisor in the eleventh century did much to uphold English identity was another great contributor to the projection of that identity. His *Sermon of the Wolf* survives to this day as testimony to the English notion of self.

Then there was Edward the Confessor (1042-66), whose long reign and personal background allowed the Anglo-Saxons to bridge the chasm created by the Norman Conquest. Matthew Parker and his circle and those who followed him had a genuine as well as political and religious interest in the affairs of the Anglo-Saxons and for centuries the palaeographers and philologists toiled with considerable success to understand and demonstrate the usefulness of the study of Old English, a study inextricably linked with the fortunes of the Anglo-Saxons over the centuries. And all this time, when Anglo-Saxon documents were being rescued from soap sellers and shoemakers to help build a church in a brave new country the Arthurian legend remained just that. Nobody picked up a copy of Geoffrey of Monmouth and tried to create something real and lasting out of it. King Arthur never drove a political debate in the centuries after his death with far-reaching consequences. King Alfred, however, did.

By examining the numerous histories of England published in the centuries gone by, it will have become clear that the Anglo-Saxons have fared very well indeed. Despite the occasional manifestation of the Brut myth and the clamour regarding the Norman achievement, there has been what would appear to be a continuity of acceptance of the contribution to English history made by the Anglo-Saxons.

The American story has also been a demonstrative one. It has shown how the Anglo-Saxons, with their love of freedom, became the role model for a fledgling nation. It has thrown the racial aspect of the argument into the forefront and we have had to examine all that has come to mean. But race was only ever a small part of the story, warped out of all proportion by those who sought to abuse the appeal of the Anglo-Saxons.

Today, there is every indication that there is still a genuine admiration for the Anglo-Saxons amongst the English people in the early years of the twenty-first century, but it seems that not enough people are writing about them or delivering the real message of English history to a popular audience. This is all that needs to be changed. History will do the rest.

When I was young, I was taught at school that English history began in 1066. What had gone before was a series of unlinked histories of minor and competing kingdoms. If *The Anglo-Saxons* does nothing else, then it must kill this theory stone dead. I was not told about King Alfred. Nobody seemed to know about or care for King Athelstan. English history seemed a folly to me. Now perhaps, the Anglo-Saxon contribution can be recognised once again. This book has, I hope, given answers to some long-standing questions.

APPENDIX

The entries below comprise those people who have left their mark on Anglo-Saxon studies in one way or another before the advent of a myriad of scholars in the twentieth century, but who have not necessarily fallen into the general narrative of the present volume. Many of them are no less important for this exclusion and so are given their due here. In some cases the evidence has shown that they may have had only a passing or accidental interest in Anglo-Saxon affairs, whilst others were the active friends and colleagues of those whose work has been examined above.

THOMAS ASTLE (1735-1803)

A palaeographer and collector of manuscripts and charters. His collection of charters now forms the central part of the Stowe MSS in the British Library. They include the *Liber Vitae* of the New Minster and Hyde Abbey, Winchester, and the Stowe charters. There is a commemorative stone to Astle at St Mary's Church, Battersea, London SW11.

GEORGE BALLARD (1705/6-55)

An antiquary and collector of manuscripts, Ballard numbered among his acquaintances Elizabeth Elstob, the famous Anglo-Saxonist whose story is outlined earlier, as well as Thomas Hearne and Richard Rawlinson. He also transcribed the Old English *Orosius*.

DAINES BARRINGTON (1727-1800)

The fourth son of the first Viscount Barrington, Daines Barrington specialised in law. In 1773, he published a translation of the Old English *Orosius*.

STEPHEN BATMAN (d. 1584)

A Cambridge graduate, Batman worked in close association with Archbishop Parker as a chaplain and librarian and some of his work was published by John Day. He produced a useful work entitled *A Note of Saxon Wordes*.

ROBERT BEALE (1541–1601)

Clerk of the Privy Council and diplomat, Beale was also an antiquary who collected artefacts and manuscripts. He also produced an Anglo-Saxon glossary.

JOSEPH BOSWORTH (1789–1876)

A clergyman and Rawlinson professor of Anglo-Saxon at Oxford (1858–76), he also founded the professorship of Anglo-Saxon at Cambridge in 1867. His *Dictionary of the Anglo-Saxon Language* (1838) was widely used for a long time.

RICHARD CAREW (1555–1620)

A Cornish poet and antiquarian, Carew was also an accomplished scholar. He entered Parliament in 1584 and served under Walter Raleigh, then Lord Lieutenant of Cornwall. As well as producing a significant survey of Cornwall, Carew also wrote an influential piece in 1605 entitled *Epistle Concerning the Excellencies of the English Tongue*. He numbered amongst his friends William Camden and Sir Henry Spelman.

DAVID CASLEY (fl. 1718–31)

Mainly known for his transcription of the Anglo-Saxon Poem *The Battle of Maldon*.

THOMAS DACKOMB (1496–c. 1572)

A sixteenth-century manuscript collector and keen antiquary whose collection comprised a number of Saxon texts.

WILLIAM DUGDALE (c. 1605–86)

Born in Shustoke, Warwickshire, Dugdale became in 1639 the Rouge Croix Pursuivant in the Herald's College and Charles I employed him to deliver royal warrants during the English Civil War demanding the submissions of garrisons. Having studied at the Bodleian, he wrote in 1655 his *Monasticon Anglicanum*, outlining the history of the English monasteries from their origins to the Dissolution. It was not a popular work with the Puritans and found a market within the Roman Catholic community of the English gentry and overseas.

Dugdale was also an eminent county historian, being an expert upon the subject of his home county Warwickshire. In 1656 he produced a sumptuous and well-researched volume on the antiquities of that county and two years later wrote a history of St Paul's. His *Monasticon* project continued to absorb him in the following years and he added a second and third part to it in 1661 and 1673 respectively, dealing with the lesser orders in the first case and the Cathedrals and Collegiate Churches in the latter, all of which brought him further consternation form the puritan element. Dugdale died in 1686, 10 years after completing a large body of work which some noted was not entirely accurate, on the English baronage.

HENRY ELSYNGE (1577-1635)

Parliamentary historian, antiquary and Clerk of the Parliaments. Elsynge produced *Modus tenendi Parliamentum* (1624-5) and along with his son Henry (1606-56), produced a draft *House of Lords Proceedings.*

FREDERICK WILLIAM FAIRHOLT (1813-66)

Illustrator and engraver of antiquities. Made many fine drawings of Saxon and other antiquities between 1835 and 1852.

EDMUND GIBSON (1669-1748)

Bishop of London and antiquary, Gibson had a passion for ecclesiastical history and acquired some material from George Hickes. As well as compiling a life of Sir Henry Spelman he also published *Chronicon Saxonicum* in 1692, the (E) edition of the *Anglo-Saxon Chronicle* with a Latin translation.

RICHARD GOUGH (1735-1809)

A prolific writer and antiquary who wrote a work entitled *Remarkable Events of the Saxon Heptarchy.*

SIR MATTHEW HALE (1609-76)

Wrote a *History of Common Law* in the 1660s where Edward the Confessor's laws were taken as the benchmark and the continuity from the Anglo-Saxon period to the Norman period was stressed.

THOMAS HEARNE (1678-1735)

Born in Berkshire, Hearne was forced to work hard as a labourer when he was young. In 1693 he was sent to a free school in Bray to learn Latin. After this he studied at St Edmund's Hall at Oxford where he took a degree. After studying at the Bodleian he obtained the post of Assistant Library Keeper, where he undertook cataloguing projects.

In 1715, he was appointed to the post of Esquire Bedell, but chose to remain at the Bodleian to the annoyance of University College who forcibly ejected him. Hearne said of this that he was 'debarred the Library on account of the oaths [ie, as a non-juror] and new keys were made and the lock of the Library door altered, tho' he hath got the old keys by him, having not made any resignation or consented to the putting of anyone in his place.'

ROBERT HEGGE (c.1597-1629)

Historian and antiquary of the bishopric of Durham who in 1628 wrote *The Legend of St Cuthbert*.

JEAN MABILLON (1632-1707)

A French historian of Frankish charters, his work was read in England and had some bearing on English scholars' approach to palaeography.

SIR FREDERIC MADDEN (1801-73)

For 40 years Madden was a keeper of manuscripts at the British Museum. A contemporary of Kemble, he differed in his views, preferring a more native English and less Germanic interpretation of early English history. He also kept what became a 43-volume diary between 1819 and 1873 which has become an important resource for Anglo-Saxon scholars.

WILLIAM MUSGRAVE (1660-1753)

Musgrave, an antiquary, was closely associated with the publication of the discovery of the Alfred Jewel.

SIR JOHN PRISE (c.1502-55)

Sir John Prise was one of the earliest Welsh humanists, with a sharp and enquiring mind. He firmly held to the *Brut* theory of British history and numbered among his own collection a 1517 copy of Geoffrey of Monmouth's *Historia Regum Britanniae* which he bought for 1s 6d in 1530. He acquired for himself many ancient books and manuscripts, most of them Welsh or Latin. There are over a hundred such documents to have passed through his hands in one way or another.

The work of Polydore Vergil in his *Anglica Historia* (1534) challenged the Geoffrey of Monmouth view of British history and this seemed to spur Prise into devoting himself to his great subsequent repost, something which he apparently worked on with Leland's help. By 1545 the first draft of his book *Historiae Brytannicae Defensio* was completed although not published until a few years later by his son Richard. In one of his dedications, Prise says of his long-standing interest in British ancient history 'From my youth I have been exercised in the old language and antiquities of the British.'

JOHN RASTELL (d. 1536)

Rastell was born in London and became a printer, author and lawyer as well as a member of parliament. He was the son-in-law of Thomas More. He wrote extensively on matters of law and doctrine and had a chequered history on both sides of the religious argument of his day. But his great contribution to contemporary understanding of English history was his *The Pastyme of People, the Chronydes of dyvers Realmys and most specially of the Realme of England* (1529), a chronicle dealing with English history from the earliest times to the reign of Richard III.

RICHARD RAWLINSON (1690-1755)

Like Hickes and Hearne, Rawlinson was a non-juror and had to tread carefully. He was a great traveller and antiquary but was known for his colossal collection of manuscripts which ran into the thousands. He bequeathed his collection to the Bodleian. Rawlinson was also instrumental in the setting up of the chair in Anglo-Saxon at Oxford which still bears his name.

JOSEPH RICKMAN (1776-1841)

Rickman was one of the first scholars to look at the subject of Anglo-Saxon architecture with an academic eye. His contemporaries were dismissive of the subject. An essay on architecture appeared in his 1817 publication entitled *An Attempt to Discriminate the Styles of Architecture in England from the Conquest to the Reformation.*

GRIMUR JONSSON THORKELIN (1752-1829)

Born in Iceland, Thorkelin is best known for his work on *Beowulf.* In 1878 he had a transcript made of it known as *Thorkelin A,* which was followed up two years later by *Thorkelin B.* When he published the poem in 1815 he believed that it had originally been a Danish work.

THORESBY, RALPH (1658–1725)

The first Leeds citizen to be elected to the Royal Society of London, Thoresby was a keen antiquary and correspondent with a number of leading Anglo-Saxonists.

KARL VERNER (1846–96)

Verner was a German philologist who developed an earlier sound-change theory first expounded by Jacob Grimm.

JOHN OBADIAH WESTWOOD (1805–93)

Westwood left a career in law to pursue entomology and archaeology. He became well known for his detailed illustrative work, particularly in the realm of Anglo-Saxon material culture.

BROWNE WILLIS (1682–1760)

Willis is one of a number of English antiquaries whose personality pervades his work to the amusement of modernity. Willis was fascinated by the ecclesiastical history of England, in particular with its built heritage. He had an equal fascination with antiquities and numismatics. Educated at Westminster and Christchurch, Oxford, he became friends with John Phillips who wrote a poem about cider which included a passing reference to Willis who seemed to admire the drink more than others. Willis sat in parliament for a while and was also instrumental in the restoration of a number of churches. He was also part of the movement which led to the revival of the Society of Antiquaries in 1717.

His extraordinary character was often commented upon. For example, he is known to have given most of his wealth away. But what remains in the mind are the frequent references to 'old wrinkle boots' (he rarely seems to have taken them off), and the lingering smells which he omitted. A Dr Sneyd Davies came to visit him around 1751 and described his house thus:

> There is many a Saxon bust….Amongst his manuscripts, written all of them in his own hand with incredible assiduity, you will see a laborious Dictionary of Lords, Abbots, Parliament-men, gentlemen, Clergymen, and Parish Clerks ever since the *Saxon* invasion …
>
> The territory around him has been remarkable for considerable actions heretofore; but is now disfigured with pits, dug not for marle, gravel, or earthly use, but in search of *Roman* spears and *Saxon* stirrups.

GLOSSARY

ADVENTUS SAXONUM

A name given to the first coming of the Germanic settlers in Britain in the fifth and sixth centuries AD. We borrow the term from the Venerable Bede (*c*.673-735) who wrote in the early eighth century and who himself was following Gildas whose invective against the British tribal leaders for letting in the barbarian host has coloured historical thinking for centuries. The period which the Adventus covers represents one of a complex intermingling of cultures and not one of dramatic single invasion, although it is true to say that many of the kingdoms which rose from the ashes of Roman Britain had their roots in the dynastic aspirations of Germanic kin groups.

ÆLFRIC OF EYNSHAM (*c*.955-1020)

Ælfric was a remarkable scholar of later Anglo-Saxon England who seems to have inspired many Saxon revivalist scholars of the sixteenth to nineteenth centuries. Initially educated at Winchester, he became the abbot of the refounded abbey at Eynsham in 1005. He was famous for his *Sermones Catholici*, written in the 990s and featuring two series of 40 homilies (sermons) on the gospels, saints and other themes. Ælfric was keen on teaching in the vernacular since in the early years he considered it important to spread the proper Christian word as the country faced doom at the turn of the millennium.

Ælfric's topics varied widely and included the meaning of the Viking raids, the interpretation of dreams and the nature of Danish paganism, to name but a few. He also produced a grammar of Latin and a much quoted volume of colloquies (classroom-based 'conversations') on trades which has given historians an insight into the nature of merchant life and other trades of the tenth century.

Ælfric's legacy was profound. His insistence on the vernacular led many later scholars to use this feature of his work as a weapon in their own battle with Rome.

BEOWULF

A famous Anglo-Saxon poem of disputed date, 3182 lines in length. It is set in Scandinavia and is a story of the Geats, the Swedes and the Danes. Beowulf himself becomes the king of the Geats, after defeating the monster Grendel. Later, the hero overcomes a dragon but is fatally wounded and the poem ends with his funeral. The work contains many references to a mythical and magical Germanic world and the survival of the manuscript went a long way to keeping alive a half-forgotten literary era.

GLOSS

Usually takes the form of interlinear or marginal writing on texts in Latin with Old English being the medium for translation and interpretation.

HAGIOGRAPHY

The cult of saints as expressed in the written form. Usually takes the form of a 'Life' of a saint.

HEPTARCHY

A phrase used to denote the political organisation in terms of the kingdoms of early Anglo-Saxon England. The most influential exponent of the heptarchy concept was Henry of Huntingdon who, following Bede, observed that Kent, Sussex, Wessex, Essex, East Anglia, Mercia and Northumbria comprised the main power blocks.

HEPTATEUCH

The name given to the first seven books of the bible, comprising Genesis, Exodus, Leviticus, Numbers, Deuteronomy, Joshua and Judges.

HOMILY

Widespread vernacular sermons, of which Ælfric and Wulfstan share the bulk of the honours in terms of their authorship of the survivors. Strictly speaking, a homily is an exposition of the periscope read during the mass, but Wulfstan in particular used his to deliver grave messages to his flock in times of national crisis.

GLOSSARY

LEXICOGRAPHY

Dictionary making, or the study of the vocabulary of a language.

OROSIUS

The Old English *Orosius* is a translation of Orosius' world history the *Historiæ aduersum paganos* dating from King Alfred's reign (AD 871–899). It also contains an interesting account of the visit of a Scandinavian sailor to Alfred's court and describes in exceptional detail the nature of the northern European coastline and the navigational aids used by Othere, the royal guest.

PHILOLOGY

The study of ancient languages and literature.

SOLOMON AND SATURN

An Anglo-Saxon work written in the form of a dialogue between Solomon, king of Israel, and the Roman God Saturn in which riddles predominate. Both characters question each other on a range of topics including pagan and Christian lore.

VERCELLI BOOK

Dating to the mid-tenth century, the Vercelli book is an anthology of religious prose and verse in Old English. Written probably in the south-east of England it had reached Italy by AD 1100 which is where it acquired its name.

BIBLIOGRAPHY

The following material will provide the Anglo-Saxon scholar with a good grounding in the subjects covered in *The Anglo-Saxons: the Verdict of History*. Without the work of these scholars, this volume would not have been possible.

Akerman, J.Y. 1847 *An Archaeological Index to the Remains of Antiquity in the Celtic, Romano-British and Anglo-Saxon Periods*. London. Marks a turning point on the road from antiquary to archaeologist.

Allen, G. 1880 Are We Englishmen? *Fortnightly Review*. pp472-91. A curious but necessary read for students of racial theory.

Ashdown, M. 1925 Elizabeth Elstob, the Learned Saxonist. *Modern Language Review* 20. pp125-46. An early paper on a much ignored scholar.

Browne, T. 1658 *Hydriotaphia, or Urn Buriall, or, A Discourse of the Sephulchrall Urnes lately found in Norfolk*. London (ed. Huntley Meredith. F.L., New York, 1966). One of the earliest publications on Anglo-Saxon material culture.

Burrow, J.A. 1981 *A Liberal Descent. Victorian Historians and the English Past*. Cambridge. A good overview of the Victorian view.

Chadwick, H.M. 1905 *Studies on Anglo-Saxon Institutions*. Cambridge. Seminal work which looked for the first time at institutions that would not be returned to for years.

Chadwick, H.M. 1907 *The Origin of the English Nation*. Cambridge. Another classic from a heavyweight.

Clarke, N. 2005 Elizabeth Elstob (1674-1752): England's First Professional Woman Historian? *Gender and History* 17. pp210-20. A welcome and recent offering on Elstob.

Colbourn, H.T. 1965. *The Lamp of Experience*. Chapel Hill. University of North Carolina Press. For all students of American Anglo-Saxonism.

Crick, J. 2003 St Albans, Westminster and some Twelfth-Century Views of the Anglo-Saxon Past. *Anglo-Norman Studies* 25. pp65-83. How identities were forged by the medieval monasteries.

Dickens, B. 1939 John Mitchell Kemble and Old English Scholarship. *Proceedings of the British Academy* 25. pp51-84. A classic account of a famous academic life.

Douglas, Revd James 1793 *Nenia Britannica, Or a Sepulchral History of Great Britain, from the earliest period to its general conversion to Christianity.* London, printed by John Nichols, for Benjamin and John White. Another groundbreaking publication from a leading early archaeologist.

Evans, S. 1958 *Geoffrey of Monmouth. History of the Kings of Britain.* London. Classic translation of the great twelfth-century work.

Faussett, B. 1856 *Inventorium Sephulcrale: an Account of some Antiquities dug up at Gilton, Kingston, Sibertswold, Barfriston, Beakesbourne, Chartham, and Crundale, in the County of Kent, from AD. 1757 to AD. 1773.* (ed. Roach Smith, C.) London. Classic account of the excavations.

Fisher, D.H. 1989 *Albion's Seed: Four British Folkways in America.* Oxford. The Anglo-Saxon diaspora as it descended on the west.

Frantzen, A.J. and Niles, J.D (eds) 1997 *Anglo-Saxonism and the Construction of a Social Identity.* Collection of valuable material on a wide variety of subjects.

Freeman, E.A. (1867-79) *The History of the Norman Conquest of England, its Causes and its Results.* Oxford. In six volumes. Required reading, despite Round's objections.

Fritze, R.H. 1983 'Truth Hath Lacked Witnesse, Tyme Wanted Light': The Dispersal of the English Monastic Libraries and Protestant Efforts at Preservation, ca 1535-1625. *Journal of Library History.* pp274-91. Readable account of the traumas of the destruction.

Godfrey, J. 1979 The Defeated Anglo-Saxons take Service with the Eastern Emperor. *Anglo-Norman Studies* 1. pp63-74 and 207-9. The story of the exiles analysed.

Gooch, G. 1952 *History and Historians in the Nineteenth Century.* London. More on the Victorian attitude.

Grandsen, A. 1974 *Historical Writing in England c550-c1307.* London. Excellent and essential companion to the medieval historian.

Grandsen, A. 1992 *Legends, Traditions and History in Medieval England.* London. Another valuable review of how medieval England saw the past.

Green, J.R. 1874 *A Short History of the English People.* London. Not that short, but important for expressing the views which would become widely held.

Green, J.R. 1881 *The Making of England.* London.

Green, J.R. 1883 *The Conquest of England.* London.

BIBLIOGRAPHY

Greenway, D. 2002 *Henry of Huntingdon. The History of the English People 1000-1154.* Oxford. Good translation with introductory material.

Guest, E. 1883 *Origines Celticae (a fragment) and other contributions to the history of Britain.* London.

Hill. C. 1958 *Puritanism and Revolution: Studies in Interpretation of the English Revolution of the 17th Century.* New York. Often cited and seldom improved upon, this was a seminal work.

Hill, P. 2004 *The Age of Athelstan. Britain's Forgotten History.* Stroud.

Hobsbawm, E.J. 1990 *Nations and Nationalism Since 1780.* Cambridge.

Horsman, R. 1976 Origins of Racial Anglo-Saxonism in Great Britain Before 1850. *Journal of the History of Ideas* 37. pp387-410.

Horsman, R. 1981 *Race and Manifest Destiny: the Origins of American Racial Anglo-Saxonism.*

Hume, D. 1763 *History of England.* London. The leading eighteenth-century work.

Jones, E. 1998 *The English Nation: The Great Myth.* Stroud.

Kaufmann, E. 1997 American Exceptionalism Reconsidered: Anglo-Saxon Ethnogenesis in the 'Universal' Nation, 1776-1850. Based on a paper delivered at the British Association of American Studies Annual Conference held at the University of Birmingham, 4-7 April, 1997. http://www.birbeck.ac.uk/polsoc/download/eric_kaufmann/WASP_reconsidered.pdf.

Kemble, J.M. 1849 *The Saxons In England.* London. Classic work from the leading light.

Kemble, J.M. 1856 On Mortuary urns found at Stade-on-the-Elbe, and other parts of North Germany, now in the museum of the Historical Society of Hanover. *Archaeologia* 36. pp270-83.

Kemble, J.M. 1863 *Horae Ferales; or Studies in Archaeology of the Northern Nations.* London.

Keynes, S. 1999 The Cult of King Alfred the Great. *Anglo-Saxon England* 28. pp225-356. A paper of great significance in the piecing together not just of Alfred's story, but of the whole journey of the Anglo-Saxons throughout history.

Kingsley, C. 1875 *The Roman and the Teuton.* A series of lectures delivered before the University of Cambridge.

Lappenberg, J.M. 1845 *A History of England Under the Anglo-Saxon Kings* (trans. Thorpe, B.). London.

Lucy, S. 2000 *The Anglo-Saxon Way of Death. Burial Rites in Early England.* Stroud.

MacDougall, H.A. 1982 *Racial Myth in English History – Trojans, Teutons and Anglo-Saxons.* Montreal. Good coverage of one particular aspect of the story, but with a disappointing and unnecessary conclusion.

Miles, L.W. 1902 *King Alfred in Literature*. Baltimore.

Murphy, M. 1981 Edward Thwaites, Pioneer of Old English. *Durham University Journal* 73. pp153-59.

Mynors, R.A.B., Thomson, R.M. and Winterbottom, M. 1998 William of Malmesbury. *Gesta Regum Anglorum. The History of the English Kings*. Oxford Clarendon Press. The standard work on Malmesbury.

Nicholas, T. 1868 *The Pedigree of English People*. London.

Palmer, J.K. 1885 *The Saxon Invasion and its Influence on Our Character as a Race*. Transactions of the Royal Historical Society 2. pp173-96. An extraordinary paper, not to be missed.

Paxton, J. 2002 Forging Communities: Memory and Identity in Post-Conquest England. *Haskins Society Journal: Studies in Medieval History* 10. pp95-109. The noble art of forgery and propaganda in twelfth-century England with particular reference to Peterborough.

Peardon, T.P. 1933 *The Transition in English Historical Writing 1760-1830*, New York.

Prest, W. 1995 William Lambarde, Elizabethan Law Reform, and Early Stuart Politics. *Journal of British Studies* 34. pp464-80.

Pulsiano, P. and Treharne, E. 2001 *A Companion to Anglo-Saxon Literature*. Oxford. A useful guide.

Raven, J. (ed.) 2003 *Lost Libraries: the Destruction of Great Book Collections Since Antiquity*. Cambridge.

Reynolds, S. 1985 What do we mean by Anglo-Saxon and the Anglo-Saxons? *Journal of British Studies* 24. pp395-414.

Richter, M. 1984 Bede's *Angli* – Angles or English? *Peritia* 3. pp99-114.

Rouse, R.A. 2005 *The Idea of Anglo-Saxon England in Middle English Romance*. Cambridge.

Shepard, J. 1974 Another New England? Anglo-Saxon Settlement on the Black Sea. *Byzantine Studies* I. pp18-39.

Steensma, R.C. 1976 'So Ancient and Noble a Nation': Sir William Temple's History of England. *Neuphilologische Mitteilungen* 77 . pp95-107.

Sturdy, D. 1995 *Alfred the Great*. London.

Strong, Sir R. 1978 Recreating the Past. *British History and the Victorian Painter*. New York.

Temple, A.G. *England's History as Pictured by Famous Painters*. London. 1896-97.

Thomas T. 2003 *The English and the Normans: Ethnic Hostility, Assimilation and Identity 1066-c1220*. Oxford.

Wiley, R.A. 1979 Anglo-Saxon Kemble: the Life and Works of John Mitchell Kemble 1807-1857, Philologist, Historian, Archaeologist. *Anglo-Saxon Studies in Archaeology and History 1*. BAR Series 72. pp165-273. More on the great man.

BIBLIOGRAPHY

Wormald, P. 1983 Bede, the Bretwaldas and the origins of the gens Anglorum. In Wormald, P. (ed) et al. *Ideal and Reality in Frankish and Anglo-Saxon Society.* pp99-129.

Wright, C.E. 1949-53 The Dispersal of the Monastic Libraries and the beginnings of Anglo-Saxon Studies. Matthew Parker and his Circle: a Preliminary Study. *Transactions of the Cambridge Bibliographic Society* 1. p208-37.

Wright C.E. 1960 Humfrey Wanley: Saxonist and Library-Keeper. *Proceedings of the British Academy* 46.

NOTES

PREFACE

1. Herbert Butterfield (1900-79) was an historian and philosopher whose 1931 volume *The Whig Interpretation of History* won him lasting fame. He also wrote an intriguing book outlining the ways in which English history had variously been interpreted entitled *The Englishman and His History* in 1944.

I SURVIVING HASTINGS

1. This point is first commented upon as early as 1605 by Richard Verstagen in his *Restitution of Decayed Intelligence.* Verstagen identified (as many would continue to do after him) the Saxons with the English.
2. Procopius. *History of the Wars,* VIII.xx. 4-8.
3. See Campbell, J. 1995 The Late Anglo-Saxon State: A Maximum View. *Proceedings of the British Academy* 87. Also supportive of the view that the Anglo-Saxons had already created a nation state is Wormald, P. 1994 Engla Lond: The Making of an Allegiance. *Journal of Historical Sociology* 7.
4. Anna Comnena *The Alexiad,* ed. R.A. Sewter, tr. (Baltimore. Penguin Books 1969). p147.
5. *The Ecclesiastical History of Ordericus Vitalis,* M. Chibnall, ed. and tr., Vol. 2 (Oxford University Press, 1969), p 203.
6. A recent survey of the scholarship surrounding the Anglo-Saxon exodus to Byzantium is expertly detailed by Nicholas C.J. Pappas of the Sam Houston State University. Pappas, Nicholas C.J., 2005 *English Refugees in the Byzantine Armed Forces: The Varangian Guard and Anglo-Saxon Ethnic Consciousness.* http://www.deremilitari.org/RESOURCES/articles/pappas1.htm
7. Civitot, near Nicea.
8. *The Ecclesiastical History of Ordericus Vitalis,* M. Chibnall, ed. and tr., vol. 2 (Oxford University Press, 1969), pp. 202-5.

9. *Miracula Sancti Augustini Episcopi Cantuariensis*, in Acta Sanctorum, May, VI, p. 406; translated in Vasiliev, *The Opening Stages of the Anglo-Saxon Immigration to Byzantium in the Eleventh Century*. pp6-61.

10. The Saga of Edward the Confessor, in *The Orkneyingers' Saga*, G.W. Desent, tr. Vol. 3, Roll Series (London, 1894), pp 427-28.

11. The identity of this man is not certain. Siward Bearn has been the most popular candidate. He had held many properties in Gloucestershire and had been involved in the fenland uprising in 1071. He was, however, imprisoned until the late 1080s and it is this fact among others that some scholars have taken to imply that the events in the *Edwardssaga* are telescoped in time. See Shepard, J. 1974 Another New England? Anglo-Saxon Settlement on the Black Sea. *Byzantine Studies* I. pp18-39. Pittsburgh.

12. *The Saga of Edward the Confessor. In The Orkneyingers' Saga*, G.W. Dasent. Tr. Vol3, Rolls Series (London, 1894). pp427-28.

13. Known as The 'Warang Sea' on a Syrian map of around 1150, although this may allude to the Russian influence in the area and not to the English.

14. A Turkmen group who were rated amongst the most fearsome of their kind. Theirs was the legend of the assassins.

15. The most thorough research into this aspect of the English exodus to the eastern Empire is still Shepard, J. 1974 Another New England? Anglo-Saxon Settlement on the Black Sea. *Byzantine Studies* I. pp18-39. Pittsburgh.

16. Shepard, J. 1974 Another New England? Anglo-Saxon Settlement on the Black Sea. *Byzantine Studies* I. pp18-39. Pittsburgh. p32.

17. The Saxi are sometimes taken to have been the people of Saksia, and not the English. However, the people from Saksia were Muslim and not Christian, were conquered by the Mongols and had not remained undefeated like the Saxi. Saski is also on the lower Volga, and it is unlikely that the friars had got their geography wrong.

18. Much work has been carried out on this subject lately. An in-depth analysis of the whole 200-year period can be found in Thomas, Hugh. M. 2003 *The English and the Normans. Ethnic Hostility, Assimilation and Identity 1066-1220*. Also, John Gillingham's *The English in the Twelfth Century* (2000) picks up on themes published in other papers relating to an early date for adoption of a sense of Englishness by the Normans.

19. Johnson, C. (ed.) 1983 *Diologus de Scaccario*. Oxford. p53-54.

20. See Frederick, J. 2000. The South English Legendary. Anglo-Saxon Saints and National Identity. In Scragg and Weinberg (eds). *Literary Appropriations of the Anglo-Saxons From the Thirteenth to the Twentieth Century*. Cambridge. pp57-73.

21. A point brought out by R. Bartlett under the general discussion of the Europeanisation of Europe in the medieval period. See. Bartlett, R. 1993

The Making of Europe. Conquest, Colonisation and Cultural Change 950-1350. Harmondsworth.

2 MEDIEVAL ENGLAND LOOKS BACK

1. Rule, M. 1884 Eadmer *Historia Novorum in Anglia.* p9.
2. William of Malmesbury, *Gesta Regum Anglorum.* vol I. Book iii. Para. 245.
3. *The Ecclesiastical History of Ordericus Vitalis,* M. Chibnall, ed. and tr., Vol. 2 (Oxford University Press, 1969), p273.
4. Gwynn Jones's Introduction to the 1958 version of Geoffrey's *History of the Kings of Britain* contains the statement 'The *Historia* is one of those works whose happy destiny it has been to meet the needs of a waiting world.' See Jones, G. 1958 Monmouth. *History of the Kings of Britain.* vi.
5. Although some argue for 1136.
6. *Ailred* S.C. lib. Ii, c. 17: P.L. CXCV, col. 565.
7. Although Edward I was not averse to seeking historical precedent for his actions, whatever the source. The submission to Edward the Elder in 921 of a multitude of Northern power groups was used in the English king's justification for his Scottish campaigns.
8. See Paxton, J. 2002 Forging Communities: Memory and Identity in Post Conquest England. *Haskins Society Journal* 10. pp95-109 for a full account of the meaning of the Relatio Heddæ.
9. See Hill, P. 2005 *The Road to Hastings. The Politics of Power in Anglo-Saxon England.* Stroud. p190.
10. Swanton, M.J. 1997 *The Anglo-Saxon Chronicle.* London: J.M. Dent p.262.
11. This exercise is taken from Mitchell, B. and Robinson, F.C., 1986 *A Guide to Old English.* (Fourth Edition). Oxford. p163.
12. This aspect of the king's legend, and its effects on medieval writers is covered in full in Hill, P. 2004 *The Age of Athelstan. Britain's Forgotten History.* pp195-208.
13. See Mitchell, S. 2000 Kings, Constitution and Crisis: 'Robert of Gloucester'. In Scragg, D and Weinberg, C. (eds) *Literary Appropriations of the Anglo-Saxons From the Thirteenth to the Twentieth Centuries.* Cambridge. pp39-56, for an expanded account of Robert's motivations and the assertion that Robert saw the Anglo-Saxon area as a source of cultural inspiration.
14. Grandsen, A 1992 *Legends, Tradition and History in Medieval England.* p301.

3 THE RISE OF THE SCHOLARS

1. See Fritze, R.H. 1983 'Truth Hath Lacked Witnesse, Tyme Wanted Light': The Dispersal of the English Monastic Libraries and Protestant Efforts at Preservation, ca 1535-1625. *Journal of Library History* 18.3 p277.

2. Oliver Lawson Dick (ed.) 1949 *Aubrey's Brief Lives*. London. pp. xxxvi-xxxvii.

3. Lambarde's relationship with Nowell is assessed in Grant, Raymond J.S. 1996. *Laurence Nowell, William Lambarde, and the Laws of the Anglo-Saxons.* Amsterdam/Atlanta, GA. More importantly, the relationship of Nowell's transcriptions and their influence upon the *Archaionomia* is examined.

4. William Agarde, for example, was still able to casually refer to the Trojan foundations of Britain.

4 THE COMMON MAN SPEAKS

1. Burton, K.M. (ed.) 1948 The Dialogue Between Pole and Lupset. pp110-11, 117, 175.

2. The seminal work on the theory of the Norman Yoke and its impact on seventeenth century political thought is still Hill, C. 1958 *Puritanism and Revolution: Studies in Interpretation of the English Revolution of the 17th Century.* New York. The line of argument followed here is inspired by Hill's chapter on The Norman Yoke.

3. *The Life of Alfred, or, Alured. The First Institutor of Subordinate Government in this Kingdome, and Refounder of the University of Oxford. Together with a parallel of our soveraigne Lord K. Charles Untill this Year. London. 1634.* Powell portrays King Alfred as an exemplar of kingship and closely associates him with King Charles.

4. *A Treatise of the Antiquity, Authority, Uses and Jurisdiction of the Ancient Courts of Leet, or View of Frank-Pledge, and of Subordination of Government Derived from the Institution of Moses, the First Legislator; and the First Imitation of him in this Island of great Britaine, by King Alfred and Continued Ever Since.* London, 1642.

5. John Hare is often accredited as being the father of the myth of the Norman Yoke. This passage is taken from his *St Edward's Ghost or Anti-Normanism* of 1647. Hare believed that the Germanic qualities of liberty in the English had been rent asunder by the Normans and his work is littered with ravings on the subject. If anything, he might qualify for the fatherhood of a much more sinister thing, that of the racist overtones in Anglo-Saxonism which gained ground in the nineteenth century as English and American boots trod the globe. Hare considered the Germans as 'the most illustrious and primer nation of Christendom' and the Saxons were 'their most noble tribe'. See Brailsford H.N. *The Levellers and the English Revolution.* Edited and prepared for publication by Christopher Hill. 1976. Nottingham p141.

6. From *The Earth is the Common Treasury of All Mankind. A Watchword to the City of London and the Armie 1649.*

NOTES

5 COLLEGES AND KINGS

1. The historical evidence for the Oxford claims to an Alfredian origin is published in Parker, J. 1885 The Early History of Oxford 727-1100. *Oxford History Society* 3. Oxford. 24-32. See also Keynes, S. 1999 The Cult of King Alfred the Great. *Anglo-Saxon England* 28. pp225-356 for an in-depth analysis of how the myth was capitalised upon and how Oxford adorned its walls with various busts and engravings throughout the seventeenth and eighteenth centuries.

2. A seventeenth-century copy exists in the Roxburghe Ballads in the British Library [Rox.I. 504-5].

3. Plot, of Borden in Kent, took up Natural History and Antiquities at the age of 30. He apparently had a poor moral reputation, but this did not stop him from playing an instrumental role in the setting up of the Alfred statue.

4. Also known as Richard Rowlands.

5. George Hickes, however, with some degree of justification, considered Verstagen's philology to be extremely wayward.

6. Baker was in prison having saddled himself with the crushing debts of his wife's family. He died in prison in 1645.

6 THE END OF AN ERA

1. See Graham, T. 2001 Anglo-Saxon Studies – Sixteenth to Eighteenth centuries. In Pulsiano, P. and Treharne, E. *A Companion to Anglo-Saxon Literature.* p427. For a comprehensive coverage of all the key players in the struggle for the Old English language in this era.

2. Full title *Heptateuchus, liber Job. Et Evangelium Nicodemi.*

3. Norma Clarke in Clarke, N. 2005 *Elizabeth Elstob (1674-1752): England's First Professional Woman Historian?* Gives Elstob's dates as 1674-1752.

4. Ralph Thoresby, *Letters of Eminent Men.* London: Colburn and Bentley 1832, 2: 163-4.

5. Despite the fact that William Elstob's Laws never saw publication, it remains likely that they were of some influence. David Wilkins had been working on a similar project and attempted for some years to seek permission from Elizabeth to see William's work. The permission was finally granted by a reluctant Elizabeth in 1719 at a time when his own prospectus was already out. It remains likely that some influence over Wilkins was exerted at the last moment from this viewing. More definite is the influence of the work on John Fortesue-Aland who had been revising his grandfather's *Difference Between an Absolute and Limited Monarchy.* See Collins, S.H. 1982 The Elstobs and the End of the Saxon Revival. In: Berkhout, C.T. and Milton McGatch (eds) *Anglo-Saxon Scholarship. The First Three Centuries.* Boston.

6. B.L. Dept. of Printed Books. 695. 18.

7 IN THE AGE OF EMPIRE

1. Sometimes known as Rapin de Thoyras.

2. Mortimer, T. 1764-66 *A New History of England.* Vol. I. p63

3. From a review of Anglo-Saxon language and literature, *North American Review* 33 (1831) pp325-50.

4. Burleigh, A.H. 1969 *John Adams.* New York. pp148-9.

5. Lemisch, L.J. (ed.) 1961 Edict by the King of Prussia. In *The Autobiography and Other Writings.* New York. pp261-6.

6. Although even this identification is not without its critics. See Fisher, D.H. 1989 *Albion's Seed: Four British folkways in America.* Oxford. p787.

7. Quoted in Adams, C.F. 1875 *Familiar Letters of John Adams to his Wife Abigail Adams, During the Revolution.* Boston. p211.

8. Longfellow, H.W. Anglo-Saxon Literature. *North American Review* 47. p126.

9. It was, of course, easier for Longfellow to take this view, living in the Eastern United States than it would have been for a similar-minded contemporary living in the west where a genocide was still taking place. See Mora, M.J. and Gómez-Calderón 1998 The Study of Old English in America (1776-1850): National Uses of the Saxon Past. *Journal of English and Germanic Philology.* pp322-36.

10. Ibid. p333. Mora and Gómez-Calderón on frequent occasions cite Klipstein's reviewer who reviewed his *Analecta* in the *North American Review* (1851), this particular quote being the most unforgettable.

8 CENTRE STAGE

1. Many of the plays written about the Anglo-Saxons are given detailed attention in Scragg, D. and Weinberg (eds.) 2000 *Literary Appropriations of the Anglo-Saxons. Cambridge Studies in Anglo-Saxon England.* Cambridge.

2. *Gentleman's Magazine* 1806. Vol. II. p430-1.

3. For a good account of a long period of artistic representation of events from Anglo-Saxon history see Strong, R. 1978 *Recreating the Past: British History and the Victorian Painter.* New York. pp114-8 and pp155-7 which include paintings depicting Anglo-Saxon historical events exhibited at the Royal Academy 1769-1904.

4. A comprehensive study of the engravings and other illustrations in the histories of this period is given in Keynes, S. 1999 The Cult of King Alfred the Great. *Anglo-Saxon England* 28. pp225-356.

5. Callcott, Lady Maria. 1835 *Little Arthur's History of England.* (1975 edition). p46.

6. Scott's last novel, incidentally, *The Count of Paris* (1832) also included a Saxon theme incorporating the heroic activities of Hereward the Wake.

7. Attributed to Dean Merivale. See Merivale, J.A. 1899 *Autobiography of Dean Merivale.* London. p81.

8. Quoted by Margaret Armstrong. *Fanny Kemble, A Passionate Victorian*. New York. 1938. p5.

9. In 1834 Kemble began a series of lectures at Trinity on the History of the English Language, which concentrated on texts such as *Beowulf*. After an initial high attendance Kemble is supposed to have commented 'I'll soon thin them'. See Dickens, B. 1939 John Mitchell Kemble and Old English Scholarship. *Proceedings of the British Academy* 25. p66.

10. Kemble's papers are now widely dispersed although this was not always the case and in recent times some detailed work has been carried out to trace the whereabouts of each of them.

Professor Simon Keynes of Trinity College Cambridge has put together a list of the various archives in which Kemble papers can be found. See http://www.trin.cam.ac.uk/chartwww/KemblePapers.html

11. *A Lecture on the Israelitish Origin of the Anglo-Saxons*. London. 1864. B.L. 4515.aa.4.

12. This being *British Medical Journal*. November 1883. p861.

9 UNEARTHING THE ANGLO-SAXONS

1. Lucy, S. 2000 *The Anglo-Saxon Way of Death*. Stroud. p6. Lucy's book, although concentrating mainly on the subject of the excavations of pagan period Anglo-Saxon cemeteries over the centuries provides an extremely good overview of the prevailing attitudes towards Anglo-Saxon archaeology across time.

2. From Thomas Wright's *The Celt, The Roman and the Saxon*. 1852. London. p399.

3. Lucy, S. 2000 *The Anglo-Saxon Way of Death*. Stroud. p7.

10 THE MODERN AGE

1. As reported by Miller in 'Towers Triumphant' 2002. http://www.nationalreview.com/miller/miller121802.asp

2. See Tolkien, J.R.R. 1955 *The Return of the King*. Appendix F. p414. London.

3. It is strongly contended in some quarters that an 'Insular Celt' is an invention of the Victorian era. See. James, S. 1999 *The Atlantic Celts – Ancient People or Modern Invention?* London. p17.

ORGANISATIONS AND RESOURCES

Listed below are worldwide and UK-based organisations and resources which researchers and people with a general interest will find useful in the support of their Anglo-Saxon studies.

BIBLIOGRAPHIES

Simon Keynes's Bibliography
http://www.wmich.edu/medieval/research/rawl/keynesbib/home.htm
Professor Keynes's invaluable online resource is also accompanied by an up-to-date bibliographical handbook available from Trinity College, Cambridge.

Anglo-Saxon Studies, a Select Bibliography (Boçgetæl Engliscra Gesiþa)
http://bubl.ac.uk/docs/bibliog/biggam/
A good all-round bibliography including a section on books for children.

JOURNALS

Anglo-Saxon England
Edited by Malcolm R. Godden and Simon Keynes. *Anglo-Saxon England* is the foremost regular publication of its kind. Published by Cambridge University Press.

Anglo-Saxon Studies in Archaeology and History (ASSAH)
http://users.ox.ac.uk/~assah/index.htm
The popular annual journal concerned with the archaeology and history of
England and its neighbours during the Anglo-Saxon period (*c.*AD 400-1100).
Published by the Oxford University School of Archaeology and typeset and
distributed by Oxbow Books.

The Heroic Age, an Online Journal of Early Medieval Northwestern Europe
http://members.aol.com/heroicage1/as.htm
The website includes hundreds of links to other useful places on the Internet.

LANGUAGE AND LITERATURE

Electronic Beowulf
http://www.uky.edu/~kiernan/eBeowulf/main.htm
The online guide to the British Library's award-winning double CD visual
Beowulf package, with links and other extras.

Labyrinth Library of Old English Literature
http://www.georgetown.edu/labyrinth/library/oe/oe.html
Transcripts, databases and links.

WENDERE Downloadable Old English/Modern English Dictionary
http://www.spiritone.com/~mcrobins/mark/oldenglish/wendere.htm
Easily searchable dictionary based around a Microsoft Access database.

Yamada Old English Fonts
http://babel.uoregon.edu/yamada/fonts/english.html
Useful resource of downloadable Old English fonts for a variety of platforms.

SOCIETIES

Angelcynn
http://www.geocities.com/athens/2471/
An Anglo-Saxon living history society concentrating on the period AD 400-900.

Ða Engliscan Gesiðas
http://www.kami.demon.co.uk/gesithas/
A society for people interested in all aspects of Anglo-Saxon language and
culture.

ORGANISATIONS AND RESOURCES

Early English Text Society
http://www.eets.org.uk/
Founded in 1864 to bring the mass of unprinted early English literature within the reach of students and to provide sound texts from which the New English Dictionary (subsequently the Oxford English Dictionary) could quote. The website includes a useful list of a long history of the society's publications.

Haskins Society
http://www.haskins.cornell.edu/
An international scholarly organisation dedicated to the study of Viking, Anglo-Saxon, Anglo-Norman, and early Angevin history and the history of neighbouring areas and peoples.

International Society of Anglo-Saxonists
http://www.isas.us/
ISAS was formed to provide all scholars interested in the languages, literature, arts, history, and material culture of Anglo-Saxon England.

Mearcinga Rice
http://www.ealdriht.org
A group dedicated to the study, revival, and practice of the pre-Christian religion of the Angles of the kingdom of Mercia.

Raven's Warband
http://www.millennia.demon.co.uk/ravens/index.htm
A re-enactment site specifically for the earlier period of Anglo-Saxon history.

Regia Anglorum
http://www.regia.org/
Formed to re-create the lives of the people who dwelt in Britain around a thousand years ago; from the time of Alfred the Great to that of Richard the Lionheart.

The Sutton Hoo Society
http://www.suttonhoo.org
Formed to promote research and education relating to the Anglo-Saxon royal cemetery at Sutton Hoo in Suffolk. As part of this work the Society works with the National Trust in providing the guided tours on the burial site.

Theod. Early Anglo-Saxon Living History
ttp://www.theod.org.uk/history.php
Concentrates on re-living the era of the Angles in Northumbria from around AD 450– 750.

SOME USEFUL WEBSITES

Anglo-Saxons.net
http://www.anglo-saxons.net/hwaet
Questions, timelines, people, maps and charters. An invaluable online resource
for Anglo-Saxon enthusiasts.

Beowulf
http://www.lone-star.net/literature/beowulf/index.html
An online adaptation of the famous *Beowulf* text.

Britannia
http://www.britannia.com/history/h50.html
Useful links, lists and timelines covering the whole of the Anglo-Saxon period.

Prosopography of Anglo-Saxon England
http://www.pase.ac.uk/
A comprehensive online database of all things Anglo-Saxon, particularly strong
on people, places and relationships.

The Orb
http://www.the-orb.net/encyclop/early/pre1000/asindex.html
An online reference book for medieval studies including many links to Anglo-
Saxon resources.

University of Arizona Department of English
http://www.u.arizona.edu/~ctb
C.T. Berkhout's invaluable resource list of scholars and their work.

INDEX

INDEX

If you are interested in purchasing other books published by Tempus,
or in case you have difficulty finding any Tempus books in your local bookshop,
you can also place orders directly through our website

www.tempus-publishing.com